Childminding

A COURSEBOOK FOR THE
CACHE CERTIFICATE IN CHILDMINDING PRACTICE (CCP)

Sheila Riddall-Leech

Heinemann Educational Publishers
Halley Court, Jordan Hill, Oxford OX2 8EJ
Part of Harcourt Education Limited

Heinemann is the registered trademark of
Harcourt Education Limited

First published 2002
2006 2005 2004 2003
10 9 8 7 6 5 4 3

A catalogue record for this book is available from the British Library on request.

ISBN 0 435 40158 0

Typeset and illustrated by Techtype, Abingdon

Printed and bound in Great Britain by The Bath Press Ltd

Websites
Please note that the examples of websites suggested in this book were up to date at
the time of writing. It is essential for tutors to preview each site before using it to
ensure that the URL is still accurate and the content is appropriate.

Tel: 01865 888058
www.heinemann.co.uk

Contents

Contents (continued)

Contents (continued)

Contents (continued)

12 THE PROFESSIONAL APPROACH TO CHILDMINDING (ICP, DCP, ECP)

Note:

This provides a key to how the chapter contents match the 3 units of the CCP award:

ICP – Introducing Childminding Practice (Unit 1)
DCP – Developing Childminding Practice (Unit 2)
ECP – Extending Childminding Practice (Unit 3)

This book is dedicated to my late, much loved father who introduced me to the wonderful world of books and reading, and to all those I love.

Acknowledgements

The author and publisher would like to thank the following organisations and individuals for permission to reproduce photographs and copyright material:

Haddon Davies – pages 11, 46, 54, 76, 267
Gerald Sunderland – pages 77, 113, 122, 127, 132, 134, 136
Gareth Boden – page 109.

Foreword

Thousands of childminders in England and Wales are signing up for units of the Certificate in Childminding Practice – the first nationally accredited training course for childminders. This course book – which recognises both the importance and professionalism of today's childminders – will provide lots of ideas and support for students and help childminders enjoy their work even more! Happy studying!

Gill Haynes OBE
Chief Executive
National Childminding Association

Introduction

This book has been written especially for people who care for other people's children in their own homes, in other words, childminders. People become childminders for a variety of reasons. Many childminders enjoy working for themselves, in their own homes and because of the flexibility that this can give. Childminders enjoy working with people, especially children. They give a very valuable service to a great many children and their parents. It can be a very demanding job, but at the same time very rewarding. It is a skilled job that requires not only a love of children, but also a good understanding of children. It is important that childminders, like other professional childcare workers, can get training and develop their skills and knowledge. It is hoped that by working through this book you will be able to get more knowledge and work towards a qualification that has been designed especially for childminders.

Working with the National Childminding Association (NCMA), the Council for Awards in Children's Care and Education (CACHE) has developed a qualification especially for childminders. It is called the CACHE Level 3 Certificate in Childminding Practice. The course is split into three units:

- Unit 1   Introducing childminding practice (*What you do*)
- Unit 2   Developing childminding practice (*How you do it*)
- Unit 3   Extending childminding practice (*Why you do it*)

This book follows the syllabus for the CACHE Level 3 Certificate in Childminding Practice. Throughout the book you will find information and activities to help you complete each unit and write your assignments. There are case studies that will help you think about your own work and ask yourself 'Why do I do this?' or 'Why do I need to know this?' There are suggested activities to help you build on your own experience and understanding and to try out new ideas. As most childminders are female, I have referred to the childminder as 'she' throughout the book, but I do recognise the excellent work done by male childminders.

The grids on pages xi–xii will guide you through the contents of the three units. If you plan to take Unit 1 only, the first grid will show which sections to read.

There has been a strong move by the government to encourage more people to become childminders and gain a nationally recognised qualification. I hope that this book will help you achieve this.

Sheila Riddall-Leech
CACHE Lead Examiner Certificate in Childminding Practice

How to use this book

This book has been written to support the CACHE Level 3 Certificate in Childminding Practice. This award has three units:

- **Unit 1 Introducing childminding practice**. This unit is designed for childminders as they begin their career in childminding. There is one assessment for this unit that you must successfully complete in order to be accredited with this unit. This assessment will be marked by your tutor.

- **Unit 2 Developing childminding practice**. This unit covers some of the topics of Unit 1 in more detail and also introduces new topics. At the present time there are two assessments for this unit, both of which must be successfully completed in order to gain this unit. Both of these assessments will be marked by your tutor.

- **Unit 3 Extending childminding practice**. It is intended that this unit will extend your knowledge and skills in all areas of your childminding. There is one assessment for this unit. If you pass this assessment and have already passed Units 1 and 2 you will be awarded the CACHE Certificate in Childminding Practice, which is a Level 3 qualification.

The book has 12 chapters that cover the syllabus for the full award. Some of the chapters cover more than one unit. Each unit has **learning outcomes** as set out in the syllabus. These are what you should be able to do when you have finished the unit. The learning outcomes are what you will be assessed on for each unit. To help you find your way around this book, each of the learning outcomes, for each unit, is listed in the table on page xi, with details of which chapter you can find the relevant information.

Features in the book

There are special features throughout the book to support you. These are:

- **Learning outcome activity**
  These include discussions of ideas, answering questions, describing your experiences, researching how things happen.
- **Good practice checklist**
  These are the key aspects of good practice that you should know.
- **Case study**
  Examples of 'real' situations based on experience, followed by questions to check your understanding and to explore ideas.
- **Check your knowledge**
  At the end of chapters these will test your understanding of the text. The questions are varied and include: true or false exercises, 'what would you do if . . .' , and multiple choice questions.

Learning outcome	Source of information
Unit 1 Introducing childminding practice	
1 *Identify the factors involved in keeping children safe through the safe and healthy environment you will provide for the children, and the actions you will take in a case of suspected abuse.*	• Chapter 1 Keeping children safe • Chapter 10 Child protection
2 *Describe how you will establish an appropriate routine for your childminding day and the play activities which you will provide in your childminding setting.*	• Chapter 3 Providing play and other activities for children in a home-based setting • Chapter 4 Routines
3 *Describe the way you will settle children into your childminding setting and the positive methods you will use in managing their behaviour.*	• Chapter 2 Helping children to settle into your childminding setting • Chapter 7 Managing children's behaviour
4 *Explain how you will establish your childminding business and initiate relationships with parents.*	• Chapter 8 Treating children and their families with equal concern • Chapter 9 Working with parents and other professionals • Chapter 12 The professional approach to childminding
Unit 2 Developing childminding practice	
1 *Reflect on the role of the childminder in providing play and other learning activities for children across the age range, from babies to school-age children, in a context of equal opportunities and anti-discriminatory practice.*	• Chapter 4 Routines • Chapter 5 Children's development and learning • Chapter 8 Treating children and their families with equal concern
2 *Examine the main issues involved in taking a professional approach to being a childminder, and in communicating effectively with parents.*	• Chapter 4 Routines • Chapter 9 Working with parents and other professionals • Chapter 12 The professional approach to childminding
3 *Evaluate a range of strategies for promoting children's positive behaviour and for dealing with unwanted behaviour.*	• Chapter 7 Managing children's behaviour
4 *Explain the main difficulties involved in taking action in the case of suspected child abuse.*	• Chapter 10 Child protection

Learning outcome	Source of information
Unit 3 Extending childminding practice	
1 *Reflect on the knowledge and skills required to provide early years education in a childminding setting.*	• Chapter 4 Routines • Chapter 5 Children's development and learning • Chapter 6 Planning and supporting children's learning and development • Chapter 8 Treating children and their families with equal concern
2 *Reflect on the knowledge and skills required to provide a childminding service to 'children in need' and their families.*	• Chapter 7 Managing children's behaviour • Chapter 8 Treating children and their families with equal concern • Chapter 9 Working with parents and other professionals • Chapter 10 Child protection • Chapter 11 Working with children with additional needs
3 *Reflect on the role of the childminder in working with other professionals and the importance of continuing your own professional development.*	• Chapter 9 Working with other parents and other professionals • Chapter 12 The professional approach to childminding

CHAPTER 1
KEEPING CHILDREN SAFE

Introduction

You must enjoy being with children and caring for them, otherwise you would not have thought about becoming a registered childminder. These are probably the most important reasons for choosing this job. It is natural that you want to provide the best possible care for the children and a good place to start is with ways of keeping children safe. When you become a registered childminder you take full responsibility, in every way, for the children that you care for. That responsibility is for all the time they are with you. You don't get a break, you will need 'eyes in the back of your head', lots and lots of patience and a good sense of humour! But that is why being a childminder can be a rewarding job, as well as a demanding one.

Anyone who looks after other people's children in their home must be registered with the Early Years Directorate of OfSTED in England or the Care Standards Inspectorate registration in Wales. This is a legal requirement under the Children Act of 1989. You will need to demonstrate to your local department that your home meets all of the legal requirements to provide a safe and secure environment for the children that you care for.

If you are to take your responsibilities seriously and be professional, it is essential that you understand how to keep the children safe at all times and how to prevent accidents. Obviously accidents can, and do, happen – that is life – but there are important things that you can do to reduce the chances of an accident happening to you, or to the children that you are caring for. It is quite frightening to read the latest research from the Royal Society for the Prevention of Accidents (RoSPA) that most serious accidents in the home happen in the kitchen and on the stairs, and that most accidents occur in the living room or dining room areas. RoSPA research shows that children 0–4 years old are most at risk from an accident in the home. Most accidents happen between late afternoon and early evening, in the summer and during school holidays. Boys are more likely to have accidents than girls. Every year almost 68,000 children have an accident in the kitchen, and 66% of these accidents involve children under four years old. It makes you think!!

Learning Outcome Activity 1 (ICP)

Accidents in your home

Ask yourself the following questions and write down your answers:

- What accidents have happened in your home?
- Where did they happen?
- Was anyone hurt?
- In what way were they hurt?
- Did they need to go to hospital?

When you have written down your answers ask a friend, or neighbour, or another course member the same five questions.

Then compare the answers, and discuss both sets of answers.

What do your answers tell you about your home?

You will need to think about the possible dangers and chances of accidents

- in your home
- in your garden
- with some of the playthings and equipment that you could use
- when taking children outside of your home and garden, for example in the car and crossing roads
- when you are preparing food and meals
- of keeping pets and animals where there are young children
- of some of the activities that you could plan to do with the children.

Making your home safe

Learning Outcome Activity 2 (ICP)

Making your home safe

To get started see if you can spot the dangers in the drawing opposite. The drawing shows a sitting room with possible causes of accidents or dangers to children. There are six possible dangers in the picture, write them down.

Can you say why each one is a danger or possible cause of accident, and what you could do about it?

Figure 1.1 *A roomful of potential dangers for a child*

In the drawing you should have spotted:

1 **The wires and cables from the television and video are trailing across the floor to the electrical socket on the wall.**

   This is a danger because a child, or an adult, could trip over the wires. A crawling baby could become entangled in them. Sudden pulls and tugs of wires and cables could cause the television to fall over.

   ### What to do:

   What you could do is make sure that no wires or cables trail from electrical appliances to the sockets. Try to position your television or lamps, for example, as near as possible to the electrical socket. It is a good idea to fix wires and cables along the skirting boards or along the edges of the wall with the correct size of flex pins. These are available from all hardware or DIY stores. Many electrical appliances also have short, coiled flexes which reduce the risk of them trailing.

2 **There are houseplants that young children could very easily get hold of, play with or even eat.**

Most houseplants, if not poisonous, would if eaten make a child feel unwell. Some houseplants have leaves and flowers that can cause skin irritations when touched.

What to do:

What you should do is make sure that houseplants are well out of the reach of the children in any of the rooms that they will use. You should also make sure that the plants are stable and will not fall over. It is a good rule to give away or get rid of any plants that you know are poisonous. Check with your local garden centre if you are unsure about a plant.

3 The fire does not have a protective guard around it

Fire is one of the most serious and potentially the most dangerous cause of accidents in the home. Toys, books, clothing and soft furnishing can easily catch fire. Fire spreads very quickly.

What to do:

What you can do is make sure that any fire, or heat source, has a firmly fixed safety guard all the way around it. Children should never be left unattended in a room where there is a heat source. You must fit smoke alarms and have, at the very least, a fire blanket. Ideally you should have both a fire blanket and a fire extinguisher.

4 There are hot drinks left unattended on low level tables

Drinks that are left unattended can very easily be knocked over by children. It is possible to get a bad scald or burn from a hot drink. The hot liquid retains its heat for much longer than you realise. Tea and coffee can still cause burns and scalds fifteen minutes after they have been made. ROSPA research shows that mugs or cups of coffee or tea being knocked over cause most of the burns and scalds that happen to children under five.

What to do:

Never leave hot drinks where children can reach them or where they can be accidentally knocked over. You should never have a hot drink in your hand, or within reach, if you are sitting with a child on your knee or next to you.

5 The baby seat is left unattended on the low level table, next to a hot drink

Apart from the dangers of burns and scalds, this baby seat could very easily be knocked or pushed off the table. Such a fall, even though it is not from a very great height, could easily hurt and injure the baby.

What to do:

You should never leave a child unattended, regardless of whether they are in a baby seat or not. Baby seats should never be placed on tabletops or work surfaces.

6 There are lots of small objects, ornaments and candles around the room that a young child could easily reach

Young children put things in their mouths. It is an effective way for them to feel the object and find out about it. Unfortunately, putting things in their mouths can cause choking, poisoning and injury.

What to do:

Make sure that all small objects, ornaments and decorative things, such as candles, air fresheners or pot pourri, are well out of the reach of young children. Not only do children enjoy putting things into their mouths, they often put them into their ears, noses and eyes.

Carrying out a 'risk assessment'

Take a walk around the rooms in your home that you will let the children use. For each room complete a 'risk assessment' exercise, using a chart like the one shown here. List the possible dangers and ask yourself:

• Why is this a danger?
• What can I do about it?

Room	Possible danger	Why it is a danger	What I can do about it
Kitchen	1.	1.	1.
	2.	2.	2.
	3.	3.	3.
	4.	4.	4.
	5.	5.	5.
	6.	6.	6.

Room	Possible danger	Why it is a danger	What I can do about it
Dining room	1. 2. 3. 4. 5. 6.	1. 2. 3. 4. 5. 6.	1. 2. 3. 4. 5. 6.
Play room or Sitting room	1. 2. 3. 4. 5. 6.	1. 2. 3. 4. 5. 6.	1. 2. 3. 4. 5. 6.
Hall and stairs	1. 2. 3. 4. 5. 6.	1. 2. 3. 4. 5. 6.	1. 2. 3. 4. 5. 6.
Bathroom and toilet	1. 2. 3. 4. 5. 6.	1. 2. 3. 4. 5. 6.	1. 2. 3. 4. 5. 6.

The rooms that you will use may be different from the examples given above; if that is the case, just change the chart to suit you.

You must remember that making your home safe is not just about checking for dangers and being sure that there is nothing dangerous around. It is also about always being on your guard and aware of possible hazards at all times. It is also about teaching children ways of keeping safe by setting a good example yourself in the ways you work and behave.

How can you set about getting your home ready for children and making it safe place for them? You need to work out a safety checklist for each room that the children will be using. Start with one room at a time and make the job manageable.

Let's start with some general suggestions to prevent accidents in any room in your home.

GOOD PRACTICE *Safety within the home*

- Never allow children into any room at any time without being supervised.
- Check furniture and appliances for sharp edges, such as the cooker, washing machine, table tops, shelving, and protect them if needed.
- Use short, coiled flexes on electrical equipment and fix wires and cables to walls, or to floors or skirting boards, so that they do not trail.
- Check that the plugs on electrical appliances are not cracked; replace them if they are.
- Make sure that the wires or cables from electrical appliances are not frayed or worn.
- When checking any electrical appliance be extra careful. Don't put yourself at risk. Switch off at the socket before you touch the appliance. Make sure your hands are always dry before handling anything electrical. Never put your fingers or anything other than the plug into an electrical socket.
- Fit child-resistant socket covers on all power points.
- Make sure that all sharp and small objects are kept out of sight and reach of children.
- Have a fire blanket in your kitchen, and ideally a fire extinguisher in another part of the house. Make sure that you know how to use them.
- Use a harness fitted securely to a highchair.
- Make sure that safety gates used across doorways and the stairs are fitted securely.
- Don't leave hot drinks or food unattended.
- If you use a table cloth make sure that the edges don't hang over the table.
- Try to keep the floor space as free as possible, make sure that rugs and mats will not slip or cause a child to trip and fall.
- Mark big areas of glass with stickers, such as glass doors, and make sure that this glass is either safety glass or covered with safety film.
- Fit window locks.
- Make sure that there are no trailing cords from curtains or blinds.
- Make sure that all areas of your home are well lit, especially on stairs.
- Fit a smoke alarm.
- Have a fire drill for your home and practise it regularly with the children at different times of the day.
- Buy toys and equipment that have a recognised safety symbol on them, such as the Kite mark.

Safety in the kitchen

- Keep the doors to washing machines and tumble driers shut.

- Keep oven doors shut. Make sure that children cannot touch the oven door if it is hot.

- Make sure that the doors to the fridge and freezer are securely shut.

- Make sure that children cannot get hold of plastic bags, cleaning materials and alcohol. These should also be kept out of sight and reach.

- Make sure that you turn pan handles away from the edge of the cooker.

- Make sure that all hot objects are positioned well away from the edge of work surfaces and kitchen units.

Safety in the dining room

- Avoid using table clothes that hang down over the edge of the table.

- Never leave the children unattended whilst eating.

- Never leave a baby propped up with a feeding bottle.

- Never leave hot food or drinks unattended.

- Make sure that children can safely and correctly use cutlery. Don't allow children to play with knives and forks.

- Make sure that children can safely reach the table by using either a high chair with a harness, specially designed booster seats or cushions.

- Don't allow children to walk about or wander around when eating or drinking.

- Keep alcohol out of reach of children or in a securely fastened cupboard.

- Keep cigarettes, matches and lighters out of reach of children.

Safety in the play room or sitting room

- Keep the floor space as free as possible.

- Don't use pillows for children under eighteen months. Use a firm mattress.

- Store toys carefully. Don't allow children to climb up and reach for things.

- Check all toys regularly for missing bits, broken pieces or sharp edges.

- Secure any doors that lead to outside areas.

Hall and stairs

- Use securely fixed gates to prevent children climbing the stairs unattended. It is recommended that you use gates with the safety standard number BS 4125.

- Remove any toys or objects that have been left on the floor.

- Make sure that your hall and stairs are well lit.

- Don't put anything that can be climbed on under a window.

- Check that your carpets are not frayed or loose.

- Make sure that banisters and balustrades are strong and firm and do not have any footholds for climbing and fill in gaps between rails.

RoSPA research shows that in any one year 54,000 children between 0 and 4 years old have accidents on the stairs.

Bathroom and toilet

- Medicines and tablets should be kept in a locked high cupboard.

- Cleaning materials and air fresheners should be kept out of reach of children.

- The hot water temperature should not exceed 54°C.

- When running a bath or water for washing turn the cold water tap on first and test the water before letting a child use it.

Learning Outcome Activity 3 (ICP)

A safety checklist

Try to put together a personal safety checklist for your home. Look at each room in turn and make a chart like the one on pages 5–6.

Remember, you will have to review this checklist regularly, if you are to keep high safety standards in your home. Your registration officer will expect you to have done this sort of risk assessment.

Making the outside play area and your garden safe

Is this a safe garden for children to play in?

The following are what you can do:

GOOD PRACTICE *Safety in the garden*

- Make sure that children do not play outside unsupervised.
- Make sure that all garden tools, equipment and any chemicals are stored away from children. These should really be in a locked shed, or garage or other building.
- Make sure that tricycles, bikes and other toys are not broken or damaged and cannot harm the children, for example, check for sharp edges, loose parts and missing pieces.
- Make sure that any large play equipment, such as swings, slides and climbing frames, are set up properly and that the ground underneath has safety mats or wood chippings so that children do not land on a hard surface.
- Make sure that children cannot get out of the garden. Have you got a secure gate or fence?
- Make sure that the children cannot get at any rubbish, dustbins, or wheelie bins.
- If you have pets, make sure that areas where the children play are free of pets' waste and excreta.
- Cover or fence any areas in your garden where there is water, including water butts and ponds.
- Cover sand pits when not in use, to stop animals getting into them.
- Don't use a trailing clothes line.
- Make sure that any plants in your garden are not harmful to children if touched or eaten.

Learning Outcome Activity 4 (ICP)

Checking plants

1 Find out which plants in your garden and indoors are poisonous to children.
2 Find out which plants have leaves or sap or flowers that could cause skin irritations. Check plants that you have in your garden and also in the house.
3 Write down what you have found out and keep it somewhere safe so that you can refer to it in the future.

A good place to find out this information is at your local library, or garden centre or from the Internet.

Poisonous plants in your garden and indoors should be removed. Many childminders find this aspect of safety a contentious issue. What can you do about any poisonous plants, shrubs and trees in your neighbour's garden that overhang into your garden? Discuss this with other course members, other childminders and your neighbours.

Choosing and using equipment that is safe

The equipment that you use in your home and how you look after it is another very important part of keeping children safe. It is your responsibility as a professional childminder to choose equipment and toys that are safe for using with the children that you care for.

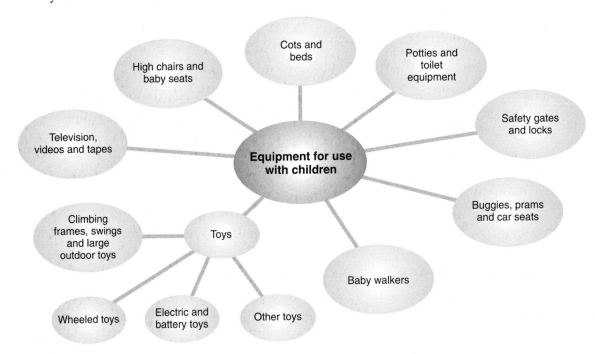

Figure 1.2 *Examples of equipment that should be checked for safety before being used with children*

☐ **High chairs and baby seats** must have securely fastened safety harnesses. These should also be adjustable so that they can still be comfortably fastened around a baby as he or she grows.

- High chairs should not wobble, the legs should be level and the whole chair should be stable. Table-mounted high chairs are not recommended as they are not stable.

- Baby seats should not be placed on table tops or work surfaces. There should be no loose pieces of fabric, coverings or broken pieces. A young child could easily put small pieces into their mouth and choke.

- Children should not be left alone in either a high chair or a baby seat.

☐ **Baby walkers** can be very dangerous pieces of equipment as babies can easily overbalance in them. There is evidence that baby walkers actually hinder children's development and childminders are advised not to use this piece of equipment.

☐ **Cots and beds** are potential areas for accidents, especially as children can fall out of them.

- Cots with sides that slide down should have secure fastenings that cannot be undone by little fingers. Beds for young children often have side rails to prevent the child falling out, but these can often be used by children for climbing.

- Young children should never be put into a top bunk, which is accessible only by a ladder.

- Mattresses for cots and beds should fit snuggly around the frame of the bed or cot. Look for the Kite mark or BS number on the label to check if the mattress meets safety standards. The covering and filling of the mattress should also be flame retardant and should have a label to say so.

- It is not good practice to use pillows for children and babies less than eighteen months old; a firm mattress is usually enough.

☐ There are many novelty **potties and toilet seats** available to encourage children to develop bladder and bowel control. Most of these are made of plastic, therefore you must check and make sure that the plastic has not cracked or split.

- Toilet seats designed for children should fit firmly over the adult toilet seat, and don't forget that children using these seats will also need a step so that they can reach the toilet safely.

☐ **Safety gates and locks** are a very important part of your equipment. Gates across doorways and stairs make it so much easier for you and the children to stay together.

- All gates should fit securely and the fastening should be firm and childproof.

- It is a good idea to fit window locks to all windows in the rooms that children will be using. There is a wide range of window locks available, in a range of colours and finishes, so you can match them to your décor. Locks can be bought from hardware and DIY stores. Most are fitted very easily. Don't forget to look for the safety labels.

☐ **Buggies**, **prams** and **car seats** may not always belong to you, as some parents may bring their child to you in one and leave it at your home. Even so you must check that there are no broken or damaged pieces or parts and that the harnesses are secure and will fasten and hold the child safely. You must let the parents know if their buggy, pram or car seat is putting their child at risk, because it is not safe.

☐ Many childminders use **television**, **videos**, **DVDs** and **tapes** to support children they care for, to help their learning and at a time of rest and quiet.

• Your television, video and tape recorder or stereo should not have trailing cables or wires and should be put where they cannot be pushed or knocked over by a child.

• If you buy or rent tapes, it is always good practice to watch or listen to them first, so that you know what they are about and to make sure they are suitable for the children in your care.

☐ **Toys** are involved in over 40,000 accidents a year according to RoSPA. Many accidents involving toys happen when people trip over them and when babies and young children play with toys intended for older children.

• Make sure toys are safe. A European Directive was introduced into British law by the Toys Safety Regulations 1995 as part of the Consumer Protection Act. Despite this, illegal and unsafe toys can still be found in many places, so shop with care. Look for the European Community (CE) symbol that means the toy meets European standards. Look also for the 'Lion Mark'. This is the logo of a voluntary association – the British Toy and Hobby Association – and indicates that toys meet statutory safety standards.

• Toys such as **climbing frames** and **other equipment that you may have outside** must be checked regularly for sharp points and edges and damage caused by the weather. Make sure that slides and swings are tough and will not collapse.

• **Wheeled toys** such as bikes, scooters and pedal cars must also be checked regularly to make sure that there are no loose parts, and that the toys have not become dangerously worn.

• Many toys are **battery-powered**, which is usually a good safe source of power, provided the batteries are used correctly. Batteries should always be fitted into the toy correctly and then covered up. Spent batteries should not be burnt, but disposed of carefully, especially smaller mercury disc batteries. These could easily be swallowed by young children or find their way into ears and noses.

• All toys should be bought or borrowed from recognised outlets.

• Try to avoid toys with loose pile fabric or hair. Young children can choke on such material.

• If you have toys with many small parts or pieces make sure that young children cannot get at them, so keep them in secure boxes or containers.

• Beware of loose ribbons on toys and long ties on dressing-up clothes. Children can get ties and ribbons fastened tightly round their necks, with dreadful consequences.

It is good practice to look for one of the safety symbols or logos shown below, before you buy a piece of equipment or toy. Some pieces of equipment or fittings in your home will have a BS number printed on the label; for example, furniture that has glass incorporated into it should have a label with BS 73767 and BS 7449.8. This means that the glass has been approved to British safety standards.

Can you identify what these symbols relate to?

GOOD PRACTICE *How to keep children safe*

- Anything that is broken, or has a frayed or damaged flex, or has pieces missing, or has loose pieces, should be removed so that the children cannot get hold of it.
- You must decide if the toy or equipment can be repaired safely or thrown away and replaced. Obviously this decision will be based partly on the type of toy or equipment and the cost of either the repair or the replacement.
- You should check very regularly for possible hazards, and don't forget to look at items of furniture as well as toys and equipment. Some childminders check every piece of equipment used by the children at the end of each working day; it will be up to you to decide how often you check, but remember accidents can happen when you least expect them.
- It is far better to be constantly aware of safety issues than having to visit the accident and emergency department at the hospital. If you buy new things, you should read the labels for potential dangers and hazards, and don't forget to look for the Kite Mark or European Community logo.
- It is also very important that the toys and equipment that you use are suitable for the age of the children, as in the following cases:
  - high chairs and baby seats and carriers should have adjustable harnesses and should only be used for young children.
  - safety gates should fasten securely and be used to stop children going up or down stairs on their own or stop them going into rooms alone.
  - toys that are designed for older children should be stored away from younger children when not in use.
  - toys with small pieces should not be within reach of young children who could easily put things in their mouths and choke.
  - electric sockets, when not in use, should be covered with safety sockets so that children cannot investigate the holes with little fingers or toys.
  - fireguards should be securely fixed around heat sources, such as electric or gas fires. Did you know that it is actually illegal to leave a child under 12 in a room with an open fire?

You can probably think of many other examples to add to this list.

Learning Outcome Activity 5 (ICP)

Making sure that toys and equipment are safe

Have a look at the toys and equipment that you are planning to use.

Can you decide which things are suitable for:

- all of the children in your care
- for children under two years old
- for children between three and five years old
- for children between five and seven years old
- for children above seven years old.

Make a checklist like the one shown here to write down your decisions.

Toy/Equipment	Age group	Safety notes
Lego	4 plus	Keep away from the babies as they could choke on the bits. Keep in a big plastic tub with a well fitting lid.

This will help you to become more aware of possible dangers and make your personal safety checklist more effective. If you are unsure about any toy or piece of equipment, it is always good practice to be more cautious, rather than take a chance that it will be all right.

Keeping children safe outside your home

You may have to transport children in your own car or on public transport. You may also want to take children out in buggies or prams, or for a walk along the road to post a letter, or to go to a pre-school group or to the shops. In these cases, you could find yourself having to cope with a lively toddler and a baby in a buggy and trying to cross a busy road.

Don't forget to obtain the parent's permission to take children out and it is good practice to tell them if you are

How can this childminder keep the children safe?

planning a special trip, for example during the school holidays, or to somewhere different. Written permission is always best.

Taking children in your own car

If you are going to use your own car you must be aware of the following points.

- Make sure that your car insurance is valid for business purposes and that it is fully comprehensive. (NCMA can advise you on this.)
- All adults must wear seat belts in the front and in the back.
- All children in the car must wear secure child restraints, which are appropriate for the age, weight and size of the child.
- All children should have a seat. *Never* allow a child to stand up in the car or sit on someone's knee.
- Child locks should be used on the doors.
- Make sure that children get out of the car on the pavement side and not out on the roadside of the car.
- Think about how you drive, be careful and alert. Set a good example to the children when dealing with other road users.

Using public transport

If you use public transport you will need to:

- make sure that the children stand well back from the edge of the pavement or station platform
- make sure young children are wearing safety harnesses and that older children are taught to hold your hand
- plan your journey carefully so that you know where the bus stops are, which platform the train arrives and leaves from, how to get up and down stairs, or across busy roads
- make sure that when on the bus or train the children sit down at all times next to you; if there are no seats left, make sure that if the children are standing they are not in danger of falling over and that if possible they can hold on to a safety rail or you.

Walking with children

When out walking with children you must be very aware of their safety and be very alert. There are many things that you can do to teach children how to keep safe; even young children can be made aware of dangers and begin to learn about keeping themselves safe.

- It is good practice to use **personal restraints** on toddlers and young children. Many types are available including reins, harnesses and straps that have a wristband at both ends for the child and the adult. Whatever you choose it should have a Kite mark or other recognised approved safety symbol on the restraint.

- Set a good example to the children when **crossing roads**. Never cross in a rush or hurry, or in a place where you cannot see traffic coming in both directions. Always use a zebra or pelican crossing and show the children how to cross a road safely. Traditionally, children were taught to look right, look left and look right again, and if clear, then it was safe to cross. However this does not work for one-way streets, and for very busy roads in today's towns and built-up places. A good thing to teach children when crossing a road is – *Stop, Look and Listen*. Only cross when you are sure it is safe, and always use a pelican or zebra crossing if there is one nearby. *Never run* across the road.

Children need to learn how to cross a road safely

- Treat **buggies and prams** like all other equipment you use with the children. They should be regularly checked, especially the brakes and folding mechanisms, and kept in good working order. They should be fitted with harnesses, which you should always use. Do not have the buggy or pram sticking out into the road while you wait to cross. It could be hit by a vehicle, and the fumes from vehicles could affect the child.

- In large **open places**, such as parks or even shopping centres, you should arrange with older children what to do if you get separated. Some childminders and children look for a prominent building or special point, such as an information desk or a park bench, and agree to meet there. Young children should always be wearing personal restraints, such as safety harnesses, so that they cannot wander off and become separated from you.

Dealing with other people

Children need to know what to do if a stranger approaches them. Talk to them about 'stranger danger' and work out what they should do. Children should be helped to understand that not everyone they meet, however friendly they seem, can be trusted. They should be taught not to speak to strangers and never go off with someone they do not know. Don't frighten or scare the children, but firmly explain to them how to cope in such situations. Remember to discuss with the children's parents what you and the children have decided in such emergencies, so that the parents can use the same tactics with the children.

Organisations such as Kidscape produce many useful leaflets and books to help teach children ways of keeping themselves safe. Kidscape have a website, details of which can be found at the end of the book. NSPCC also has useful materials.

Think about what you need to have with you when you go out with the children. It depends on where you are planning to go and how long you plan to be out. You might take with you some form of personal identification, relevant emergency telephone numbers, a mobile phone, and a first-aid kit.

CASE STUDY

Anna has been a registered childminder for six months. Apart from her own six-year-old, she has responsibility for twins aged two-and-a-half years. During the school holidays Anna and all the children often walk to the local park, to feed the ducks and play in the adventure playground.

1 How can Anna make sure that the walk to the park is 'stress free' for everyone?
2 What can Anna do to make sure that all the children have fun, and remain safe whilst feeding the ducks?
3 What particular dangers should Anna be aware of in the adventure playground?
4 What should Anna take with her in case of an emergency?

Think about your answers and discuss them with other childminders.

Making sure that your home is a healthy place for children

As a professional childminder you and your home are open to scrutiny. This scrutiny will be from parents, social service registration officers, OfSTED and other professionals that you could come across whilst working with children, such as health visitors, medical personnel or social workers.

It is very important that you have high standards of personal hygiene. It is also vital that your home is a safe and hygienic environment for children and that you do everything that you can to prevent the spread of infection. As part of the registration process your home will be checked for its cleanliness.

The children will copy and learn from what you do and say. The way you behave, such as washing your hands after going to the toilet, will teach the children that this is the correct thing to do. You will need to establish routines that encourage hygiene and help children to learn safe ways to care for themselves. Routines will be discussed in more detail in Chapter 4.

Hand washing

Washing your hands and teaching children to wash their hands properly is one of the most effective ways of preventing the spread of infection.

- Hands should be thoroughly wet before applying soap. Ideally this should be liquid soap as soap bars have a tendency to retain bacteria if they sit in water.

- The surfaces of both hands should be vigorously massaged with the lather, special attention being paid to the finger tips, thumbs and between the fingers. If you wear a wedding ring you should wash underneath it.

- Rinse your hands well under running water and dry them with a paper towel.

The hand-washing process should take no less than 30 seconds.

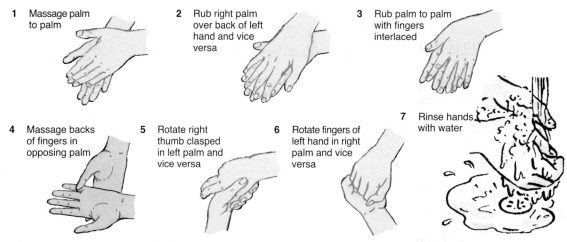

Figure 1.3 *You should follow these steps in washing your hands thoroughly*

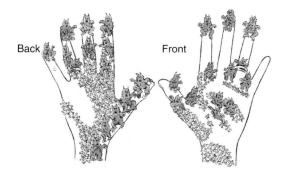

Figure 1.4 *You need to wash your hands thoroughly to make sure there are no germs left on them*

It is good hygiene practice to use disposable plastic gloves when dealing with faeces, urine and blood as well as washing your hands with hot water and soap.

Figure 1.5 *These are occasions when you should wash your hands*

Learning Outcome Activity 6 (ICP)

When do you wash your hands?

Keep a written diary for one complete working day of how many times you wash your hands.

Then check your diary with the spider chart above and see if there are any times when you should have washed your hands and you didn't.

Keeping your home clean

You must do everything possible to keep your home clean and hygienic to prevent the spread of infection. Children can easily pick up infections. Touch, food, water, animals, droplets in the air, cuts and grazes can spread infection. The kitchen and bathroom are the rooms most likely to hide germs that cause infections and so must be kept thoroughly clean.

Keeping a clean home will stop germs from multiplying. Using everyday things like soap and water and allowing in fresh air and sunlight will destroy many germs. Cleaning products will also help you to keep the home germ-free, but remember many of these are harmful to children and pets and must be kept out of a child's reach at all times, even locked away if necessary when not being used. Antiseptic cleaners and wipes are forms of weak disinfectant and do help to prevent germs from multiplying. However, they do not destroy germs and bacteria and can be dangerous to children.

GOOD PRACTICE *Keeping your home clean*

- It is good practice to clean and disinfect floors, equipment and toys regularly. Many childminders clean and disinfect kitchen and bathroom floors at least once a day.
- High chairs and changing mats need to be cleaned every time they are used.
- Rubbish bins must be kept covered and should be emptied at least once a day. Rubbish bins can be a source of germs and bacteria and for this reason it is very important to keep them thoroughly clean.
- Animals and domestic pets should not be allowed in the kitchen. Your much-loved family pet does not know how to wipe its feet or wash its paws! It will bring into your kitchen dirt and germs from outside no matter how careful you are.
- As well as keeping the bathroom floor clean, don't forget that germs can breed around damp towels and face cloths. Each child must have its own towel and face cloth. These should be washed and thoroughly dried, frequently. Many childminders change the children's towels and face cloths each day.
- We often think that soap is germ-free. Actually a soggy piece of soap sitting on a wash basin can be a source of potential infection. If you and the children use pieces of soap make sure that it is a clean piece and does not sit in its own little puddle of water on the wash basin. You might decide it is better to use a dispenser with liquid soap. Remember to keep the dispensers clean as well.
- Your toilet must be kept clean. Children should be taught to flush the toilet each time they use it. They should be taught to put toilet tissue into the toilet carefully before they flush it. As children wash their hands after they have flushed the toilet this means that the toilet handle is a source of potential infection, so make sure it is wiped and disinfected regularly. The toilet seat needs special attention, as does the actual bowl, both inside and out. If you have a carpet around the toilet it could very quickly become smelly and a source of germs. Think about the flooring in your bathroom and consider a washable mat or floor covering around the toilet.
- Nappies and other soiled clothes or products should be disposed of hygienically. You can buy specially designed covered containers that will help you dispose of nappies by wrapping and sealing each one separately in anti-bacterial film. When the container is full the bag is lifted out and put in an outside bin. This equipment can be bought at large supermarkets, chemists and nursery stores. On the other hand, many childminders use plastic bags for each item, which they then fasten securely. Each plastic bag is then put in an outside bin. You need to decide what is best for you, as long as you dispose of nappies and soiled things hygienically.

Learning Outcome Activity 7 (ICP)

Preventing spread of infection

Someone in your family, or one of the children that you are care minding, has developed cold sores.

How could you prevent the spread of the infection to other people and children?

Make a note of your answer, and then read through this part of the chapter again to check if you have the right answer.

Food hygiene

Part of your job as a childminder will be to prepare and give children food and drinks. The way that you prepare, cook and serve the food will help the children you care for learn sensible eating habits, and should also encourage them to try out various foods. The food that you provide needs to supply energy so the children can grow and develop. If you are not very careful about how you prepare, store and handle food, you could pass on to the children many different forms of food-borne illnesses. There are some very straightforward tips that you should always follow so that you can be sure that the food you give to the children is safe.

GOOD PRACTICE *Tips on food safety*

Shopping for food

- Don't buy or open cans of food that are swollen or dented.
- Don't buy any food product if the packaging is soiled – it could have leaked.
- Don't buy food if you think that it has been repackaged or tampered with.
- Check food for the 'sell by date' or 'best before' date. If the date has expired it does not always mean that the food is not fit to eat. It tells you that the food now does not meet the manufacturer's or supermarket's quality standards. In effect you could be buying inferior quality food.
- Don't buy food from a fridge if it is not cold to the touch. Most refrigerated food should be stored at a temperature less than 7°C.
- Frozen foods should be solid. If the packaging is soiled it shows you that the food has thawed out in the past and then been refrozen. Don't buy frozen foods that are stacked above the 'load line' in the freezer. These foods will not be stored at the correct temperature and could be thawing out.
- Don't forget you should always take frozen and refrigerated foods home as soon as possible and not leave them in your car whilst you do other shopping. Your car can get very hot, even when there is no sun.

GOOD PRACTICE *Tips on food safety*

Storing food safely

- Cover all food that is left out.
- Check that the refrigerator is no higher than 5°C and that the freezer is set at −18°C.
- Make sure that air can circulate round the refrigerator, and don't try and overfill it.
- Never refreeze food that has thawed out.
- Never store raw meat next to other food. Wrap it up well and put at the bottom of the refrigerator if you can
- Raw meats can 'leak' or drip juices onto foods stored below them. These juices nearly always contain harmful bacteria. Store meat in leak-proof containers.
- Store cans and packets in a cool dry place. Don't store these foods above your cooker. Foods in cans should always be eaten within one year of purchase or before the expiry date on the label.
- Look carefully at the 'best before' dates on food, and don't risk eating food that is out of date. It is better to be safe than sorry.
- Don't store food or juices in cans once they have been opened. Once a can has been opened, air can get to the contents and affect the quality of what is in the can. It is good practice to transfer what is left from the can into a leak-proof container, cover and store in the fridge.
- Take care to protect fruit, vegetables and salads. Many people store salads in the fridge, but what about fruit and vegetables? These are often left out in the kitchen and can be touched by anything and anyone. This is a health risk.

Preparing foods

- Be careful not to cross-contaminate food. For example, do not use the same board to cut raw meat, chop vegetables and then slice bread. The juices from the meat can contaminate the other foods. In the same way don't use the same knives, plates or other utensils for different foods.
- Don't thaw out foods on a kitchen work surface. Use a leak-proof container and make sure the food is completely thawed through.
- Plastic chopping boards are easier to keep clean than wooden ones. If you worked in a day care centre or restaurant preparing food, you would need different coloured plastic boards for different types of food.
- You must follow the manufacturer's instructions on labels when thawing, heating or cooking food. Just as foods must be properly thawed, they must also be cooked thoroughly. Harmful bacteria are not destroyed in food until the food has been cooked to a temperature of 71°C (boiling point is 100°C).

CASE STUDY

Jenny is a childminder for Tom, aged five, Ahmed, aged three, and a baby of eight months. She has to prepare Tom a pack lunch for school. Tom has decided that he wants a cheese sandwich, an orange that is peeled and cut up and a carton drink. Jenny gets her wooden bread board and butters the bread; she uses the same knife and board to cut the cheese and the finished sandwich. She puts the sandwich and carton drink in Tom's lunch box. Jenny wipes the board with a cloth and then cuts up the orange, wraps it in plastic wrap and puts that next to the sandwich.

1 How many times do you think Jenny has not followed good practice?
2 Can you decide what she did wrong, and what should she have done?

General safety at mealtimes

Snacks and mealtimes can be very good learning opportunities for children, especially if they are involved with preparing the food. You must be a good role model and so the children will learn from you good, safe practices.

- Both you and the children should always wash your hands before eating or preparing food.

- Children should never be left unsupervised when preparing food or eating and drinking.

- If you are using knives and forks, make sure that you teach children safe ways to handle and use them. Do not let children wave any eating tools around.

- Make children sit down when eating or drinking. This will reduce the chance of them choking or tripping over.

Keeping children safe around animals

You need to make sure that the children in your care are not in danger from any animals you keep in your home.

- Your elderly, much loved dog might be the soppiest animal in the world around you when you are about, but might react violently to being touched by someone else when you are not there or by being around a lively noisy group of young children.

- No childminder should ever have a pet in the house that is not tolerant of children.

- You should teach children how to care for animals, and encourage them, if appropriate, to clean out cages and feed the animals.

- Children should be taught to wash their hands after touching animals and not to kiss pets. It is not good practice to allow pets to lick faces.

- As with sick children, sick animals need time and special attention. You will need to consider this when childminding. What will you do with the children if you have to take a sick cat to the vet?

- Both children and pets need fresh air and exercise, so you will need to think about whether you have enough time to walk the dog and look after the children.

- You will need to keep animal feeding bowls separate from those used by humans and wash them separately.

- Don't forget to clean up any 'pet accidents' straightaway and dispose of everything hygienically.

- If you or members of your household keep exotic pets make sure that they are securely and appropriately housed so that children cannot get access to them.

- Children should not be left alone with pets and animals, no matter how tame and friendly you think the animals are, or how careful you think the children will be.

There are often horrific stories in the newspapers about children who have been bitten and injured by dogs. Hamsters and rabbits can bite children, especially if they stick their fingers through the cage. Cats will scratch if play gets too boisterous. Animals can be unpredictable in their behaviour, especially if provoked or hurt or think that they are in danger. You can teach children how to care for and how to treat animals, but 'at the end of the day', you are responsible for keeping the children safe.

CASE STUDY

Jenny, Tom and Ahmed are cleaning out the hamster cage on the outside patio. The telephone rings and Jenny tells Tom and Ahmed to wait until she comes back. While Jenny is on the telephone, Tom runs in to tell her that the hamster has bitten Ahmed's finger and he is crying.

1 How could Jenny have avoided Ahmed being bitten?
2 What should she have done about the telephone call?

The balance between safety and independence

It is often not easy to get the balance between keeping children safe and allowing them to learn and develop independence. Young children love to explore, which is one of the ways that they learn. Older children want to be able to go the local shop on their own, for example, and so gain confidence and independence. But children need to be educated from an early age about safety and ways to cope in emergencies. How they learn about safety will be from you, the childminder, and their parents. Everyone in a home is relaxed, and often feel safe because they are at home. Yet most accidents happen in the home, and during the summer months. Research has shown that boys are more at risk than girls. Young children are most at risk because they want to explore and be independent, but they cannot anticipate dangers. It is better to teach young children a safe way to crawl up and down stairs, than have them fall down. It is even better to have a secure stairgate that can only be opened by an adult and so the children can only go up and down stairs with supervision.

Teach children to use a handrail when going up and down stairs. Many childminders teach toddlers to crawl up stairs on their hands and knees and to come down again on hands and knees, but backwards. Always supervise children when they are going up or down stairs.

Dealing with accidents, emergencies and first aid

Preventing accidents

An accident is something that happens that is not expected, or planned, and is not caused deliberately. Accidents can be prevented, or at least their effects can be limited. As a childminder your responsibility is to try to prevent accidents from happening, and if they do happen, then you must know what to do.

RoSPA estimates that as many as 20 children die each year as a result of falling from windows, balconies or stairs; and that 42% of all accidents involve a fall.

The chart below gives examples of the most common accidents that can happen to children. It shows some possible causes of accidents and what you can do to prevent such accidents.

Potential accident	Possible cause	Prevention
Cuts and grazes	• sharp objects such as scissors, knives • sharp edges on furniture and equipment • damaged or faulty toys • broken glass	• make sure that sharp objects are out of reach of children • protect furniture edges, especially corners • remove or throw away damaged or faulty toys • mark large areas of glass, such as patio doors with stickers, use plastic cups for children's drinks

Potential accident	Possible cause	Prevention
Falls	• falling between two levels, such as high chair to floor, bed to floor	• use harnesses or personal restraints in high chairs. Fit safety rails to beds and make sure that cot sides are securely held in place
	• tripping over toys left on the floor	• make it part of your routines to encourage children to put away toys when they have finished playing
	• falling up or down stairs and steps	• fit secure stair and doorway gates. Never let children climb up and down stairs unsupervised
	• falling out of windows	• fit window locks and move furniture from underneath windows to stop children climbing
Burns, scalds and fire	• hot drinks being knocked over	• do not leave hot drinks within reach of children
	• matches and lighters	• keep matches and lighters out of children's reach
	• fires and heaters	• fit secure guards around any heating source. Have a fire blanket or extinguisher handy
	• water too hot	• domestic hot water should never exceed 54°C
	• kettles, irons and electrical equipment	• fit coiled flexes to equipment and do not allow flexes to trail over the edge of work surfaces
	• cookers	• oven doors can be fitted with protective guards or fitted with heat-resistant covers. Pan handles should be turned away from the edge of the hob or cooker
Poisoning	• cleaning materials	• store in a secure cupboard that children cannot open
	• plants – both indoors and garden plants	• either keep out of reach, or better still destroy poisonous plants

Potential accident	Possible cause	Prevention
	• medicines	• store in a locked high cupboard
	• cosmetics	• keep out of reach of children
Suffocation and choking	• pillows	• don't use pillows for babies under eighteen months
	• small pieces of toys	• keep toys with small pieces away from small children
	• skipping ropes	• discourage children from using ropes for anything else other than skipping
	• cord and ties on clothes and furnishings	• avoid clothes with ties. Make sure cords from furnishings and blinds do not hang down
	• plastic bags	• keep away from children. Store out of reach, preferably knotted, so that they cannot be easily opened
	• nuts	• do not give to young children
Electric shocks	• electric sockets	• fit covers to all electric sockets that are not in use. Don't overload sockets with too many plugs
	• damaged electrical equipment	• check equipment for frayed or damaged flexes and replace if necessary
Drowning	• bath	• do not leave children in a bath unattended
	• paddling pools	• do not leave children in paddling pools unsupervised
	• ornamental ponds	• cover or fence ponds
	• buckets or bowls of water	• don't leave any amount of water in a bucket or bowl

Remember accidents can happen anywhere, at anytime and usually when you least expect them, so be prepared.

Coping with an emergency

An emergency, like an accident, is unexpected. It can involve only you or several people. Emergencies often are the result of accidents. Even though you cannot predict accidents and emergencies you can be prepared. The best way to cope is to have a personal emergency plan, so that you are prepared for the worst. Such a plan will help you remain calm and more able to cope.

Putting together a personal emergency plan

- You will need access to a telephone, either a landline or a mobile phone. If you rely on a mobile phone, make sure it is fully charged during the times that the children are with you. Also, check that the mobile has good reception. If you do not have a telephone in your home, make sure you know where the nearest public call box is and keep a phone card or coins handy, to be used only in an emergency. (Remember emergency services can be contacted on landlines and public call boxes by dialling 999; many mobile phone services use 112.)

- Next, make sure that you have an up-to-date list of essential telephone numbers. This list should include:

  - the contact numbers of the parents of the children and an emergency contact number if they are not available

  - telephone numbers of the children's doctors

  - your own doctor

  - the nearest police and fire stations

  - the nearest hospital with an accident and emergency department

  - the name, address and telephone number of someone who you could call to cover for you if you have to leave your home. (You will have to reassure parents that you would never leave their children unattended, and if possible, they would always be left with another qualified person.)

- You must make sure that your records of the children are up to date.

- When putting together an emergency plan you will need to decide what are the most important things to do first. These first actions are known as the 4Bs:

  - Breathing – your first priority is to check that the child is still breathing

  - Bleeding

  - Breaks

  - Burns.

It is very important that you do not attempt to resuscitate a child unless you have been specially trained to do so. Call an ambulance if you are in any doubt.

Learning Outcome Activity 8 (ICP)

In case of an emergency

Mentally 'rehearse' an emergency.

This will help you plan what you need to do first and will help you feel more confident and more able to reassure the children in a real emergency.

A personal emergency plan could be something like this

1 Don't panic, keep calm, take a few deep breaths.
2 Deal with the emergency following the 4Bs.
3 Check if it is possible to contain the emergency without harm to you or the children, for example, use a fire blanket, or fire extinguisher.
4 Check the safety of all of the children and if possible remove them from the immediate area; never leave them unattended.
5 If necessary make telephone calls to emergency services or doctor. Make sure you are talking to the correct person, identify yourself and explain clearly why you are calling.
6 Contact the parents of the child or children. If you leave a message, make sure that it is brief, but gives all the necessary information without causing the parents to panic. Remember to leave a contact number for the parents to get in touch with you.

A personal emergency plan is exactly that – it is personal to you and it must work for you. It is good practice to write out your personal emergency plan, so that other people can follow it if something was to happen to you. You should also look at your plan regularly and change it if necessary. This is especially important for keeping up-to-date records of the children. The National Childminding Association has produced a form that you and the parents can complete with details of address, telephone numbers, emergency contacts, medical details and other useful information. You could make up your own forms if you wanted, but make sure that you include all details about the children that you need to know in order to keep them safe. There is more about keeping records in Chapter 12.

Why does a childminder need a relevant first-aid qualification?

Another way you can make sure that you are fully prepared for any situation, accident or emergency is to have an up-to-date and relevant first-aid qualification. It is very reassuring for parents to know you are professional and caring enough to get as many recognised qualifications as you can. Many local authorities insist that all childminders registered with them have a specialist first-aid qualification. These qualifications are very important and will teach you how to deal with emergencies and some first aid. Most qualifications last only for three years, so all childminders will need to keep their qualification up to date.

The Red Cross and St John's Ambulance run courses especially for people who work with young children. Their telephone numbers are usually in the local telephone directory, or at the library. Their addresses are at the end of this book. If you have difficulty in finding out about courses contact your social service department, or your local college may be able to help. These courses also will help you to put together your own first-aid kit. You can buy from a chemist or supermarket a first-aid kit that is already put together, however some of the items in these kits are unlikely to suit your needs. Many childminders make up their own first-aid kits, which means they can put in what they need and know how to use it.

Learning Outcome Activity 9 (ICP)

Making up a first-aid kit

1   What would you put in your first-aid kit?
    Make up a first-aid kit list that would be right for the children that you care for and for you to use.

    Check your list against the one below.

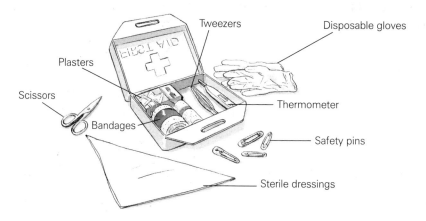

2   Have you thought about possible allergies to plasters?
3   What could you use instead of plasters?
4   Have you thought about the different types of thermometers you would need, and which would be the easiest for you to use and read?
5   Have you remembered to include disposable plastic gloves, for both the children and your protection?
6   Where would you keep your first-aid kit?
7   What sort of container would you use to store the items?
8   How often would you check your kit?

Every time you use the first-aid kit you should get into the habit of making a note of the items that you used and add them to your shopping list, if necessary; and when you have finished using the kit, do a quick check to see if everything you need is there and usable. You could stick a list of contents of the kit on the lid of the container, and then simply do a quick check against the list.

You may find that your registration officer from the local authority has a list of the suggested minimum requirements for a first-aid kit; it is worth asking.

Your first-aid kit should be used only for your childminding business. Any medication that you keep to give to members of your family should not be given to the children you are caring for. You must have written permission from the children's parents before you give any first aid or medication. This written permission can be part of your record keeping and included on the form mentioned earlier in this chapter. Any medication for children that you have been asked to give to a child by parents must be kept out of the reach of children, stored at the correct temperature (read the label), and disposed of carefully when the course of treatment is finished.

REMEMBER

The most important way of keeping children safe and reducing the risk of accidents is by YOU setting the best possible example, at all times, to the children.

As mentioned earlier, having an up-to-date first-aid qualification is essential for all childminders. However, it is important that you are aware of your own limitations and in an emergency only carry out things that you are competent to do.

In an **emergency** situation where you have to give first aid, follow this routine.

• Stay **calm**. This helps you to assess the situation.	*Childminders*
• Deal with a **dangerous** situation first.	*Don't*
• **Remove** child, other children and yourself from danger.	*Rush*
• **Talk** to the injured child to see if he or she responds.	*Things*

Remember **C D R T**

Then follow the ABC routine that you should have learnt on your first-aid course.

• Check the child's **airway**.	**A**
• Check the child's **breathing**.	**B**
• Check the child's **circulation.** Is there a pulse?	**C**
• Put the child into the recovery position – see the drawing on page 34.	

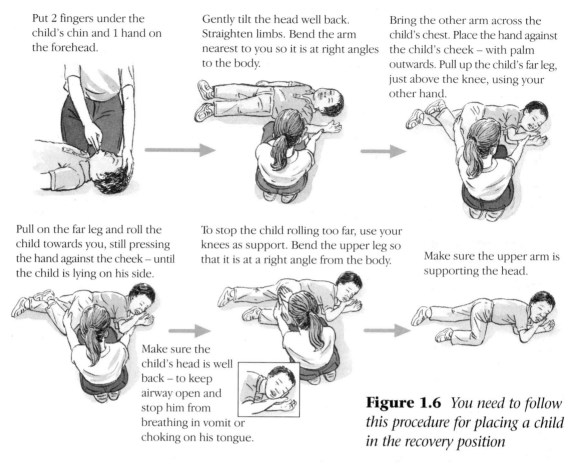

Put 2 fingers under the child's chin and 1 hand on the forehead.

Gently tilt the head well back. Straighten limbs. Bend the arm nearest to you so it is at right angles to the body.

Bring the other arm across the child's chest. Place the hand against the child's cheek – with palm outwards. Pull up the child's far leg, just above the knee, using your other hand.

Pull on the far leg and roll the child towards you, still pressing the hand against the cheek – until the child is lying on his side.

To stop the child rolling too far, use your knees as support. Bend the upper leg so that it is at a right angle from the body.

Make sure the upper arm is supporting the head.

Make sure the child's head is well back – to keep airway open and stop him from breathing in vomit or choking on his tongue.

Figure 1.6 *You need to follow this procedure for placing a child in the recovery position*

If the situation that you are dealing with is not an emergency or a crisis situation, you still need to remember **C D R T**. Many accidents can be dealt with easily provided your first-aid box is complete and you know what to do. The chart below gives you a list of the sort of first aid to carry out when dealing with common minor accidents with children.

Accident	First-aid treatment
Grazes of all kinds	Rinse the area with plenty of clean cool water to make sure the grazed area is dirt-free
Minor burns	Run under a cold tap for at least 10 minutes Chemical burns need at least 20 minutes Do not cover burned area
Nose bleeds	Tip the child's head forwards and pinch just below the bridge of the nose
Bruising and sprains	Put something cold over the area (a bag of frozen peas, wrapped in a small, clean towel is ideal) Keep the sprained area raised and try to stop the child using that part of the body

Accident	First-aid treatment
Head injuries	Put something cold over the injury (a bag of frozen peas, wrapped in a small, clean towel is ideal) Watch out for signs of concussion, such as headaches, drowsiness, vomiting If in doubt seek medical help
Objects in the nose or ears	Do not try to remove the object – get a doctor to remove it

It is not really possible to cover every common accident that you may encounter. If you are not sure what to do, seek help.

CHECK YOUR KNOWLEDGE

Answer the following questions.

1 Why do you need to check the kitchen especially for hazards and dangers?

2 Name three accidents that can happen in the kitchen. How could these be prevented?

3 How can children be accidentally poisoned?

4 What are the main details that you should have on record about children you are minding? Why do you need this information?

5 How many poisonous plants have you identified in either your garden or home? What should you do with them?

6 What is the 'Kite mark' and where are you likely to see it?

7 What do you need to remember if you are out with a child in a buggy?

8 What temperatures should a refrigerator be set at?

9 Why is it important to teach children to care for animals?

10 Can you explain why the young child's need to explore can sometimes result in that child having an accident?

11 What are the 4Bs?

12 How do children learn how to keep themselves safe?

CHAPTER 2
Helping children to settle into your childminding setting

In any new situation that we face there are bound to be insecurities and worries. They may be about things that seem to be quite minor afterwards, but at the time seem very important to you. You can do simple things to reduce your worries. For example, when starting a new job, you could do the journey from home to work before you start, so that you know how long it will take, where to park or which bus stop to get off at. It then becomes one less thing to worry about.

One of the best ways to cope with new situations is to plan ahead as much as possible. When you are taking children in to your home for the first time, it is important to remember that they could be feeling just like you did when you started school or that new job. Just as you could have done certain things to reduce your own concerns, there are things you can do to help a child to settle.

Settling any child into a new place takes great care and thought. It should not be rushed and you should allow the child and parents to set the pace. Having established routines can help settle a child as they can quickly learn what is to happen at certain times of the day. They begin to feel secure and so will settle.

Managing the first meeting with parents or carers

The first thing to consider when settling any child is your relationship with the parents or carers. It cannot be stressed how important this meeting is for you, the parents and the child. This meeting is the start of your professional relationship with the parents. You should spend some time getting to know them; a quick telephone call in response to 'have you any vacancies' is not enough. You should talk to parents face to face and spend time to answer their questions. Mothers returning to work after the birth of their first child are often very anxious about leaving their baby, so your job is to be as reassuring as possible.

If they cannot come to you, think about going to the parent's home. Whatever happens do not miss out the first visit.

Sometimes childminders can start to care for a child at short notice and so the first meeting and preparations could be rushed. In such cases you will need to think of ways, such as making a 'must do' list, to make sure that all the important points are covered and all essential information is exchanged.

GOOD PRACTICE *The first visit*

- It is always good practice to invite the parents and the child to visit you in your home before the child starts coming to you. First impressions are very important and so you should be professional and welcoming.
- Agree a definite time for the first visit. This means that you can organise your day so that you have the time to give to the parents and the child.
- If you have other children, including your own, or other family members, don't forget to tell them that you have parents coming to visit.
- Offer the parents tea or coffee if appropriate.
- Start off by talking about everyday things such as the weather or something that is in the news that day. This helps to put people at ease and build confidence.
- Be business-like but at the same time friendly.
- Show the parents the rooms that the children will be using and don't forget to show them the garden if the children will be playing there.
- Explain what kinds of activities you will be doing during the day.
- Show them your business documents such as registration and insurance documents. Better still, show them your information file.
- Explain to parents why you need them to complete specific information about their child and give them your welcome pack.
- Agree what would be good times for you to share information about the child. Not every parent or childminder has time at the end of the meeting to chat. Some childminders give parents a brief outline of what the child has been doing during the day. This is especially useful for parents of babies and young children as it can give information about what they have eaten and when, how often they have had a soiled nappy or how successful the toilet training has been that day. This also provides parents, children and you with common information and helps to build good relationships.

Putting together a welcome pack

It is a good idea to put together a 'welcome pack' for parents that includes relevant information about you, how much you charge and a form for parents to complete with information and details about their child. The idea of a welcome pack is that parents can take it away with them and keep it as a reference. Some childminders make a booklet about their business. What you give to parents is up to you, but it should include:

- Your full name.

- Your full address including your postcode.

- Your telephone number, both land line and mobile if you have one.

- Details of the days and times that your business is open, including details of your holidays.

- Details of your charges for a full day, part-time/sessional, holidays and additional hours. Include exactly what parents will get for their money. Will your charges include nappies, food and drinks? Don't forget to include any extras that you may wish to charge for and make it very clear who will pay for such things as pre-school sessions and after-school activities.

- A brief outline of how you plan to organise your day. This helps parents know where you are likely to be if they want to get in touch with you.

- A brief outline of some of the activities that you plan to do with the children.

- Brief details of when you were registered and inspected last.

- A detailed registration document for parents to complete and return to you *before* you start to care for the child.

Much of this information will have to be regularly revised and kept up to date, for example your own holiday dates.

Learning Outcome Activity 10 (ICP)

Compiling a welcome pack

- Start to make your own welcome pack.
- Think what you are going to include.
- Think about how you will make it. Can you use a computer to compile some things, or devise your registration form?
- Will you use a form that is already made for you, such as the one produced by the NCMA?

Putting together an information file

Many experienced childminders will have built up an information file, which they show to parents at the first meeting. This file can include:

- the registration certificate

- OfSTED or Care Standards Inspectorate reports for Wales (CSIW)

- a copy of the police check

- details of insurance policies, including house, contents, car, public liability
- details of the daily routine
- brief descriptions of some of the activities that they do with the children
- a personal emergency plan
- what to do when a child is unwell
- any policies you have developed such as for managing children's behaviour
- certificates of training attended and qualifications gained.

Some childminders also include letters that parents have written in the past about their childminding service and business.

Learning Outcome Activity 11 (ICP)

Compiling an information file

There is no reason why you should not start to build up your own file, even though you may be a new childminder and just starting off in your business.

- Start to collect together information that you will include in your information file.
- Think about how you are going to present it. Will you use an A4 file? Will you use plastic wallets to protect important documents?

Preparing yourself

As well as having to cope with parents feeling anxious and perhaps guilty about leaving their child, you will feel certain emotions yourself. You naturally will be concerned about the other children that you care for, and your own children if you have any. You will need to think about how a new child could affect them. You may worry about what strangers will think about you and your home. You may worry that you will not like the new child.

All of these worries are perfectly normal, but being able to recognise your own concerns and do something about them will in the end make you more professional and more able to offer a high quality childminding service. You should remember that you can learn from parents. Not every parent will bring his or her children up in the same way as you, if you have any. You must respect each parent as an individual and recognise that although their ways could be different from yours, they are equally acceptable and valid. Be open to new ideas and different ways of doing things.

Think about the sort of questions that you will need to ask the parents about their child. Write down your questions so that you will not forget anything important. Write down the parents' answers as well, which will help to stop any misunderstandings.

Think about how you will introduce the new child to the other children that you care for and also to the other people that live in your house. Don't forget to introduce the parents too. Make all of your introductions clearly, don't rush your words, and take your time. Allow the child time to hear the name of the person being introduced, to think about it, and possibly repeat it before moving on to the next person. Be consistent in your introductions, for example don't ask one child to say 'Hello', another one to say 'Hi', and then have your partner say 'Good morning'.

Preparing for the separation from parents

The parents must return the registrations form to you before you start to care for the child. From this you can find out as much as possible about the child before they are left with you. For example, you will find out if they have allergies or a medical condition, which will enable you to know what to do in an emergency. You will also have to find out who may or may not collect the children and who may or may not have contact with them.

Practical ways to help settle a child into your home

- If possible parents should be encouraged to stay with their child for a while, especially during the first week, but this obviously depends on the parents' work commitments.

- As both the child and the parents become more confident and reassured, the length of time that a parent stays can be gradually shortened.

- If parents cannot stay with their child, don't let them just drop the child off and go, especially at the beginning. Suggest that for the first few days they can bring their child a little earlier so that they can come into your home and help to settle the child.

- Once parents decide that they are going, make sure that the goodbyes are not long drawn-out affairs, as these can be distressing for everyone concerned.

- Encourage the parents to develop a routine for saying goodbye and ensure that they stick to it.

- Parents should not leave suddenly when the child is not looking as this can lead to insecurity and distrust in the child. Children tend to be more clingy and insecure when parents disappear suddenly.

- Once the parent has gone you should try to give the child as much attention as possible. You may need to adjust your routine to allow you to spend more time with the new child.

- It is a very good idea to give the child an activity to do immediately after their parent has left. This should be something that they would do at home and are familiar with. Any activity that you offer should be fairly easy and straightforward and one that does not involve too much concentration

- Some childminders find it very useful if a child brings with them a special toy from home that both of you can play with during this time.

- Don't force them to play or join in play, let the child set the pace at the start.

- A child that is distressed might need cuddles, or their comforter at this time. Remember that some children only like close contact with their mother and you should always take your cues from the child.

Learning Outcome Activity 12 (ICP)

Helping a child settle

You have been asked to care for a boy, Josh, who is eighteen months old, as his mother is returning to work full-time. At the first meeting the mother makes it very clear that she cannot stay with Josh at all during the first week he is with you. Josh's mother takes the view that she is paying you to look after her child and that it does not need two of you to care for Josh. At the first meeting Josh seemed to be very clingy and you are worried that he could be very upset when his mother leaves.

1 How could you help Josh's mother to understand about the benefits of spending time to settle him?
2 What sort of compromise might you suggest to her?

Practical ways to settle a baby into your home

In many ways it is easier to settle a young baby than an older child. However you still need to plan carefully. Many of the keys to good practice for older children apply to babies.

GOOD PRACTICE *Settling a baby into your home*

- The first visit is always very important. Babies learn about the world through their senses and so they will build a mental picture of you and your home through the smells, sounds and shapes they experience. During the first visit they will be bombarded by new smells, sights and sounds; the next time these will not be so new.
- The first visit is the time to ask questions about the baby, such as the baby's feeding pattern, the way they sleep, what types of nappies are used, the comfort objects they have.
- It is also very important that you and the parent care for a small baby together at the beginning. This helps the baby to get used to being handled by different people. It also reassures the mother that you are capable of caring for her baby. If the baby is being breast-fed it will give the mother time to adjust, perhaps by expressing milk for you to store and give to the baby, or to wean the baby on to a bottle and formula milk.

GOOD PRACTICE *Settling a baby into your home (continued)*

- You will have to adjust your routine to cater for both the mother and new baby and the needs of the other children that you care for.
- When a baby is about eight months old, he or she will have become aware of strangers and may start to miss her mother or another familiar adult. This can make the baby feel unsure and upset about being left by the mother. You may need to prepare the parents that their baby may be distressed at first at being left, and so you should be very reassuring to both the parents and the baby. You should also remember that parents are likely to miss their baby very much and they may need a lot of reassurance.

Comforters

During the first visit you should ask the parents if their child or baby has a comforter. In particuar, ask when the child receives the comforter and if it has a special name. Make a note of the answers so that you will not forget. Unless you write down the name of a comforter you may not be able to remember it, especially when the child is asking for it and getting upset because you don't understand.

When using the comforter keep to the routine the parents have already established with the child or baby. Don't try to change this use, even if you don't agree with it. A comforter can offer a baby or child security, a link between home and this strange place. If you have very good reasons for wanting to change how often the child has the comforter, discuss it with the parents after a few weeks.

Remember that when the child is not using the comforter it should be kept away from other children. Some children use a blanket or an item of clothing as a comforter, or a favourite toy, and will get very distressed if another child gets hold of it. The way you treat the comforter is very much a reflection of your attitude to the child, and they will pick up on this very quickly. If the comforter is an object that requires sterilising, follow the same routine as you would for keeping other things clean and germ-free.

Saying goodbye

As mentioned earlier, it is not a good idea for a parent to suddenly disappear from your home when their child is not looking. The child will not understand where their parent has gone and this can cause distress. This can result in children becoming clingier to their parents when they arrive, as they don't trust them not to suddenly disappear. A clinging child can be distressing for both the parent and the child. In these circumstances settling a child can be hard work and often distressing for you. In the same way, if a child has fallen asleep on the way to your house and is still asleep when the parent leaves, he or she could be hard work to settle when awake, especially in the early weeks of their care.

Why is it important for parent and child to wave goodbye?

It is good practice to encourage the parents to develop a routine for saying goodbye to their children. This is something you should raise at the first meeting! Parents should work out their own special routine of saying goodbye. Encourage the parent to make their goodbyes quite short and to say the same thing each time they leave. By doing this the child will begin to understand what to expect and what is going to happen next. They will then settle into your care better, and will feel secure and safe. If children are showing signs of being distressed at being separated from their parent, some childminders suggest that the parent leaves a small personal item, such as a scarf 'accidentally on purpose' when they leave the child. It is hoped that by doing this the child will understand that the parent will come back to collect the item and the child.

Long drawn-out goodbyes can be stressful for everyone. They take up more time than necessary, and if a child is already unsure about their parent going, delaying the actual parting will not help. Parents should remember to give their child a KISS!

Keep It Short and Simple (or Sweet) – KISS

A suggested routine for settling a baby and saying godbye could be something like this:
- Parent and child arrives at your house.
- You greet both child and parent.
- They both come in.
- Parent removes child's outdoor clothing.
- If appropriate, both you and the parent take the child through to the room that they will be in.
- Parent says that they are going now and that they will come back at lunch-time or tea-time, or at another agreed time in the day.
- Parent and child say goodbye in their own special way.

- You pick up the child or hold their hand, or whatever is appropriate.
- Go with parent to the door.
- Child and parent wave goodbye.
- Close door and immediately start to occupy the child with an activity.

CHECK YOUR KNOWLEDGE

1 What would you do if the parents do not want to visit you and seem to be happy with a telephone conversation?

2 Make a list of all the questions that you would expect a parent to ask you at a first meeting.

3 Why should you plan a familiar activity for the child just after the parent has left?

4 Can it be easier to settle a baby of three months or a child of two-and-a-half years? Why?

5 Why do you and the parents need to agree a definite time for the first visit?

6 How would you explain to parents the reasons for establishing a routine for saying goodbye?

7 How can comforters help a child settle?

CHAPTER 3

Providing play and other activities for children in a home-based setting

What is play?

To **play** can mean amusing yourself, having fun either on your own or with others, and sometimes 'messing about'. You can probably think of other meanings. Some educationalists and theorists think it is one of the most complicated ideas to try to understand. Fredrick Froebel (1782–1852) set up a kindergarten in Germany where he was able to test his ideas about play. He believed in outdoor and indoor play and is recognised as inventing finger play and many songs and rhymes. Many of Froebel's ideas still influence modern day thinking about play.

Play is one of the most important ways that children learn. Some people think that children play naturally, but in fact children learn how to play. Children will learn from their parents, from you, from older children and from doing the same things over and over again. We all like to play, whatever our age. Everyone should be able to play, in some shape or form, regardless of their age or whether they have an additional need. Play should be fun and can be relaxing as well as stimulating. It is a very important part of children's lives. When children play they are in control, they can put right their mistakes and can experiment and explore.

How a childminder can help children play

To help children get as much as possible from play you must understand how valuable play can be. You will need to know how to plan and organise play opportunities for all children, and you can get involved with those activities. As a childminder you should give all of the children in your care activities that they will enjoy, that will stimulate them and help them to learn. You will have to plan into your routines opportunities and time to play and sometimes things to play with and the space to play. You will have to learn when to become involved in the children's play and when to step back and let them get on with it.

Remember children need:

Figure 3.1 *What children need for play*

In 1979 the United Nations produced the 'Declaration of the Rights of the Child'. In this important document Principle 7 states:

'The child shall have full opportunity for play and recreation, which should be directed to the same purposes as education; society and the public authorities shall endeavour to promote the enjoyment of this right.'

Children have a right to play and you as a professional childminder have a duty to support and encourage that right.

Why do children play?

All children play in some way whatever their age. A baby plays with 'toys' such as her own fingers and toes. Some experts say that a baby's first toy is her mother's breast as she becomes familiar with the smell of the mother's skin, learns to find the nipple, suck and get satisfaction as she is fed. When children play they behave in different ways. Sometimes their play will be noisy and energetic; sometimes it will be quiet and thoughtful. Sometimes children will describe what they are doing and discuss and plan how to play and what to do next.

Playing with a baby gym on the floor will help a baby learn to control their arm muscles so that they can pat at the objects hanging down. This is a new skill. A child playing with a bat and ball will learn how to co-ordinate their movements and hit the ball. This can be developed so that they can play a sport, get greater control of their movements and become more skilful.

Skills can be developed in many different ways when a child is playing; for example if a baby has learnt how to control the muscles of the arm to pat a dangling toy, they can extend that skill so that they can grasp and hold the toy. A child who has

Figure 3.2 *Reasons why babies and children need to play. Children can do all of this when they are playing*

learnt how to fit two construction bricks together can use that skill to build a bigger model.

If you learnt to drive, can you remember how many times you practised reversing round a corner before you could do it without touching the kerb? In the same way children need to do things over and over again before they are really capable. This practising of skills is part of play.

Children need to learn about their world and the people in it. They need to understand how they fit into society and the roles of other people. Children can do this through role-play, dressing up and pretending to be somewhere or somebody else.

Exploring is part of learning. Children can find out a great deal from playing in water, in sand, feeling different materials, helping you cook and looking at changes and differences. They can do all of this from play activities that you can provide.

Stages of play

Play develops as children develop. From being a baby playing on her own, a child will develop to play alongside another child or an adult, watching and perhaps copying them but not getting involved. As the child develops and learns he or she will want to play with other children or adults and so will learn to share and co-operate; later the child will start to plan games and start to use rules. This development in play is usually known as '**the stages of social play**'. These are four stages of play:

The four stages of play

1 **Solitary play** – from a tiny baby to about two years old

At this stage children play on their own. They need to have an adult nearby for encouragement and will happily play games with an adult, such as finger rhymes and peek-a-boo.

2 **Parallel play** – from about two to three years old

Children become more aware of each other and will play alongside another child. At this stage the children do not play together and are often unwilling to share their toys.

3 **Associative play** – from about three years and above

At about this time many children start at pre-school groups or nursery. Children will watch each other very carefully. They copy each other when playing, but do not always play together.

4 **Co-operative play** – from about three years and above

By the time children are three years old, they enjoy the company of other children. They are willing to share their toys and want to play together. Children at this age get a great deal of satisfaction from sharing and co-operating. They talk about their play and share ideas.

Learning Outcome Activity 13 (ICP)

The four stages of play

Think about four of the activities that you plan to do with the children in your care.

Write down which stages of play the activities will encourage; for example play with a construction set could be solitary, parallel, associative and co-operative play, whereas two children cooking with you will be playing in a co-operative way.

Types of play

Play can be inside your home or outside in the garden or away from your house. Play can be organised by children, adults or a combination of both. Sometimes children need lots of toys and 'props' to play with; sometimes they don't need anything other than themselves. Watch a baby play with her toes! How many times have you given a child a toy in a box or package to play with and they have spent more time playing with the packaging than with the toy?

There are two main types of play that children in your care will be involved in. These are:

1 **Spontaneous or free play** – when children play in an 'unplanned' way. They decide what to do, how to play and what things, if anything, they will use. It is up to you to provide the space, time and things for the children to play with.

2 **Structured play** – when play is planned by you. You decide what the children will do, and you work alongside the children. This type of play happens mostly when you want to develop a particular skill, such as learning the names of colours. You might collect a few red objects and encourage the child to find more red things around the room.

As well as spontaneous and structured types of play, there are also different categories of play.

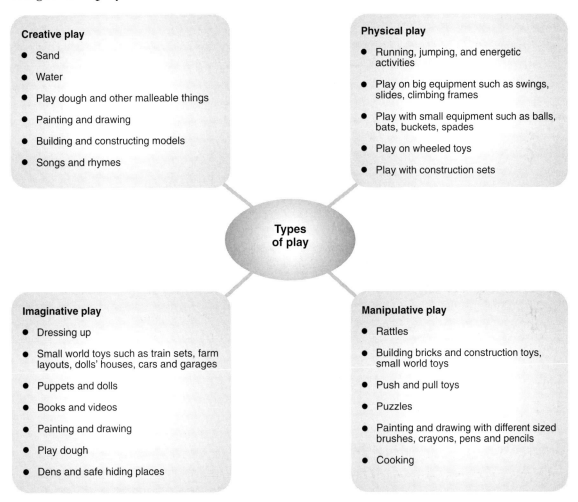

Creative play

- Sand
- Water
- Play dough and other malleable things
- Painting and drawing
- Building and constructing models
- Songs and rhymes

Physical play

- Running, jumping, and energetic activities
- Play on big equipment such as swings, slides, climbing frames
- Play with small equipment such as balls, bats, buckets, spades
- Play on wheeled toys
- Play with construction sets

Types of play

Imaginative play

- Dressing up
- Small world toys such as train sets, farm layouts, dolls' houses, cars and garages
- Puppets and dolls
- Books and videos
- Painting and drawing
- Play dough
- Dens and safe hiding places

Manipulative play

- Rattles
- Building bricks and construction toys, small world toys
- Push and pull toys
- Puzzles
- Painting and drawing with different sized brushes, crayons, pens and pencils
- Cooking

Figure 3.3 *These are the types of play that children get involved in*

CASE STUDY

Dan is a registered childminder who, working with his wife, cares for Matt, aged three-and-a-half, and Amy who is eleven months. They also care for three other children before and after school. Matt's favourite activity is playing with Duplo. Dan often puts the Duplo out on the floor and lets Matt and Amy play spontaneously. Amy's play is mostly manipulative. She picks up the pieces and handles them, passing them between her hands. She feels the pieces with her fingers, hands and tongue. She is aware of Matt but makes no attempt to interact with him. Matt likes to build models on his own and will often make up stories about his models. He likes to show Dan his creations and sometimes asks Dan to help him make something more complicated. Most of the time, Dan sits alongside the children to make sure that Amy plays safely with the Duplo and sometimes to pass pieces to Matt. Sometimes Dan can extend Matt's play by asking questions about what he is doing. Often Dan and Matt will play together, sharing ideas and having fun.

- Dan has given the children space, time and things to play with.
- He is providing opportunities for spontaneous play.
- Duplo is allowing the children to play creatively as they explore the shape and size of the pieces and also as Matt creates models. Putting the pieces together helps Matt develop his hand and eye co-ordination, which is part of physical play.

Write down how Dan is encouraging manipulative and creative play with Amy and Matt.

How play helps a child to develop

Play helps the all round development of children. Children develop at different times, and at different ages. All children are unique and you should not compare the development of one child at a certain age with that of another child at the same age. Children's development can be affected by many different things, such as premature birth, brothers and sisters, diet and characteristics that they may have inherited from their parents, like body size. Many parents become concerned because their baby is not sitting up at the same age as their friend's baby. This is perfectly normal and you should reassure the parents that there is nothing wrong with their baby. However if you do think that there could be a problem, tactfully suggest that the parents make an appointment with their health visitor.

Play and the areas of development

Children's development can be broken down into five main areas. These are shown in the chart opposite.

Area of development	Examples of what can be developed through play
Physical	height, weight, sight, hearing, taste, touch, smell, muscle control, movement and co-ordination of hands, eyes and feet
Intellectual	memory, attention span, concentration, the way children think about things, ideas about numbers and the world around them
Language	ways to communicate, including talking, body language and gestures, facial expressions, reading, writing, signing
Emotional	feelings and emotions, how to build relationships, independence, confidence, feeling secure
Social	learning to share, co-operate, take turns, building relationships and friendships, understanding the needs of others

Examples of how play can help physical development

Playing with sand, water, clay or even mud will help a child understand about the world around them, and using spades to dig and buckets or pots to fill will help them develop physical skills such as control and co-ordination. Playing with puzzles and jigsaws will help children develop their fingers, grasp and dexterity. This area of physical development is often called **fine motor skills**. Playing outside in the garden on bikes, climbing, running and jumping will help a child develop their bodies and muscles. This area is called **gross motor skills** development. Being outside in the fresh air will help children stay healthy, another important part of physical development.

Examples of how play can help intellectual development

Children will often play in a pretend or make-believe way, they will perhaps pretend to be someone else, or go under the table and be in an imaginary world of a cave or a hidden place. Playing like this helps children become more imaginative and creative, and so develops their intellectual skills. Counting with you, talking about colours and what they can see around them, looking at a leaf or a ladybird are all ways that you can help a child to develop intellectually.

Examples of how play can help language development

Children often talk or sing to themselves when playing alone, this is a good time for them to try out sounds and words that they have heard. Reading books together is a very good way for a child to learn new words and understand how books work. Watching a television programme or video together and then talking about what has happened will help a child use language in different ways as they ask questions, explain why something has happened or describe an event or character.

Examples of how play can help social development

Playing with other children helps a child learn social skills such as how to share, take turns and co-operate. Playing finger rhymes with a baby helps them begin to understand how to take turns. Playing board games helps older children understand not only how to take turns but also learn about rules and fair play.

Examples of how play can help emotional development

Copying what adults do whilst playing, such as 'cooking dinner', helps children understand the world of adults and so helps their emotional development. Playing in this way will also help children begin to learn about the needs of others. If you mind a child who has an additional need, the other children will learn through playing with him or her how to be more tolerant and understanding. Listening to stories about other people feeling different emotions, such as happy or sad, will help children understand their own feelings.

You should never underestimate the '**power of play'**.

Learning Outcome Activity 14 (ICP)

Helping children to develop through play

1 Take a few moments to carefully watch a child playing. The age of the child does not matter.

Ask yourself:

- What is the main area of development that this play activity is encouraging?
- If I became involved could I encourage more development and if so how and what?

2
- Think of a play activity that you could do to help a child of three to learn to count.
- Think of a play activity that you could do to help a five-year-old improve their hand and eye co-ordination.

Write down your answers.

You will find that some books that you read will divide children's development into different areas, but I think that the five areas above are easy to remember. Chapter 5 looks at children's development and learning in much more detail.

You should remember that sometimes a child will play in a way that you would have expected of a younger child, such as just watching other children playing rather than joining in as they usually do. There are lots of reasons for this, such as the child might not feel well, it could be a new group of children and the child is unsure or shy, it could be a new game that is being played and again the child might lack confidence. Take your cues from the child and don't try to force them to play in a way that they are not happy about. Remember play should be fun.

Some other ways that play can help a child to develop

- **Confidence**. Play should help a child to become confident. Children develop confidence if they succeed in what they are doing and make their own choices about what they do. Activities that you plan should help children become confident whatever their age and so you must make sure that the children can actually do the things that you or they plan or be able to achieve them with a little help from you.

- **Co-ordination**. If you watch a young child playing with a construction set, you will see how they have to line up the pieces to successfully join them up; this is called co-ordination and is a very important skill that children learn. Co-ordination is needed for almost everything we do that involves our hands and feet, such as holding a cup and drinking, getting food into your mouth, playing football. Many simple and straightforward play activities involve co-ordination such as running round the garden.

- **Competence**. When you plan activities for children you want them to learn and, hopefully, become better at doing things. Getting more skills and becoming more capable is called competence. It does not necessarily mean getting cleverer, but getting more able to do something. This could be holding a rattle for longer, being able to feed themselves, going to the toilet on their own and sorting out their clothes.

- **Being creative**. When a child is given the chance to play in a creative way, they learn how to make connections between things that they find out and so gain more understanding. Babies and young children use their senses of sight, smell, touch, hearing and taste to help them play and learn in a creative way. Older children build on this learning and so it is very important that you provide activities that will help to extend a child's imagination and creativity.

- **Communication**. Play helps children to communicate with each other, often in a non-threatening way. They do not always have to talk, but can use body language, facial expressions, gestures and signs to let other children and adults know what they want to do. Watch children dressing up and see how they communicate with each other. Children playing together will talk to each other to organise and plan their play. A baby can often wave bye-bye, or shake their head, earlier than they can say the words.

- **Concentration**. We all need to concentrate at some time. It might be listening carefully to a telephone message from a parent changing a pick-up time, to helping a child with a tricky piece of homework. To be able to concentrate is very important and there are many play activities that you can organise that will help the children in your care to develop concentration.

- **Co-operation**. Play helps children to learn how to take turns, to share and to co-operate with each other and with adults. Co-operation is an important social skill. A child should be encouraged to willingly help another child, or adult, and understand why they should.

How does reading together help a child to develop?

CASE STUDY

Angi is caring for two children, a toddler, Jessie, who is twenty-one months, and a four-year-old who goes to the local nursery each morning. Jessie's parents are concerned that she doesn't seem to being saying very much and asked Angi if she could spend some time encouraging Jessie to talk. Angi knew that Jessie liked teddies and this was one of the few words that she said clearly.

Over several mornings, when the other child was at nursery school, Angi and Jessie went to the local library to find several picture books about teddy bears. Angi made sure that at some point during the morning she sat down with Jessie and looked at the books together. To begin with Angi did most of the talking about the pictures, but after a few days Jessie began to add words that she had heard Angi say. Jessie began to say things like, 'Where's Teddy gone?', and try to describe what the teddies in the pictures were doing. Angi listened carefully to what Jessie said and made sure that she gave Jessie enough time to say what she wanted. If Jessie just said one or two words, Angi repeated the words but added some more and so helped Jessie learn more.

Angi told the parents about the books and they took one book home with Jessie each night and used it as a bedtime story. They told Angi that Jessie really enjoyed these story times and that she was saying a lot more.

This is a good example of how a simple everyday play activity, like reading a book together, can help a child to communicate.

Play activities in your home

Play is all about encouraging the children that you care for to develop and learn in every way possible. It is not necessary to buy expensive toys and play equipment to encourage development. There are many things around your home and routine things that you do that will help children of all ages develop through play. You must remember that whatever you give the children to play with must be safe and not be likely to harm them in any way.

Figure 3.4 *These kinds of play activities a child can do in the home will help their development*

All of the above activities are things that you probably do every day in your home; the list could be extended. I have only included the main ones. They are also excellent play activities and opportunities for development for children.

Cooking with you helps children to understand the sequence of how things happen. It helps them learn to count, weigh and measure. Older children will learn how things change when they are cooked – the beginnings of science. Younger children will learn how to use different utensils and tools and so become more skilful. You and the children will talk about what you are doing and so the children will develop their language skills. Obviously, cooking with children will take longer than if you were doing it by yourself; but think about what they are learning and how worthwhile the extra time is. Remember, play is about helping children develop and learn. It can be structured – that is, led by you – or spontaneous – that is led by the child.

Preparing food, like cooking, can be a play activity. Children can count the number of vegetables needed to feed everyone at dinner time. They can talk about the different vegetables and compare and match colour textures and sizes. Younger children will learn through touching, smelling, feeling and tasting different foods. Both cooking and preparing food are good opportunities to help children learn about the needs of others; you could talk to older children about different diets, why some people do not eat certain foods, allergies and likes and dislikes of food. There are opportunities for both spontaneous and structured play when cooking

Setting the table is a good way to help children to count and match. You could ask questions like, 'Have we enough spoons for everyone?' or 'Can you put the red mugs on everyone's place mat?' If you occasionally 'make a mistake', such as giving a child one spoon too many to put out, children will find your silly mistakes fun and so help make the activity more amusing. This is probably going to be a more structured play activity.

Getting dressed can be a game for all children. Older children can decide what to wear and so learn how to make choices and decisions. Babies and young children will learn the names of different parts of the body if you give a 'running commentary' as you dress them. You can say things like, 'Put your arm in here' or 'Let's just pop this over your head'. Allowing children to get themselves dressed helps them to develop self-help skills such as learning how to do different fastenings on clothes. There are opportunities for both structured and spontaneous play when getting dressed, although spontaneous play will make the activity much longer, especially if the child decides halfway through that they are going to be a monster with a green head and red claws, in other words a green top on their head and red socks on their hands!

Helping to tidy up can become a chore and not much fun. However try making the activity into a challenge – such as who can do it quickest, or how many children will it take to put the Lego away in the box. Tidying things away helps children to sort and match. Tidying a room will also provide opportunities for children to copy what you do and so learn from you. You could all have a duster or cloth to wipe the furniture and sing as you do it!

Washing hands and face is much more fun if you sing a rhyme as you do it. If a rhyme does not immediately spring to mind, then make one up, play around with words and make silly endings such as 'washy, washy, cleany cleany'. Let children help you sort out clothes before putting them in the washing machine or hanging them up to dry. Ask the children questions to encourage them to match up socks, or different coloured clothes. Make the matching and sorting into a game.

Making shopping lists together will help children learn about writing for different reasons. It will help their memory skills and make them feel you value their views and opinions about what to buy. Shopping lists do not have to be written in words. Children can cut out pictures from magazines to make a different kind of list, or draw pictures themselves.

Putting shopping away together will help children to sort, count and recognise different shapes and colours. Giving young children simple instructions, such as 'Put the carrots in the basket' or 'Put the biscuits on the table', will help them feel important and help them develop their memories. Talking to the children about differences in weight, for example, between a big packet of cereal and a tin of baked beans, will help them to develop an understanding of weights and sizes.

All the play activities above can be fun and enjoyable for all children. None of them need special or expensive equipment, but they are still play activities. Some childminders think that helping to sort clothes before putting them in the washing machine could be unhygienic, but it is a matter for discussion and also depends on what you are planning to wash. It is up to you to make the play activities experiences from which the children can learn and develop.

Learning Outcome Activity 15 (ICP, DCP)

The toys in your home

Have look round your home and rooms where the children play and write a list of how many things that you have already got that are normal, everyday items and are safe to use as 'toys'.

I expect you have more than you first thought.

Play activities outside your home

The play activities that can be found outside your home are extensive, depending on where you live. The spider chart below shows some of the most common ones.

Figure 3.5 *There are various activities that you can do outside your home that will help children develop*

When the weather is fine, most play activities can take place outside. As well as being able to run about and 'let off steam', playing outside can help children develop and learn in many ways. Playing outside allows children to use up energy, helps stimulate the appetite, circulation and digestion, helps them to sleep and generally makes them more able to fight off infection. In other words, being outside is good.

Travelling by bus or train can be a learning and play experience for children. It can give them a different perspective of the world; for example sitting on the top desk of a bus looking down on people and cars will let children see different things. For example, they may notice that some police cars have numbers on the roof.

If you are driving with children in the car, you must make sure that any games being played do not distract you. Cassette tapes and CDs can be used to entertain children in a car, leaving you free to concentrate on driving safely.

Outside play activities in your garden

In Chapter 1 we looked at making your garden safe for children to play in. The children's safety must always be your first thought. Sandpits can provide lots of good play opportunities, but do remember to cover the sand when it is not in use. You need not buy climbing frames and other outdoor play equipment. However, they can be very beneficial if you can afford them. Children will get lots of fun and exercise from running around outside. Think of your garden as another room in your house; there isn't really any activity that you do inside that you could not do outside.

Visits to friends

You should make sure that your childminding takes you and the children beyond the home. Some childminders will get together in each other's homes, or at a community centre or any other safe venue. These can be very useful occasions, when you can make new friends, get new ideas, share worries and concerns without breaking confidentiality. Find out whether there is a childminding group in your area that organises 'drop in' sessions. NCMA can give you this information.

The children will also make new friends, play with different people and with different things. They will learn how to get along with different people and learn new games to play. These times can benefit everyone.

Going for walks and trips to parks and sports centres

The local park will provide many opportunities for children to play and learn. The large open space enables children to run about, and there are many other chances for children to play. For example, you could organise a hunt in the park for different shaped leaves, or different coloured flowers; children could draw their favourite thing in the park; or they could learn how to care for living things by watching those who work in the park.

You might not however have a park near your home. In that case, walking along the street can provide good play opportunities. Play 'I-spy' as you walk along; make up word and number games for older children using the registration numbers of cars that pass by – for example, see who can add up the numbers the fastest, who can make a word from the letters or who can suggest another word that begins with the same first letter.

Taking and collecting other children from school

This can be an opportunity for children to learn from each other and from you about road safety. Children can be given the responsibility for stopping, looking and listening, then deciding if it is safe to cross over the road. Traffic lights can help children learn colours and sequencing. As well as playing 'I-spy' and other games, younger children can look for different coloured doors, shapes of signs, or jump over cracks in the pavement.

Shopping

When toddlers throw very noisy temper tantrums in supermarkets, their parents or childminders may quietly vow that they will never take that child into a supermarket again! However there are some things that you and the children can do to make the experience better for everyone. Several large supermarket chains provide child-sized trolleys that children can push around and collect items from a specially made up shopping list. You can set older children challenges to find certain foodstuffs or products, or add up how much things cost. It is in no way intended that childminders with the children that they are caring for, undertake a 'family-sized once-a-week' shop, but buying a few things for lunch, a picnic or a cooking session can be very good learning opportunities. Shopping in small local shops can also be fun as children can learn to ask for things themselves, learn social skills, how to handle money and find out more about the world around them.

Visits to health centres

Quite often you will need to take children to health centres if they are feeling unwell or need to have routine health checks or injections. If the child is unwell they probably will not want to play games, but you could share a story together whilst you wait.

Don't forget that before you take children outside of your home, you should have written permission from the parents (see Chapter 1). Remember, don't get so carried away by playing games that you risk the safety of the children.

Learning Outcome Activity 16 (ICP, DCP)

Places to visit outside the home

1   Complete this questionnaire for three different places that you visit with the children.

Name of place	Reason for going there	How to get there

2   Choose the place that you visit most often and list the opportunities for play. You might find it helpful to list these using the following areas of development.

Places most visited

....
....
....

Physical

....
....
....

Intellectual

....
....
....

Language

....
....
....

Emotional

....
....
....

Social

....
....
....

Play activities for babies

Babies need to be given time, space and things to play with in the same way as older children. Babies need to play with the same things over and over again so that they can learn new skills. This type of play is called **mastery play** as the babies 'master' the skills. Babies will watch other children whilst they are playing, but usually play on their own. This is **solitary play**.

Babies learn through their senses. They like to play with things that stimulate their sight, things that they can touch, feel, smell, and things that make a noise. Things that make a noise, such as rattles, don't have to be bought. Provided you give a baby a non-toxic, lightweight washable container that has no sharp edges, has a secure lid or top and is too big to swallow, you can make a rattle. I have seen many babies playing very contentedly with a screw top plastic container, into which the childminder had put some large pieces of uncooked pasta.

A baby will take many toys and playthings to his or her mouth to feel the shape and texture. Again you must make sure that anything that you give the baby is safe. Bright coloured objects will attract a baby's attention, which is why many toys that you buy are often bright coloured. However not everything that a baby plays with has to be bright. The rattle I described earlier wasn't bright, a large wooden cooking spoon is rather dull, but an interesting shape, and a baby's own fingers and toes will be very interesting to them.

Making a treasure basket

The educationalist Elinor Goldschmied spent a lot of time studying and watching babies and toddlers play. She developed the idea of a treasure basket to give babies and toddlers play experiences that would stimulate all their senses. The idea is that a baby is offered a basket or container filled with natural things or items made from natural materials. Each item in the treasure basket is chosen because it may have an interesting shape, or texture. The items should be things that are around the house and that babies don't normally come into contact with. There are usually about twenty items in the treasure basket.

It is very important that all the things can be kept clean, and are not dangerous, such as having sharp edges or being small enough to be swallowed or put in ears and noses. The baby needs to be put in a safe and comfortable position, often on the floor. They do not have to be able to sit up unaided, but can be propped up with cushions or pillows so that they do not topple over. You sit a little distance away, but near enough to be able to watch. You do not need to talk to the baby, as this will distract them from playing and exploring.

Things that you could put into a treasure basket:

a baby mirror	an orange	a fir cone
a bunch of keys	a wooden spoon	a range of brushes
a wooden clothes peg	a length of chain	a wooden cotton reel
wooden bricks	clean vegetables	pebbles
closed tin with rice or pasta inside	wooden shapes	a firmly secured ball of wool
a pumice stone	bells	corks
metal lids of different sizes	a lemon	wooden serviette rings

Learning Outcome Activity 17 (ICP, DCP)

Making a treasure basket

Look at the list of things to put into a treasure basket.

Sort the list into objects that will stimulate the five senses:

Sight	Smell	Hearing	Taste	Touch

Music, songs and rhymes

From a very young age babies will respond to sound, provided that their hearing is not impaired. Musical mobiles, wind chimes and the sound of your voice are good ways to stimulate a baby's hearing. Singing to a baby comes naturally to most people. You don't have to be a wonderful singer and you will always get a positive response, such as a smile or giggle!

Playing songs and action rhymes will help a baby develop in many ways.

- Playing with fingers and toes helps to develop their hand, foot and eye co-ordination, bouncing up and down will help strengthen muscles, which are part of physical development.

- As they become more familiar with the rhymes they will learn what is going to happen next and the different sounds, which are part of intellectual and language development.
- Playing together is fun, which will help their social and emotional development.

Learning Outcome Activity 18 (ICP, DCP)

Songs and rhymes for play

Make a list of all the songs and action rhymes that you could play with a baby.

Share this list with other course members, other childminders and friends.

See if you can learn some new ones.

Play activities for toddlers

Toddlers are obviously more mobile that babies. They want to explore and investigate. They do not have a long concentration span and need lots of different play opportunities. Toddlers learn through trial and error, such as trying to put things into boxes or containers to see what will happen. Toddlers can become very frustrated and scream with rage, but it should be easy to distract them by offering new toys or a play activity. Toddlers take more notice of other children and adults when they are playing, but still play in a solitary way. However they do like to play with adults at times, such as looking at books together, playing action rhymes and songs and 'helping' with daily activities such as picking up toys.

Toddlers like to play with push and pull toys. These can help them move more efficiently and also learn how things move and work. Toddlers can learn a lot from playing with simple construction toys. They can learn how to join things together and they will develop finger and hand control as well as hand and eye co-ordination. There are many toys that are designed to help hand and eye co-ordination, such as puzzles with lift in and out pieces, posting boxes, stacking toys and big chunky crayons. However in exactly the same way that you do not need to go to a lot of extra expense for babies, the same is true for toddlers.

Earlier in this chapter there were details of how to make a treasure basket for babies. This idea can be adapted for toddlers. You can collect empty boxes and cartons, such as large cereal boxes and cartons from the supermarket. Save and wash empty 1 litre plastic bottles that have had water or other drinks in them and empty large tins of instant coffee. At the same time put aside smaller boxes or tins that can be put inside the bigger ones. Using many of the items from the treasure basket, a toddler will happily play with all these things, fitting them together, putting things inside containers, making different sounds as they shake bottles and cartons.

Play in this way and play with the treasure basket is often referred to as **heuristic play**.

Play activities for school-age children

Many childminders look after school-aged children before and after school and during school holidays. These may be children you already know from having looked after them as babies and toddlers, or they could be the brothers and sisters of children that you are caring for. Recent government policies to encourage more parents to return to work will inevitably mean that there will be a greater need for this type of care. School-age children are more independent and will be influenced by lots of other things outside of your home and their own home. They do still need care and attention from you and you will need to make sure that you provide them with appropriate things to do and play with.

Before school

Children have a busy time at school and need to be as well prepared as possible. Before school can often be a busy time for you, as the parents and children start arriving at your home. Play activities should be simple and you should avoid activities that could tire a child or overexcite them. Older children may be asked to help with younger ones, and whilst it could be argued that this will help their social development, some children would not describe it as 'play'.

Suggested activities

- Preparing their pack lunch – the child can help and play by using cutters to make different shaped sandwiches, for example.
- A box of toys and activities including books of short stories, drawing materials and paper, hand-held electronic games, playing cards and more complex construction sets.
- 'Thinking games', for example:
  - Asking each other questions and not being allowed to answer 'yes' or 'no'. For older children this could be adapted to include words such as yesterday or tomorrow.
  - Children who can read and write could be given slips of paper with well-known advertising slogans or phrases, but with one or two important words missing which they have to supply.
  - 'I-spy', where you give an initial letter and the children name everything that they can see in a particular room or place beginning with that letter.

After school

Some children 'lose ground' a little bit, especially with social skills, when they first start school. Remember this when planning activities for these children. Many children come out of school excited by the day's activities and bursting to tell someone about them. This makes it important that you are on time when collecting a child from school. It is also important not to leave the child waiting around on their own, because of the dangers and because the child could lose confidence in you.

Suggested activities

A full school day can be very tiring for children and there will be times when they just want to be quiet and 'recover'. Activities that you plan for after school must consider the needs of the child.

- Many children will be hungry, so one of the first things is to give them a snack and a drink.
- If the child wants to talk, try to give them your undivided attention whilst they tell you about their day.
- If they need to be quiet, allow them to watch a short amount of television or read, or do some other quiet activity. Remember, it will also be towards the end of your working day and you might also be tired and not have quite as much patience as you would have at the start of the day.
- You may have agreed with the child's parents that he or she will start homework whilst with you. If this is the case you will need to make sure that the child has an appropriate place to work. Don't forget that you will need to tell the parents what their child has done.
- Thinking games that were started before school can be completed, or even new ones introduced, especially if you need to take children to after-school activities. Because school-aged children may not spend a lot of time with you during term-time does not mean that you do not have to plan play activities for them.

During school holidays

Many local authorities and sports centres organise holiday play schemes during school holidays. If children are booked into these, your responsibilities to them are the same as if they were at school. However some parents find these expensive, so they may ask you to care for their children. You will have to think about the play activities carefully as you could have children of different ages to consider. Some of the play activities you do with younger children can quite easily be extended for older children, for example, painting and art activities.

Suggested activities

- Try a 'keep-fit' session in a suitably open space or cleared room. This can involve all children regardless of their age.
- Draw round all of the children's hands and feet on paper and cut the drawings out. Let the children guess which ones belong to whom. Later the children can decorate the cutouts.
- Use an old roll of wallpaper for children to draw on. Older children can be encouraged to draw a story that develops along the roll of paper.
- Allow children to decorate plain biscuits with icing and cake decorations. Make it more interesting by sticking to a theme, such as animals, or seasons, or space monsters.
- Using old curtains, sheets and boxes, allow children to make dens, or tents, or hide-aways. Then help the children to prepare a picnic to eat inside their den.
- Special days out can be very exciting times during holidays. With careful planning these can be great times for the other children and you.
  - Visits to the local park can be turned into special occasions, especially if you arrange to meet up with groups of friends and children. You could organise a 'mini sports day' or treasure trail.
  - Trips into town centres do not have to be trips to the shops but can be to places of local interest. Look in you local paper to see if the museum, theatre or gallery are putting on special events for children. Make time to look at old buildings and perhaps get the children to draw them or you can photograph them to be copied later.

There are so many play activities that you can organise; what you do very much depends on you and the children in your care. Whatever you plan to do, you must make the children's safety your first priority at all times. Remember, if you go out on sunny days the children should be protected with hats and appropriate sun creams. You need to talk to children about 'stranger danger' and agree a meeting place, if they get separated. Don't forget to let the parents know of your plans and get their written permission to take the children out.

Learning Outcome Activity 19 (ICP, DCP)

Some activities with children

Make a note of short activities that you and the children could do together, such as sorting the washing or setting a table for a meal. These are ideal opportunities for learning and playing.

You could make a game of sorting washing by colour and 'accidentally on purpose' put a red sock in with whites, before washing of course!! Children love to point out your silly mistakes and as well as helping them recognise colours, doing something like this is fun and helps to build the children's self-confidence. Putting out on the table spoons, forks, beakers, mats and other items for a meal gives children the opportunity to count, sort and match. Again you can make it fun and so help the children learn through play.

Remember – one of the most valuable 'things' that children can play with is YOU.

Extending your play equipment

No one can expect you to have every toy, book and play thing for every situation. There will be times when you may only want to have a play thing for a short time and for a specific purpose. You may be caring for a child with a special need and so may need adapted toys. A child in your care could be going into hospital, so you could get storybooks about hospital visits and stays from your local library. You may want to have a dressing-up area of uniforms worn in hospitals and have play stethoscopes, and so on.

For situations like this, toy libraries are invaluable. They will lend toys and equipment to childminders for agreed lengths of time at a nominal charge. In most cases you have to collect and return the toys to the library. Toy libraries also have toys that are more suitable for disabled children. Ask your local Children's Information Service or Early Years Development and Childcare Partnership, or library if you have a toy library in your area. If you have difficulty contacting them, their addresses are at the end of this book.

As well as toy libraries, some childminders share toys and equipment informally between themselves. This is another good reason to meet up with other childminders in your area. Some groups of childminders have got together and successfully applied for funding from the National Lottery to set up their own toy libraries. Again the addresses should be available through your local library and at the end of the book.

Some local libraries give tickets to professional child carers so that they can borrow larger numbers of books. Ask in your local library for this service.

If you are caring for a child with special or additional needs, the relevant association can sometimes offer advice and support about play things. Some of the larger organisations have regional offices that run their own toy libraries. It is a good idea to ask the parents of the child if they are members of the association; if they are they could give you a contact name and number, which always makes it easier. Alternatively, at the end of the book are the names and addresses of some of the organisations for children with special or additional needs.

CHECK YOUR KNOWLEDGE

1 Why is play important?

2 How many types of play can you remember?

3 What could a child of two learn from playing with play dough?

4 Why is a big carton from a supermarket just as valuable as a play thing as a toy bought from a shop?

5 What play activities can you think of to do with a four-year-old whilst walking to nursery?

6 How can toy libraries help you provide a better service?

7 Is helping you shop in the supermarket an example of play? If so, why? If not, why not?

8 How can play help a child to communicate?

9 What play activities could you provide to help a three-year-old concentrate?

10 Is it true that playing with other childminders' children could help your children to develop emotionally? If so, why? If not, why not?

CHAPTER 4
Routines

This chapter is really about time management. In any business, time management is something that should be thought about very carefully. If not planned carefully, a lot of time can be wasted, or not used well. You are running a business. Admittedly it is unlikely you will employ large numbers of people; even so time management is very important if you are to be successful and enjoy what you are doing. One way for childminders to manage their time is to establish routines.

What are routines?

Routines are everyday events and activities that happen regularly in your home. Routines can be set up for daily, weekly or monthly activities and events. They are usually planned things, such as watching a favourite television programme, having a haircut, collecting children from school at the same time each day, or the activities around a child's care such as nappy changing and sterilising bottles. Daily routines often happen around the same time each day, such as getting meals ready and going to school.

Routines can provide consistency and continuity for the children and for yourself. Daily routines give a pattern and a structure to your working day, so that both you and the children know what is going to happen and what you are expected to do. They can help you cope better with a busy, hectic working day or week. Routines can also be to do with physical care, such as having meals at certain times, care of the teeth and teaching children about hygiene. A good routine, for example, when sterilising bottles, can help you make good use of your time to allow you more time to spend playing with the children. Routines can help children feel secure. Children who feel secure and have consistency and continuity in their lives, develop well, especially emotionally. An established, well thought out routine can help a new child settle into your home.

It is impossible to describe a childminder's routines in a general way as each routine will depend on the individual circumstances, such as the ages and number of children being looked after, the needs of the parents, your own family and personal likes and dislikes. You can probably think of other things that affect the way that you work and your routines.

A routine should be planned to help you. It should make your working day easier and, within reason, should be flexible. For example, you may have to decide whether it is more important to go outside to play with the children during a dry spell on a wet day or to prepare vegetables for the evening meal because that is what is on your routine at this time. Routines also need to change as children grow and develop (this will be looked at later in this chapter). Remember, whatever routine you plan, it must be right for you and the children in your care.

You should try not to change your routine too often. If you do regular activities, such as getting ready for a meal, a different way each time or with no set pattern, then the children may become confused. They may not be able to predict what will happen next and this, together with feeling confused, could affect their emotional development and possibly their behaviour. Obviously there will be times when you will change things for good reasons, and you need to be flexible enough to accommodate these cases. However there is a danger that if you change your routines too often, or make them too flexible, you could become overwhelmed by events and will lose control. Some routines should not be changed, such as sterilising bottles, as you could put the health of the children at risk. You should be managing your time and activities, not letting activities control you.

Establishing routines

Being a professional childminder is a busy and demanding job. If you can establish routines for daily, weekly and longer events, you will, hopefully, make your life run more smoothly. Routines also play a part in establishing good standards of care and hygiene, and teaching children to look after themselves, such as going to the toilet and helping them become independent. You should discuss your routines with parents.

Planning daily routines

A positive starting point for establishing a good routine for your working day is to think about your family.

Learning Outcome Activity 20 (ICP, DCP, ECP)

Working out a routine

- Make a list of all the daily routine events that involve you and your family. This can include getting your own children up and dressed, making packed lunches, loading the washing machine, going to after-school activities, and so on.
- Now put your list into a time order, starting with the first event of your day and ending with the last – usually bedtime!
- After you have done that, make a list, in time order, of the daily events for the children that you care for. This list will obviously start with the time that the children are either dropped off at your home or the first time you have contact with them, which in some cases can be at the end of the school day.

If you look carefully at your two lists and compare them, you should be able to see that there are some times in the day when several things seem to be happening at the same time. For example, near the end of the day can be a hectic time: parents are arriving to collect their child, your own child wants help with his homework, you are trying to get a meal prepared, another child is tired, cross and crying for your attention, and the telephone rings. At such times you must decide what are the most important things to deal with.

Having a routine and structure to your day can avoid many of the stresses at busy times. You could, for example, set time aside to help with homework or hear a child read; you don't have to prepare a meal at the same time as parents are due to arrive and you could have a telephone answering machine that you switch on at busy times. In the same way there may be times in the day when you are not as busy. If you know when these times are likely to be, you can do some of the jobs that you were trying to do at other times, such as start to prepare a meal.

In other words establish a routine that suits *you* and the children.

What can you do to avoid stress like this?

Learning Outcome Activity 21 (ICP, DCP, ECP)

Planning a daily routine

Earlier on in this chapter you made two lists, one for you and one involving the children.

1 Now try to put both lists together and make your own daily routine.
2 Think about how you can make time in your day for things like:
   • Arrivals and departures of children and parents
   • Taking children to and from school, playgroup, pre-school and other activities
   • Mealtimes
   • Sleep and rest periods
   • Children's play activities
   • Going out and about
   • Homework and early evening activities for older children
   • Television
   • Domestic jobs, like cleaning, doing the washing, shopping
   • Care needs such as sterilising bottles

You might find it easier to start by planning your routine following a chart like the one below.

Time	Event	Special things to remember
7:00 am	Get own two children up	Check things needed for school that day
8.00 am	Baby Matt arrives with Mum, Lin	Ask if he has slept well that night and if he has had breakfast
8:15 am	Amy and Tom arrive with Dad Partner leaves for work	Check if they need anything for school
8:20 am	Load washing machine and switch on	
8:30 am	Start to get ready for taking children to school	
8:40 am	Leave house for school	Take house keys and letters to post on way Check that TV is off

You should try to build into your daily routine a special time for each child – this is often called 'quality time', but don't you think 'special time' sounds more caring? Think about this when you are considering taking on more children. If you have children of your own, they need 'special time' as well, as do you and your partner.

Planning weekly routines

Routines are also important for weekly activities. You will need to think about things that the children do each week, such as the football club, Brownies or Cubs, dance lessons, and so on. These activities often take place in the late afternoon or early evening and could coincide with times that children could be picked up from your home. Weekly routines do need to be carefully planned, but may not need to be as tightly arranged as a daily routine. Again you might find it easier at the beginning of your childminding career to plan these events on a chart. Older children could help you make this chart and perhaps be responsible for marking the appropriate day or new events on it.

If you are studying or attending courses, meetings or training events, you will need to make sure that your routine includes time for you to work. You also need some social time, and perhaps going to the gym twice a week could be very important to you, so include it in your routine.

Planning monthly or longer routines

Think about the monthly activities and events that can be planned for, and even those that are longer, for example those during a term. Some people do a big supermarket shop once a month and that needs to fit in with other activities that are planned. You usually get plenty of notice of hospital and other medical appointments to enable you to plan around them. However, don't forget that these appointments often take much longer than you expect.

You will need time to maintain your business accounts; many childminders do these monthly, some do them weekly, it depends on the individual. You will need to set aside time in your routines to check and maintain the children's records.

Your planning will need to take into account yearly events. This could include the inspection of your childminding facilities. You will need time to prepare for this, no matter how well you are running your business. When you plan and organise family holidays, you will need to let parents know in plenty of time that you will not be able to care for their child at that time.

Making sure your routines fit in with the wishes of the parents

Parents usually know more about their child than anyone else. One of the main reasons parents choose a childminder is because they want their child to be cared for in a home that is as much as possible like their own. Parents will often hope that you follow the same care patterns as they have at home. It is very important that you make absolutely sure that your childminding routines fit in with what the parents' wish for their child. This does not just mean their rest and sleep times, and could include how much time for watching television and what programmes are suitable. You will need to think about the different cultural practices that may be involved with care of children. It may be that in order to meet the needs and wishes of several different families compromises will have to be discussed and agreed.

You may need to think about how you prepare food for some of the children. Some cultures have clear guidelines, and some quite strict rules, on handling and storing food and what meats are excluded. Do not assume everyone eats what you do or that your way is right or better. See the charts on pages 23–24 and 305.

If you care for African-Caribbean children you could find that their hair and skin is cared for in a different way to other children, so your routine must take this into consideration. You will need to establish a routine for skin and hair care in such cases. Some cultures have strong views about modesty and this could affect clothing worn by children when playing, or using the toilet. Again your routine must show that you have thought about these things.

Do not assume that because a family is part of a particular culture or group that they follow all the practices of that culture. The only way to make sure that your routines give the child the care that the parents want is for you to *ask* them. You may have to reach a compromise with the parents, especially if certain aspects of a routine could affect other children; if you do reach agreement in such cases, you must stick to it.

CASE STUDY

Paul and his wife are registered childminders. They have only one son, who is eighteen and still living at home; he is a full-time student at the local college. They live by the coast and often take the children to the beach, especially in the summer.

At the moment Paul and his wife care for four children, each day. The youngest child is three months old and the oldest one is eight. The others are four and seven years old. They have been asked to care for twin girls, aged eighteen months, whose parents are Trinidadian.

How might the routines need to be adjusted to care for the twins and can you give good reasons why the changes are needed?

Why routines need to change as children develop

If you start your childminding career caring for a baby and a toddler, you will probably have planned care routines for such activities as sterilising bottles, nappy changing and cleaning potties, plus routines that allow enough time for play and rest. As these children grow and develop you will find that bottles will be used less and less, and there will come a time when the routine for sterilising bottles will not be needed. It may be replaced by another care routine that is more suitable for the age and needs of the children. You may find that your daily routine will include one quiet time for rest and sleep. In the same way you may start off caring for a child who goes to a morning pre-school session, so that your daily routine will be planned to fit in with taking and collecting the child. There will come a time when the child will start at school, at which time your daily routine will have to change. Older children in your care may join after-school clubs as they become more independent and again this could affect your daily and weekly routines.

As children develop and grow they will want to 'help' you or do things for themselves. It is often quicker to put a child's coat on yourself, however letting the child do it for themself may help the child to learn how to do fastenings or zips and so learn independence. Allowing the child do things for themself will probably take longer, so you will have to adjust your routine for that. Again a child might want to help you prepare food or help find things in the supermarket. This is valuable learning experience for a child. However, it takes more time, and you will have to remember this when planning your day.

Learning Outcome Activity 22 (ICP, DCP, ECP)

Think about your own daily routine

List three things that are part of your routine today that will have changed by this time next year.

1 _____

2 _____

3 _____

Why will they have changed?

Routines for babies and toddlers

Looking after babies and toddlers is very rewarding. However there are many extra responsibilities for the childminder when looking after a baby or a toddler. Babies are totally dependent on their carers for everything, in this case YOU. They need lots of attention in every way to help them develop into healthy, happy children. Toddlers can be very demanding and you will need lots of patience.

Why is it important for childminders to establish routines for babies and toddlers?

When agreeing with parents to look after their baby you will need to think about many different things, such as:

- How will having a baby in the home affect not only the children that you already care for but also your own children?

- What extra equipment will you need to provide so that you can care for the baby in a professional way?

- Will you have to change your work routine and how could this affect you, your partner, other children and your children?

- How will you make sure that you keep the parents of the baby informed about how their child is developing, such as their teething and their first attempt to roll over or sit-up?

- How will you make sure that parents don't feel 'left out' of the care for their child?

There are many things you will need to consider and the above list is only a start. You can probably think of many more demands and extra responsibilities when caring for a baby.

Toddlers are often very challenging and your routines will have to accommodate their growing need for exploration and independence. You could be involved with toilet training and will need to establish a routine with the parents that will help the toddler become independent.

Routines for babies

Routines for babies depend on their needs. Babies have very definite needs, which change as they grow and develop. In order to grow and develop babies need the security of routines.

The needs of baby are:

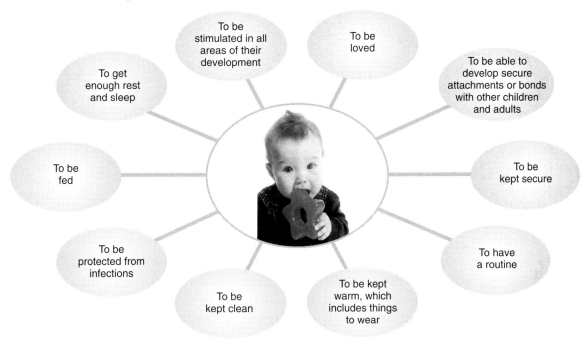

Figure 4.1 *Routines are essential for the way babies grow and develop*

How the needs of a baby affect your routines

To be loved

A baby who is shown love and affection will respond with smiles, giggles and cuddles. The more attention he or she is shown, the more smiles you will get. Making time in your daily routine to spend with a baby is not necessarily the only way to show the baby affection. Having a special time is wonderful, but this could be a nappy changing time or mealtimes. Consider having the baby with you when you are doing routine jobs, like sorting washing. Put the baby, securely fastened into a baby seat, in a position where he or she can see and hear you as you go about your work. Talk to the baby and involve them as much as possible in daily events.

To be able to develop secure attachments or bonds with other children and adults

A baby develops secure attachments, or bonds, with another person in several ways. It can be by recognising the sound of their voice, the shape of their face, their smell. It could be the person that feeds them or makes them feel warm and secure. Routines help establish these bonds.

Usually the first person a baby will bond with will be his or her mother. You should not try to break that bond, but help the baby to build another bond with you. It is a good idea if you and the mother can share the responsibility of caring for the baby before you are left in sole charge. This helps both you and the baby to get used to each other. However, this is often not possible if the mother is returning to work and time is limited.

There are lots of things that you can do to help the baby develop a bond with you. You can keep as much as possible to the same routine as the mother has, especially for feeds, rest and sleep times. Welcome the baby into your home with the same happy words each time he or she comes. The baby will learn to recognise not only the sound of your voice but also the words that you use. As the baby gets older they will need to learn how to develop bonds and relationships with other children and people. Your routines may have to change to accommodate this need. You will have to think about activities that will allow the baby to meet other people, perhaps meeting up with other childminders with babies, for example. Your routine will have to be changed to make time for such activities.

To be kept safe and secure

The surroundings for a baby are very important in making them feel safe and secure. Loud, sudden noises can startle and distress a baby. The way a baby is held will affect their feeling of security, as will the way that they are handled during changing, feeding and generally moving around. Again routines will help establish this sense of security. Routines should help you feel more confident and this will be picked up by the baby, who in turn will feel safe and secure.

In the first chapter you looked at ways of keeping your home safe and accident free. This is especially important when caring for babies. The equipment that you use for a baby must be safe, such as adjustable harnesses on high seats, properly fitted car seats or toys with no loose or small pieces. As a baby becomes more mobile and active you will have to watch them carefully at all times. You must make sure that he or she cannot hurt themself or get to places that are not safe. You will also have to think about protecting your own possessions and those of other older children that you care for. As babies grow and become more active and mobile they want, and need, to explore their surroundings. Caring for a baby who hasn't yet learnt to crawl has different safety issues for a childminder to think about than caring for a baby who is crawling. Devices like door, window and cupboard locks, stair and door gates become essential pieces of equipment when caring for a crawling baby. Babies need to have opportunities to explore in a safe environment and your routine will have to allow for this.

To have a routine

Routines are very important for both you and the baby. Routines help you to plan your day, your week and even longer. This is essential for a busy professional. For example, you may have to fit in taking and collecting children from school with caring for the baby. Routines help the baby feel secure. A baby will start to become aware of daily events and begin to understand what is going to happen. A baby may get excited when he or she sees you getting the buggy out as they know it means a trip to school to meet other children; seeing you get a feeding bottle out of the steriliser may help a baby learn that it is feeding time. This will help a baby make sense of time and the world around them. It also allows them to make sense of their surroundings, for example if the baby is always fed by you in the kitchen they will begin to associate the joy and fun of eating with the smells, sights and sounds in your kitchen.

There are many routines that affect a baby's physical care. These are:

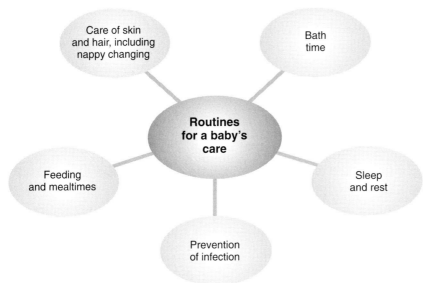

Figure 4.2 *Some of the routines that are important for a baby's care*

Routines associated with these aspects of care will be dealt with later in this chapter.

To be kept warm, which includes things to wear

Babies need to be kept warm. A low body temperature can become a dangerous medical condition. You should also remember that being too warm could be just as dangerous. Normal body temperature is 36.5°–37°C but it can vary during the day depending on the weather and what the baby or child has been doing.

It is good practice to try to keep rooms where babies and young children are in at a temperature of about 15°C (60°F). Make it part of your routine to check the temperature of the room that is used by the children.

Clothes should allow the baby to move freely, and should not be too tight, especially around the neck. When a baby is asleep, check that the covers are not restricting her movements, or making her too hot, or have fallen off so that she is cold. Make sure that you plan to keep the baby warm if needed, or protected from the sun and heat if you are outside.

To be kept clean

Babies have little immunity against infection, so it is very important that they are kept clean. You must establish good routines to keep babies clean. You should, as much as possible, follow the same routines established by the mother. You should understand how to care for a baby's skin, hair and prevent common skin conditions such as cradle cap, heat rash and nappy rash.

To be protected from infections

This is very closely linked to the need to keep a baby clean. It also involves your personal hygiene and routines for sterilising bottles and other equipment, making up feeds, changing and disposing of nappies and bathing a baby. You will also have to teach older children in your care about personal hygiene. They will need to know to wash their hands after using the toilet and before eating or handling food. They will need to know how to dispose of used tissues and aspects of personal hygiene such as covering their mouths when coughing or sneezing and not to cough or sneeze over the baby.

If you get the opportunity to train for a qualification in food hygiene, seriously consider doing it. Not only will it show parents that your are well-trained and professional in your work, but it will give you greater understanding of how to prevent infection from food and to use routines in the handling and preparation of food that ensure good, safe practices.

To be fed

Feeding times can be a time to develop relationships with the babies and children that you care for. During mealtimes you can develop the children's social skills and help them learn many things. A baby can develop language skills if you talk to her when giving her a bottle; she will learn to feel secure and loved as you hold her and care for her. Some mothers will want their babies to be fed breast milk, even when they return to work and are not caring for their baby full-time. In this case you will both need to make sure that there is plenty of expressed breast milk for you to give to the baby in a bottle. This milk will need to be kept in the freezer and will have to be defrosted carefully and brought to body temperature before giving it to the baby. Make sure your daily routine is flexible enough to meet everybody's needs, the other children, the baby, the mother and you.

To get enough rest and sleep

Realistically it is not possible to say that a baby of a particular age needs a certain amount of rest and sleep. You know from your own experiences that all babies are different, especially in their need for sleep, as are all children and adults of any age. What is important is that you find out from the parents if the baby has a sleep pattern, how the parents get their baby off to sleep and how often does the baby sleep during the day. As much as is practically possible, you should try to follow the same methods as the parents and fit them into your daily routine. However, some things may not be possible, as in the case of parents who get their baby off to sleep by driving them around in the car for an hour. As a busy childminder with other children's needs to consider this may not be possible for you, and so you should talk to the parents about other ways that you will try to get their baby to sleep.

It is worth noting that new-born babies often sleep for as much as 18 hours in any one 24-hour period. This need for sleep will decrease as the baby develops and grows, but many children still need a sleep or a quiet rest during the day, well into their third year.

To be stimulated in all areas of their development

All babies need to play. They need to have time, space and appropriate toys or activities that will stimulate them in every way. If you give a baby a shiny safe mirror or metal toy they will be stimulated by the appearance and feel of it. This will help their sensory development; they will handle the object, perhaps moving it between hands and mouth, and so develop muscle control and co-ordination; if you are talking to the baby whilst they have this object they will respond to your voice and facial expressions, an aspect of language and cognitive development; the baby will hopefully feel secure and safe which will help their social and emotional development. Babies will play in a solitary way but love to watch older children play and will be stimulated to copy their actions.

You need to understand how to meet these needs. You will need to be one step ahead of the baby so that you can predict how his or her needs will change, and plan accordingly. This is especially important when thinking about keeping your home safe and accident-free.

Routines for skin and hair

Babies have little immunity against infection, so their skin needs to be cared for very carefully. Babies' skin needs careful protection from the sun, so you should ask parents to provide a sun hat for times when you are outside and use a high factor sun protection cream, or one that has been specially formulated for babies. It is good practice to keep babies under six months old out of direct sun; use a sun shade or umbrella on buggies and prams, keep the babies covered with light loose clothing and use a sun cream with a factor of at least 15 SPF.

There are two washing routines that are used with babies:

- top and tailing
- bathing.

It more likely that you will be involved with the routine of top and tailing, that is washing hands, face and bottom, than bathing a baby, however you should also have a good routine for bathing as you never know when it could be needed.

A baby's head needs special care as the bones of the skull are still relatively soft. It may be that you will not need to wash a baby's hair, but again you never know when it may be necessary; it is surprising how much food can end up in the hair when a baby tries to feed itself!

Most childminders have their own children and will be very familiar with the care routines for babies and young children. However it is important to remember that caring for other people's children as a professional puts you in a different position from caring for your own. It is **good professional practice** to check that your existing routines are examples of good practice, so don't dismiss the next few pages, saying to yourself 'I know all this already'. Use the suggested routines as benchmarks to compare your own routines.

GOOD PRACTICE *A routine for top and tailing*

- Collect all the things that you will need before you start or have them all together in one place.
- You will need:
  - a changing mat
  - nappy changing items
  - clean cloths or cotton wool
  - bowl of warm water and cotton wool or the baby's own soft flannel
  - a baby brush and oil, if the routine involves hair care.
- Wash your hands.
- Take off the baby's outer clothes, making sure that the baby is in a safe and clean place.
- Gently clean the baby's face with cotton wool or a cloth. Take care to avoid the eyes. Throw away the cotton wool.
- Get a new piece of cotton wool and clean around the nose and ears.
- Wipe the baby's hands.
- Dry the baby with cotton wool or his or her own clean soft towel.
- Move down to the bottom and begin a nappy changing routine.
- Don't use the same cloth, towel or pieces of cotton wool for the baby's bottom.

Don't forget to talk and perhaps sing to the baby whilst you are doing this routine. It should be a pleasurable time for both of you.

Routine for nappy changing

You will need to establish a routine for changing nappies, which will help you and the baby.

Babies will tell you, often by crying, if their nappy is soiled or wet. A baby who is left for long periods of time in a wet or soiled nappy is at greater risk of infection and nappy rash. It is important that nappies are changed regularly and that the baby's bottom is washed and dried thoroughly.

Remember, you should **never** use the same cloth or cotton wool or wipe for both the face and the bottom. All parts of the baby that you wash or wipe must be dried thoroughly.

GOOD PRACTICE *A routine for nappy changing*

Suggested nappy changing routine

1   Get all the equipment ready before you start or take off the nappy.
2   Wash your hands and put on disposable gloves.
3   Pick up the baby and place on a secure, firm, safe surface that can be easily wiped down afterwards.
4   Remove the baby's clothes from the lower part of the body and undo the nappy.
5   Use tissues, wipes or cotton wool to clean the baby; don't forget to clean carefully in all the 'cracks and creases'.
6   Put the nappy, if disposable, with the tissues or wipes into a nappy sack. Make sure that you do not turn your back on the baby, or leave him or her unattended, to do this. If you have to move away, put the dirty nappy and tissues to one side, out of reach of the baby, and deal with them later.
7   Dry the baby's bottom thoroughly.
8   Apply barrier cream if used.
9   Put on a clean nappy and dress the baby.
10 Put the baby in a safe place, whilst you clean the changing area and dispose of the nappy and tissues.
11 Remove disposable gloves and wash your hands.

Don't forget that nappy changing can be an ideal playtime for the baby, and gives lots of opportunities for you to talk and play with her as she enjoys the freedom of having no nappy.

Routine for bathing a baby

Bathing the baby should be a fun and happy experience for both of you and is an ideal time for play and learning. If the baby is frightened of the sensation of water or the freedom, don't make bath time a 'battle'. Postpone the idea of a full bath for a while, it is better to have a happy baby that has been well 'topped and tailed' than a baby who is scared of water. As with all care routines you must have all the things that you need ready and to hand before you begin.

Activity Bathing a baby

1   Make a list of all the things that you will need to have ready before you start to bath a baby.
2   Put together a step-by-step routine for bathing a baby, and then compare your routine to the example given at the end of this section. If you have missed something out, decide if it is very important and whether you need to add it into your routine.

Figure 4.3 *These are the things you need to have for bathing a baby*

GOOD PRACTICE *A bath time routine*

- Have everything ready before you undress the baby.
- Wash your hands.
- Check the temperature of the room. It should be about 20°C.
- Put warm water in the bath. It should be about 38°C using a thermometer. If you check it with your elbow the water should feel lukewarm.
- Undress the baby, apart from their nappy, and wrap in a towel.
- Wash the baby's face using the routine for top and tailing.
- If you are going to use a baby bath, such as bubble bath, put it in the water now.
- If you are going to wash the baby's hair hold them firmly with one hand with their body held under your arm and hold them over the bath.
- Using your other hand, wash the hair.
- Dry the baby's hair.
- Take off the towel and remove the nappy.
- Keep the towel on your knee.
- Clean the bottom if needed, following the routine for top and tailing.
- Using both hands and supporting the baby's head, lift into the bath.
- Hold and support the baby with one hand and use your free hand to wash the baby.
- Allow the baby time to kick, splash and enjoy the bath time.
- Lift the baby out of the bath and place on the towel.
- Dry the baby very carefully and don't forget all the little creases. If the baby has dry skin the parents may want you to apply moisturising cream. Some African-Caribbean babies have oil massaged into their skin.
- Put on a clean nappy.
- Dress the baby.

It is important to remember that talcum powder can be inhaled and cause infections. Some children also have an allergic reaction to talcum powder and it can aggravate asthmatic conditions. It is safer to avoid using it.

Routine for care of the hair

The way a baby's hair needs to be cared for depends on the wishes of the parents and the baby's hair type. If you are in any doubt how to care for the baby's hair you must ask the parents. You could ask this question at the first meeting with the parents (see Chapter 2). Some parents will ask you to put oil on their baby's hair and ask you not to use shampoos or soap. You should look regularly for any signs of cradle cap on the baby's scalp and discuss with the mother how best to deal with it. In most cases it is treated by gently rubbing olive oil on to the cradle cap and then washing it off after a few hours. Remember, it is vital that you respect any cultural or religious wishes of the parents about the care of their child's hair.

Routines for feeding and mealtimes

It is more than likely that the mother will have established some sort of feeding pattern for her baby. This can be very varied, from feeding whenever the baby is hungry or at set times of the day. Whatever pattern has been established by the mother you should not try to change it without talking to her first.

If the baby is still being breast fed you will need to make sure that your routine considers the needs of the mother, as mentioned earlier in this chapter. You may have to help the mother and baby transfer from breast to bottle and later you may have to wean the baby on to solid foods. Routines will help you manage all these things better.

Keeping feeding equipment clean and safe

All feeding equipment used for feeding a baby must be kept thoroughly clean and as germ-free as possible. By doing this you reduce the risk of infection. You will find it easier if you establish a routine for cleaning and sterilising bottles and other feeding equipment, starting with washing your own hands.

There are several methods for sterilising feeding bottles and equipment:

- Chemical or cold water
- Steam
- Boiling water
- Microwave.

There isn't really a best method, all are equally as good as each other, provided that they are done properly and that you don't attempt to cut corners. Establish a routine regardless of what method you choose to use.

Chemical or **cold-water sterilising** is a fairly cheap way of sterilising. You must remember to rinse everything to remove all traces of the chemical before using. This form of sterilising can discolour metal, so be careful with your own finger rings. It can also cause rubber teats to perish. You should follow the manufacturer's instructions when using this method.

Steam sterilising is quick and simple to use, but you will need to take care when lifting up the lid of the unit. Remember that you can only put things in a steam steriliser that can take boiling water. Follow the manufacturer's instructions for use.

The **boiling water** method involves boiling the feeding equipment in a pan for ten minutes. This is possibly the cheapest of all methods, but it has hazards. See Chapter 1 for possible hazards and risks to children, especially in the kitchen.

Using a **microwave** to sterilise equipment is also quick and easy. You cannot however sterilise anything that is metal in the microwave. Equipment should be placed upside down in the microwave and again you should follow the manufacturer's instructions. Things should be left to cool down before you take them out, and be careful, anything coming straight out of a microwave is very hot.

Routines for making up bottle feeds

When it comes to making up bottle feeds of formula milk it is a good idea to establish a routine, or step-by-step approach. The following is a suggested routine.

GOOD PRACTICE *Routine for bottle feeding*

1 Make sure that the formula you are using has not passed its sell by date. Make sure that the tin is stored in a cool, dry cupboard and that the lid is firmly on.
2 Boil some water and allow it to cool.
3 Wash and dry your hands carefully.
4 Get sterilised bottles from the unit and rinse very well, preferably using cool boiled water.
5 Fill a feeding bottle to the required level.
6 Measure the exact amount of formula using the scoop provided and level off with a clean knife. Manufacturers of formula milk have found that many babies are given bottles of milk that are incorrectly mixed, being either too strong or too weak. It is very important that you read the instructions on the sides of the tin, or leaflet supplied, and follow them.
7 Add formula to the bottle.
8 Put on cap and shake very well to make sure that all of the formula is well mixed. If not using straight away, cool quickly, cover and store in the fridge. If you are using immediately check the temperature of the milk on your wrist before giving it to the baby.

Babies prefer warm feeds, although some will happily take cold milk. If you need to warm up a bottle, take care that any jugs of hot water are not within reach of other children. Milk in bottles should not be kept warm for longer than 45 minutes; after that length of time bacteria can start to breed in the bottle, and if given to the baby it could make them quite ill. Whatever is left in the bottle after the baby has finished feeding should be thrown away.

GOOD PRACTICE *For bottle feeding a baby*

- Wash your hands.
- Warm the bottle either in warm water or bottle warmer. Don't use a microwave as this does not distribute the heat evenly and could cause parts of the bottle to be hotter than other parts and so burn the baby.
- Change the baby's nappy if needed.
- Collect together everything that you will need, including bibs and clothes or tissues.
- Check the temperature of the milk on your wrist.
- Pick up the baby and sit together in a comfortable chair.
- Touch the baby's mouth with the teat and wait for him or her to open their mouth.
- Put the teat into the baby's open mouth and angle the bottle so that there is a steady flow of milk into the teat.
- Allow the baby to feed at their own pace, taking breaks as needed.
- Wind the baby by either putting them over your shoulder or in a supported sitting position and gently rub the back.
- Throw away unfinished milk.

Dealing with feeding problems

Always discuss with the parents any concerns you may have about the feeding of their baby. Many difficulties are fairly minor and often to do with wind. However, sometimes feeding difficulties can be a sign that the baby is unwell.

Colic is one of the most upsetting feeding problems. A baby will often scream in pain and draw the legs up to the stomach. It usually occurs at the same time each day, quite often in the evening. The childminder can comfort the baby by cuddling, massaging his or her stomach and gently rocking. You should advise the parents to see their doctor or health visitor for advice. In most cases a baby will 'grow out' of colic after about three months.

A baby can have breathing difficulties if they have a cold or blocked nose. This will affect how they feed and you may need to allow the baby to take longer over their feed and possibly take more frequent breaks.

If you suspect that the baby is not feeding properly because they are unwell, check their temperature. Don't try to force them to feed. Contact the parents. Write down the details of the problem for the parents. If necessary implement your emergency plan.

Pam has agreed to care for a three-month-old baby boy from 8.30 am to 5.45pm for three days a week, as his mother has returned to work. The mother has breast-fed her baby and has tried to gradually introduce him to formula milk and bottles over the last three weeks. At the moment the baby has a combination of formula milk and expressed breast milk at different times of the day when he is hungry. He is beginning to get colic, often cries, and you feel that he is not as content as he could be.

What would you suggest to the mother that you both could do to try to sort out these problems?

Write down your answers

Routines for weaning

Most parents introduce foods other than milk to their babies when they are about six months old. Up to then milk provides all the nutritional needs of a baby. When they get to about six months old babies need extra energy, and so require more iron and vitamins A and D in their diets. Introducing different foods earlier than about six months is not always good practice, as the baby's digestive system will not be mature enough to cope. Introducing food that a baby has to chew helps to develop the muscles of the face, mouth and tongue. All of these muscles are used when talking. However, if started too early the muscles will not be developed sufficiently to allow the baby to chew.

Babies do vary as to when they are ready to be introduced to different foods and it is important that you discuss with the parents when it is time to wean the baby. Quite often the bottle-feed will not satisfy the baby's hunger. The baby could also start to sleep for shorter periods of time and want feeding more often.

Getting started

Start to wean a baby at a time when they are not tired. Many people think that the middle of the day, around lunch-time is a good time. Most babies will want to drink milk first, especially if they are very hungry, so keep the baby on your knee. Offer the bottle first and then put a small amount of food on a spoon up to the baby's lips. The baby should try to suck the food off the spoon, although sometimes at first the baby might spit it out! Make sure that both the spoon and the food bowl have been sterilised and rinsed before using.

Foods to introduce first

Foods should be warm and introduced slowly. It is usual to start with some form of cereals, such as thin porridge, rice, cornmeal or millet mixed with either formula or breast milk. Many food companies make baby weaning foods that can be used successfully. Some parents introduce babies to puréed fruit or vegetables at the start. It is very much a matter of parental and baby preferences. There are, however, certain foods that it is good practice to avoid. See the spider chart opposite.

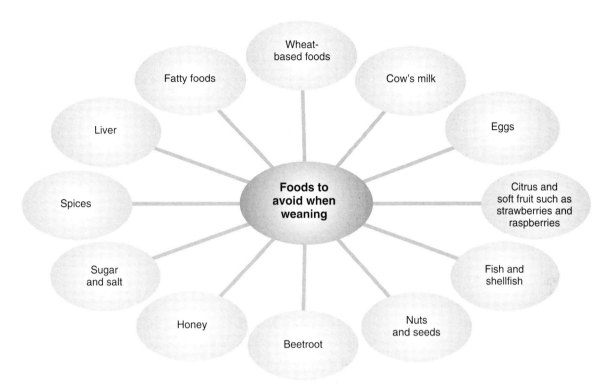

Figure 4.4 *These foods should not be fed to a baby who is being weaned*

When the baby is happily accepting the first food, gradually introduce another, such as puréed meat or dahl. Many childminders find a food blender an invaluable piece of equipment at this time. Once a baby can sit up unaided he or she can be put in to a high chair, with a harness, at feeding times. Remember no child of any age should be left unattended whilst feeding.

It is important to remember that milk should be the main part of a baby's diet when starting to wean them. Gradually as more foods are introduced, the amount of milk can be decreased and water can be also introduced, if it has not been already.

Moving on as the baby develops

By the time the baby is about six months the foods can be a bit more 'lumpy' and mashed rather than puréed. You can also start to introduce cow's milk and diluted fruit juices.

By the time a baby is about nine months old he or she can eat, more or less, the same foods as older children, provided that these foods are well mashed or minced. Finger foods, such as raw carrots, apples, toast, pitta bread, can be gradually introduced around nine months. There is a huge range of commercially produced baby foods on the market. It is up to the individual childminder, parent and baby to decide if these are better than home produced foods. One of the advantages of using commercially produced foods is that they are ready prepared and so quick to prepare. One disadvantage is that they can be quite expensive.

Difficulties when weaning

When you first start to wean a baby it is very important that you look for signs of food intolerances. It is much easier to spot these when introducing foods one at a time rather than later when the baby's diet is more varied. Signs to look for are:

- constipation

- diarrhoea

- wind or colic when a baby has not had this problem before

- eczema

- failure to gain weight and grow properly

- wheezing and breathing difficulties.

Routines for rest and sleep

All babies are different in their needs for rest and sleep and in the ways that they settle to sleep. You must ask the parents how much sleep their baby needs during the day, what position they are put in, and how they are settled. These questions should be part of your first meeting with parents (see Chapter 2). It is important that you follow the routine that has been established by the parents for rest and sleep, but at the same time be flexible. By the time a baby is about nine months old a routine or pattern for rest and sleep should have been established or else it might be difficult for you to settle the baby.

Find out from the parents where they put the baby to sleep during the day, and if possible use the same piece of equipment, such as a cot, Moses basket, or baby seat.

Find out from the parents how they settle their baby. This could be cuddling or rocking, using comfort objects like a blanket, special toy or soothers, or making a special noise or playing music.

As babies get older they will begin to learn the sequence of some events in their lives, for example, they will get to know that after eating they will have a nappy change and then go to sleep.

It will help you and the other children if you can establish a pattern for rest and sleep times. Babies who are over-tired are often difficult to settle and can become distressed. This could upset and distract older children. When a baby is asleep during the day, do not creep about and prevent other children from making any noise. Carry on as normal as the baby should be able to sleep through a normal level of noise.

GOOD PRACTICE *Helping babies to sleep*

- Check the temperature of the room and make sure it is well ventilated without being draughty.
- Make sure that the place where the baby is to sleep is comfortable, dry and clean.
- You may want to darken the room as this sometimes helps older babies sleep.
- Make going to sleep a calm and pleasant time. Don't excite the baby, and speak quietly and calmly.
- Check that the baby's nappy is clean and dry.
- Make sure that if a comforter is used the baby has got it.

Routines for caring for teeth

As soon as baby has got teeth you should introduce a routine for caring for their teeth. A baby should have his or her own soft toothbrush, which is kept only for cleaning teeth. It is not necessary to use toothpastes for babies. Establish a routine of gently cleaning teeth after the baby has been fed and before being put down to sleep. Remember to discuss your planned routine with the parents.

Routines for toddlers

Toddlers can be very demanding as they learn to become independent and confident. They need every opportunity to explore and investigate their world, whilst at the same time remaining safe and well cared for. In many ways the routines that you have established for babies can be continued for toddlers, such as nappy changing and sterilising feeding equipment. Some routines will need to be adapted as the toddler develops, just as any of your routines would have to be as children grow.

Routines for skin and hair

As with babies, toddlers' skin is delicate and needs care. Skin protects our bodies by preventing infection from entering it and helps to regulate the body temperature. Toddlers are very active and there is an increased chance of grazes and scratches as they play. They are also more likely to get sweaty and hot on warm days as they explore and play. Washing skin and moisturising it where needed is the main way to care for skin.

Allergies or other skin conditions, such as eczema, may need special care and treatment. You must always check with the parents what products you can safely use on their child.

Protecting from sun burn

Young children can burn very quickly if their skin is exposed to sunlight without protection. Toddlers and all young children should wear high factor sun cream (at least 15 SPF), a sun hat and loose clothing that covers exposed skin. Children should be kept out of the sun during the summer months between 11 am and 3 pm, as this is when the sun is at is strongest.

Care of hair

Each child should have their own brush and comb, which should only be used for that child. Never use the same brush and comb for several children. Shared brushes and combs is one way that head lice can spread. Brushes and combs should be kept clean, usually by regular washing in warm soapy water and then rinsing well. Many toddlers will have a good head of hair. This can present problems, especially if the hair is long and could get in their eyes and face, or tangled. Ask parents if you can fasten long hair back so that it does not get covered in paint, food or other messy materials. If you need to wash a toddlers' hair check with the parents that they do actually wash and shampoo the hair rather than using moisturising oils.

Dealing with head lice

As many toddlers mix with other children, there is an increased chance that they could pick up head lice. The symptoms that a child has been infected are:

- Scratching the scalp because it is itchy.
- Small scabs on the scalp.
- Small red bites on the scalp and hair line, especially at the back of the neck and behind ears.
- Tiny white or yellow eggs attached to hairs about 1 cm away from the scalp.
- Tiny brown fast moving insects.

It is best to seek advice for the best way to treat head lice and discuss it with the parents. There are many special chemical lotions and shampoos available from a chemist, or you could use electric or hand-held fine-tooth combs to comb out the eggs and lice.

You must tell the parents of children that you care for that one of the children has head lice. Parents will then have to treat their own hair and that of other family members. Head lice are very easily spread between people. You will also have to treat all your family members.

Keeping noses clean

A runny nose can spread infection to other children. If a child has a dirty nose it can in some cases cause ear infections, so it is important that you teach children to keep their noses clean. Toddlers cannot blow their noses, so if they have a cold their noses will need to be wiped frequently. A downside of this can be that frequent wiping of the nose can cause the skin around the nose to become sore. With the permission of parents many childminders find that a thin smearing of Vaseline around the nose area can help to protect the skin. Used tissues must be disposed of immediately, do not leave them lying around or use the same tissue on more that one child. If you use fabric handkerchiefs, use one per child, do not leave them lying around and make sure that they are changed, washed and dried regularly.

Routines for washing and bathing

Good hygiene practices can be taught to children at a very young age. Toddlers love to copy adult actions, so use every opportunity to teach them; for example, when you wash your hands, wash those of the toddler too and tell them why you are doing it. As with some of the routines for babies, many childminders will be very familiar with routines for toddlers, but again be a 'reflective' professional and use the routines to confirm your own good practices and perhaps update and develop your skills.

Hand washing

This is the main way of preventing the spread of infection. Young children can be taught how to wash and dry their hands properly from a very young age. Make sure that if children are standing on something to get to a washbasin or sink that they are not left unattended and that whatever it is that they are standing on or sitting on is stable. Many childminders teach toddlers to wash their hands by putting a bowl of water on a low table at child height so that there is no need for the child to balance or stand on something.

In Chapter 1 hand washing is described in detail. This is the routine that you should teach children. Makes sure that the water is not too hot; a recommended temperature is about 63°C.

Bathing

It might sometimes be necessary for you to bath a toddler, for example if you have been doing a particularly messy play activity or if they have had an 'accident' with a bowel movement. The routine for bathing a baby can be successfully followed for a toddler. Remember however that the toddler is more active and should be supervised at all times when in a bath.

Some families do not take baths and only use showers. This may be a matter of personal preference or for religious reasons. You must ask the parents what they would want you to do.

Remember that all children should have their own cloths for washing and these should be regularly washed. Many childminders put face cloths through a hot wash cycle in their washing machines and dry thoroughly.

Routines for nappy changing and toilet training

Toddlers can become aware of wet and dirty nappies and are able to let you know that they need changing. Toddlers are very mobile, so you must make sure that their nappies are secure and not likely to restrict their movements. It is possible to buy shaped nappies, both terry fabric or disposable ones, which are less bulky and more comfortable for active toddlers. Ask the child's parents what they would like you to use.

The routine for nappy changing can be followed for a toddler, however many childminders prefer to put the changing mat on the floor and do the nappy changing down there. It does rule out the danger of an active toddler falling. Before you start this routine don't forget to wash your hands and put on disposable gloves.

Toilet training

The age at which a child becomes aware of bladder and bowel activity can vary greatly. There is no correct time for children to develop this awareness and you must take your cues from the child and respect the wishes of the parents. In most cases a toddler will gain control of their bowels before they get control of the bladder. Also, you will be more aware of when a child is doing a bowel movement; they often go quiet, with a look of concentration and sometimes effort, on their faces. Quite often a child will have a bowel movement at the same time each day.

The signs that usually tell you a child is ready to start toilet training are:

- They tell you when they want their nappy changed.
- The nappy stays dry for longer.
- They want to copy other children or adults.
- They start to show an interest in potties and toilets.

GOOD PRACTICE *Toilet training*

- Discuss with the toddler's parents how this is to be done and when.
- Make sure that both you and the parents agree on a consistent approach.
- Suggest to the parents that the toddler wears clothes that will unfasten easily.
- Make the place where the potty is kept, usually a bathroom or toilet, a pleasant, sweet-smelling place – somewhere nice to be. It is not a bad idea to get down on your hands and knees in your bathroom and look at the room from a child's perspective – it can look quite different!
- Keep a potty readily available. This should be clean and preferably not used by more than one child. Some childminders use a training seat over their own toilet seat and a step to help the child get up to the toilet. Usually potties are used for younger toddlers, training seats for older ones.
- Don't put pressure on the toddler to 'perform' when sitting on the potty. It is very important that toilet training should be relaxed, so you must not get cross over 'accidents' which will always happen, especially at first.
- Praise the toddler when they do use a potty or toilet successfully, but don't make then feel inadequate if they don't. You can always try again later.

Dealing with 'accidents'

It is very important that you are as unconcerned as possible about 'accidents' and deal with them without upsetting the child. Take the toddler to a quiet place and try to be relaxed and calm. Wash, dry and change the child without drawing attention to the 'accident'.

Remember to tell parents, away from the hearing of the child, about 'accidents' and the general progress of the toilet training.

CASE STUDY

Emma is an active toddler aged 22 months. She has been walking since she was 13 months old. She is cared for during the week by Sue, a registered childminder. Sue has noticed that Emma's nappy is often dry when she comes to change her before lunch, and she usually has a bowel movement after lunch before her nap. Sue also cares for a three-year-old who is toilet trained. Emma is aware when the other child goes to the toilet and what they are doing. Sue arranges with Emma's mum to chat about the possibility of toilet training. Emma's mum finishes work early one day and comes to talk to Sue about how to go about encouraging Emma to use a potty. They decide that Emma's mum will go shopping with Emma at the weekend and buy a potty which Emma can use both at Sue's and at home. They decide that Sue will suggest to Emma that she sits on the potty after lunch, before she has her nap. They also agree that Emma sit on the potty whenever she asks to, even if it is to sit and play or look at a book. Emma's mum also buys a supply of 'trainer' nappies that make it easier for both Sue and Emma to pull up and down. They agree to chat again specifically about Emma's progress in four weeks.

Routines for feeding and mealtimes

Toddlers will be fully weaned and many will have made serious and determined attempts to feed themselves. Most toddlers eat a normal balanced diet and drink from a cup or training cup. Details of healthy and balanced diets will be covered in Chapter 5, in the physical development section.

It is also quite normal for toddlers to still have a bottle, especially just before a nap or bedtime. Bottles and training cups should still be sterilised, following the routines that you have established for babies.

All mealtimes should be social, happy times and a positive experience for all. It is important to teach all children good personal hygiene when handling food and eating. Toddlers can be taught when their hands need washing. They can learn by watching other children and you as to how to behave when sitting down to eat and will begin to understand what is acceptable and what is not.

Toddlers are very active and use up a lot of energy. Boys usually need more calories than girls to keep up their energy levels. It is good practice to give children regular small meals or snacks every 2–3 hours rather than three big meals; for example children could have breakfast quite early before coming to you and will be ready for a mid-morning snack and drink. All children should be able to have drinks of water whenever they are thirsty, especially in hot weather or after physical, vigorous play activities.

The chart below shows a routine that you could establish to feed toddlers and older children.

8:00 am	Breakfast either at home or with the childminder
10:30–11:00 am	Mid-morning snack and drink
12:30–1:00 pm	Lunch
3:30–4:00 pm	Mid-afternoon snack and drink, time to depend on when older children are collected from school
5:30–6:00 pm	Dinner or tea at home or with childminder

Problems with feeding toddlers

Toddlers' likes and dislikes of foods can change without warning, which can be very trying for a childminder. However mealtimes and feeding should not be times of stress and pressure. You should never force a child to eat.

Toddlers want to be independent and to do things for themselves. This can mean that mealtimes and feeding can take longer than you planned, but be patient and let the toddler try to use a spoon and fork themselves, for example.

If a toddler normally eats well and enjoys mealtimes, any loss of appetite or lack of interest in food could be a sign that they are not feeling well. You will need to check them carefully, possibly taking their temperature, and tell the parents of your concerns.

Talk to the parents about any difficulties that you may have and agree to work together.

Routines for rest and sleep

Many young children still need to take a nap at some point during the day, often up to the age of four. Toddlers are very active and need time to 'recharge their batteries'. Some children do not want to sleep, but you should still encourage them to rest and be quiet. Establishing a routine for naps or rest and quiet will help parents, as their toddler should then be ready for bedtime at home.

It is good practice to establish a routine of a calm and quiet time before you expect a lively toddler to sleep. This could be sitting down together to read a book, listening to music and quietly talking together. Many childminders practice this routine in the room where they want the toddler to sleep.

For settling toddlers, follow the routine for settling a baby to sleep as described earlier in this chapter.

Routines for care of teeth

Caring for children's teeth is very important and toddlers should be encouraged to have their teeth brushed after every meal. Many toddlers will want to do this for themselves, so they will find it easier if they learn a sequence of actions. This could be the following:

1 Wash and dry hands.

2 Wet tooth brush.

3 Put a small amount of toothpaste on brush.

4 Using a circular action, not a 'scrubbing' side to side movement, brush upper teeth, lower teeth, both front and back and inside edges.

5 Rinse and spit several times.

6 Rinse brush and shake off excess water.

7 Replace brush in a clean, safe place.

8 Wash or wipe mouth area.

Routines for care of feet

Toddlers grow very fast, not least their feet. Whilst it is the responsibility of parents to provide their children with shoes and socks, you may spot when shoes and socks are becoming tight before the parents. It is very important that you tell the parents about soreness, blisters or corns on the child's feet. It is good practice to let young children go barefoot whenever it is safe for them to do so.

Routines for school-age children

It is becoming increasingly common for mothers to return to work after having children. Recent government initiatives have made it easier for mothers of school-aged children to work if they wish to. This is good news for childminders as they are in a very strong position to offer flexible care to suit both school-aged children and their parents.

Sometimes parents do not return to work until their child starts school. If this is the case you could be the only other person to care for the child outside their family. In this case the child will need plenty of time and reassurance to get used to your routines. It is a good idea to encourage the parents to leave the child with you at some point before they start school, if they have not been left before. You can then help the child and the parents by making sure that the child can manage the toilet on their own and can dress themself. When at school it is important that a child has personal independence.

You can use this time before the child actually starts school to talk to them about what to expect. You can explain about school routines, what happens at playtime and dinnertime, what the toilets are like and what the differences are between school and nursery or pre-school groups.

You could be asked to care for school-aged children before school, after school and during the school holidays.

Routines for before school

It is quite possible that the school-aged child will only be in your care for a relatively short time before school, and it is also possible that this could be a very busy time for you. You will have other children to care for, parents arriving and leaving and possibly your own children to consider.

Each child in your care has an equal right to your care and time. It does not mean that because a child is older and perhaps more independent than others, that they do not need your time and care. Do not leave school-aged children to fend for themselves before school because you are too busy dressing or sorting out younger children or meeting and greeting parents.

Establish a leaving routine for the child and their parents. You could use a similar one to the leaving routine described earlier in this chapter for babies. The golden rule of keeping it short and sweet still applies. Once the parents have gone, provide an activity for the child to do, like the ones described in Chapter 3.

Before leaving for school, check that the child has got everything that they need for the day ahead. If by chance something has got left behind at home in the early morning rush, reassure the child and if needed speak to the teacher and let him or her know.

Try to make time to talk to the child about their day ahead, and it is good practice to try to remember what you talked about, so that you can ask them about it when you meet them. Don't appear to rush or hurry the child. Help them to start the busy day ahead in a calm and relaxed way, in other words be a good role model. Use care routines for washing hands and cleaning teeth before leaving for school. A suggested routine could be:

- When they arrive at your home, they remove outdoor clothes. Check with parents if the child has had breakfast or if he or she needs something to eat. Also check with parents that the child has everything needed for the day ahead, such as a reply slip from a letter, reading book, homework or PE kit.
- Say goodbye to parents and start quiet play activity or have breakfast.
- Go to the toilet.
- Wash hands, and clean teeth if they have eaten something.
- Collect things for school.
- Put on outdoor clothes if needed.
- Leave for school.

The journey to school

Children of school age need to learn how to become independent, while still remaining safe. The walk or journey to school is a good time to talk about 'stranger danger' and road safety. Children may also want to talk about problems that they have at school with friends and peers. Listen to what the child says and if you have any concerns speak to their parents.

If it is appropriate and does not distract you if you are driving, or from caring for other children, you could use the journey to school to play 'mind games' such as 'I spy', or have older children make up words from car registration number plates, or you could just talk to each other.

Routines for after school

At the end of the school day many children are tired. Their concentration and energy levels will be lower and they may not want to talk or be bothered by other children. On the other hand, some children will come out of school bursting to tell you about what they have done. However the child behaves, you must respond appropriately.

For the quiet child, allow them time to recover, sit quietly and perhaps play a game that does not require much effort. Don't push them into doing an activity if they are clearly tired, as this will only lead to upset and possible confrontation.

For the talkative child, give them your attention and let them tell you what they have been doing. Don't just 'hear' what is being said, actively listen, by giving eye contact and not doing anything else whilst the child is talking.

Most children come home from school hungry and so you will need to give them a healthy snack and drink. Many parents like children to change out of school clothes into something more casual; this is a good time for the quiet child to have 'space' as they change their clothes independently. Many children will have homework to do and you should agree with the parents when this is to be done. If it is your responsibility to make sure that homework is started, if not completely finished, then you will have to provide the child with a quiet place to work but where you can still supervise them.

A suggested routine could be:

- Come back to childminder's house.
- Take off outdoor clothes.
- Wash and dry hands and probably face.
- Have drink and snack.
- Get changed.
- Do a quiet activity.
- Start homework.
- Play with other children or friends.
- Wash hands.
- Have tea or dinner.
- Collected by parents and exchange of information between you and the parents.

Many children attend after-school or early evening activities. It could be part of your job to take the child to these activities, so you will need to adjust your routine in order for you to do this. It could be that taking a child to an early evening activity will affect the pick-up times and collection of other children. You will then have to decide what is most important or arrange with other carers or parents also going to the same activity to car share if possible. If this is what you decide, you must get the parents' permission for someone else to take their child. If there is an accident and you have not got the parents' permission, you could be held responsible for the child.

Routines for school holidays

School holidays should be fun times for children. Suggestions for play activities for school holidays are given in Chapter 3 and will be discussed in more detail in Chapter 6. It is important that all children have a structure and routine to their day at any age. You will still need to have routines for care and mealtimes during school holidays as well as routine times for rest, sleep or quiet activities.

Older children can be given the responsibility for planning their own day and building into their plan routines to encourage good personal hygiene, for example. Children can also use charts to help them plan a week's activities, drawing or writing daily details. This helps them develop a sense of time as well as giving them independence and responsibility – both important aspects of a growing child's emotional development.

Learning Outcome Activity 23 (ICP, DCP, ECP)

Gathering information for planning routines

- Talk to other childminders, parents, course members or relatives about caring for school-aged children.
- Ask them what their experiences are of getting children ready for school.
- Ask them how their child is at the end of the school day.
- Ask them what their child likes to do when they come home.
- Ask them about the school holidays, what activities they do with the children, what activities children do on their own and any problems that they might have had.

Make a note of the answers. Use this information to help you plan suitable routines when you are caring for school-aged children.

Check your knowledge

Answer true or false to the following statements, then check your answers on page 290.

1 Babies need to feel secure.
2 It is not necessary to wear disposable gloves when changing a baby's nappy.
3 It is better to boil feeding bottles to prevent infection.
4 Bath water should be about 38°C.
5 Babies can eat any form of cereals when starting to be weaned.
6 Babies usually grow out of colic.
7 African-Caribbean babies should not be bathed.
8 Mothers should be discouraged from breast feeding once they decide to ask a childminder to care for their baby.
9 You should not use the same piece of cotton wool or cloth to wipe a baby's face and bottom.
10 Feeding is a good time to develop relationships with a baby.

CHECK YOUR KNOWLEDGE

1 What is a routine?

2 How many different types of routine can you think of?

3 Can you think of three reasons why routines are important?

4 Why should you not change your routine too often?

5 When and why would it be right for you to change a routine?

6 Why must you consider the wishes of parents when planning your routines?

7 Why do toddlers need regular small meals?

8 Is it true that toddlers need more sleep than babies?

9 What are the signs that you should look for before starting to toilet train a toddler?

10 Suggest two ways that you could encourage a toddler to use a potty.

CHAPTER 5
Children's development and learning

Most people know that babies go from being tiny defenceless newborns, who stay where they are put, to walking, talking, questioning individuals in a few short years. But what happens in those few short years and why do childminders need to know?

If you understand how and why children develop and grow in the way that they do, you will know what to expect. If you know what to expect you will be able to meet each child's needs. If you know what to expect you will be able to plan better play activities and experiences for the children and you will also be able to spot potential problems.

The nature/nurture debate

There is no such thing as an 'average' child, although we often talk as if there is!

Every child is unique and different and has inherited from his or her parents characteristics which will affect their development from the moment that conception occurs. A child's development is also affected by where they live, who cares for them and the people that they meet. There is no exact way of knowing if what a child inherits from his or her parents has more of an effect on the way they grow and develop than the influences of where a child lives and who they meet. Educationalists and theorists have debated for centuries which has more effect, but no firm conclusions have been reached and the debate continues.

CASE STUDY

In Singapore, in the 1980s, the government of the day, which mostly consisted of people of Chinese ethnic origin, decided that what a child inherits (**nature**) was the strongest influence in deciding how a child would develop. As a result adults who had a university education and were graduates could have as many children as they wanted. Other people were restricted to two children per married couple. It was decided that graduates were more intelligent than non-graduates and that their children would inherit high levels of intelligence. Financial penalties were imposed if non-graduates had more than two children, such as having to pay for schooling and health care.

However the Chinese were the largest ethnic group in Singapore, therefore there were more Chinese students at the university. Graduates were able to get better paid jobs than other ethnic groups and so could afford better housing and had more spending power. They could afford to have their children cared for at nursery schools and day centres rather than using non-qualified family members. More money, better housing and trained child carers are considered to be factors of the **nurture** argument.

So what do you think? Talk to other course members and childminders about the nature/nurture debate.

Was the Singapore government right?

Can you decide what has the greatest influence on how a child develops?

What is child development?

The growth of children from babies through childhood is usually referred to as **child development**. To *grow* means to get bigger and to *develop* are the changes that happen as a child grows. Children grow and develop from the moment they are conceived until they reach adulthood. This growth and development is continuous and there is no time when growth or development stops. However growth and development does not happen at the same time in each child, and at certain times of a child's life they will grow and develop faster than at other times, for example at puberty. The fastest time of growth and development is the first nine months in the mother's womb; a child will never grow and develop as fast at any other time of their lives.

Stages of development

Children develop as they grow and although the speed at which they develop does vary, all children pass through the same stages of development. Each stage of development is clearly defined, for example a baby sits up before crawling, stands up before walking. A child must reach a certain level of development at one stage before they can pass onto the next stage. However some theorists believe that development is an unbroken progression and that stages of development are not obvious. This is another debate – stage versus continuous growth – that you might want to think about.

Assessing and measuring development and growth

Most books and articles that you read divide a child's development into different areas. One of the main reasons for this is so that development can be measured and assessed. However it is often very difficult to separate development and growth into different areas as all are dependent on each other. For example, in order to talk a child has to be able to hear, have physical control over the muscles of the face and tongue, understand that talking is a way of communicating and understand social 'rules' like not interrupting.

When development is measured health and childcare professionals can identify problems or exceptional abilities. The measurement and assessment of development is based on studies of children of all ages going back for many years. These studies have shown a likely scope and pattern of growth and development at certain ages. The results of these studies are often produced as developmental charts. This means that a child's growth and development can be checked against the likely scope and pattern as shown on the charts. Sometimes some professionals refer to developmental 'milestones', which are specific things that a child should be able to do at approximately a specific age, for example, when they can cut with scissors or stand without help.

Why does a childminder need to assess and measure children's growth and development?

As a childminder you are observing, watching and assessing the children in your care all the time, sometimes without being fully aware that you are doing it. It is almost instinctive. You have the advantage of working very closely with the children that you care for, often for quite long periods of time. You will get to know the children that you care for very well. This puts you in a very strong position to get a detailed view on how the children are growing and developing compared to other childcare professionals, such as a pre-school worker in a playgroup who may only see a child for two-and-half hours twice a week.

Any professional childcare worker needs to be able to watch children in an unbiased way and make sound judgements about what the children are doing, why they are doing it and how they are doing it. Sometimes you will do this quite formally and write down what you see a child doing, sometimes you will do it almost instinctively – for example, how do you decide that a child is ready to be toilet trained? You have probably watched them over a few weeks, made 'mental notes' and used your professionalism and experience to assess or measure if the child is ready.

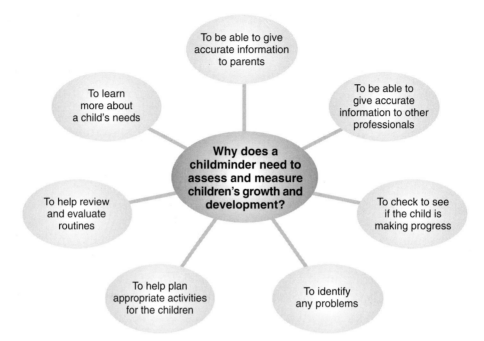

Figure 5.1 *There are various reasons for assessing and measuring a child's growth and development*

To be able to give accurate information to parents

It is essential that any information that you give to parents about their child is accurate. Sharing information with parents about how their child has been during the day and what they have been doing, shows that you care in a professional way about not only the child, but also the parents and the service that you give. Sharing accurate information with parents often will help to build relationships with them and avoid or sort out problems before they become major issues.

To be able to give accurate information to other professionals

It is often very useful if you can give accurate information about children that you care for when they start school, or move to a new care setting. Sometimes some professionals may ask you to note specific things about a child, for example, a speech therapist may ask you to listen carefully to how a child speaks and make a brief report for them. If a child becomes unwell whilst in your care, you will need to give the doctor and parents very accurate information about the child's symptoms.

To check to see if the child is making progress

It is good practice to assess a child when you first start to care for them. By doing this you will know exactly at what stage they are at and will be able to decide later if they have made progress or if there are any problems. This first assessment can form part of your meeting with the parents at the beginning. You may want to devise a record sheet like the example given here to help you make a first assessment.

Name: _____

Date of Birth: _____

Age: _____

Date: _____

Starting date: _____

Area	Special comments
Language used at home	
Any other languages spoken or understood	
Physical description	
Position in family	
Areas where child is advanced	
Areas of concern	
Social skills including toilet training, feeding self	
General personality	
Mixing with other children	

Any comments that you put in the last column can be used to help you in the future to decide if the child has made progress or has any special needs.

To identify any problems

The range of problems that you might come across in your professional career are almost too numerous to try to list. They could range from a parent asking you to take a special note of how a child is when in your care, as they think that the child might be going down with a illness, to being asked to assess a child and make a report to provide evidence for a child protection conference. By assessing a child's growth, and development you may become aware of difficulties or problems; for example you may notice that a child has suddenly become aggressive, in which case you would need to talk to the parents and try to find out why.

To help to plan appropriate activities for the children

If you know at what stage in their growth and development the children in your care are at, you will be able to plan suitable play activities for them; for example there is little point in planning a complicated cutting activity, if the children cannot handle scissors skilfully. You would be better giving them lots of magazines and catalogues to cut up and practice using scissors.

To help review and evaluate routines

Your day will be built round a series of routines and regular events, as discussed in Chapter 4. You will need to assess the children to decide if your routines are working for everybody or if they need changing. Routines need to change as children grow and develop.

To learn more about a child's needs

It is important that you understand the basic needs of children and how you can meet them. The basic needs are:

- love

- food

- shelter

- stimulation

- play.

The more information that you have about the children's needs the better and more professional you will become. You may also be able to identify early on, additional or specific needs that may require specialist help.

It is very important that any information that you keep about the children in your care is stored very carefully. They should be confidential to you and the child's parents, and possibly other professionals if appropriate. They should be accurate and factual. Ways to record and assess children will be looked at in detail in Chapter 6.

Areas of growth and development

Development is often looked at in separate areas in order to make accurate measurements and assessments. Many books divide growth and development into five areas:

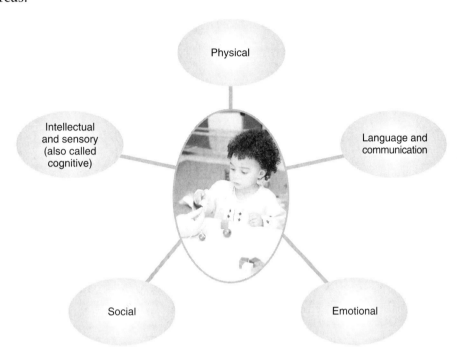

Figure 5.2 *The five areas of growth and development*

What is physical development?

Physical development is about how children get control of their bodies. It includes:

- **Fine manipulative skills**, which are small movements that are needed to write or draw.
- **Fine motor skills**, which are small movements involving the whole hand.
- **Gross motor skills**, which are movements involving all of an arm or leg, such as in throwing.
- **Locomotive skills**, which are controlled movements that children use to run, jump and walk.
- **Co-ordination skills** of hand, eye and foot, and the ability to combine more than one skill or movement at the same time. In this aspect of development a child uses perhaps their eyes to guide their hands when catching, or their eyes to guide their feet when going upstairs.

- **Balance** is a skill that require co-ordination but not necessarily from the eyes or ears. The ability to balance is developed by the body as the movements use information received from the central nervous system.

Learning Outcome Activity 24 (DCP, ECP)

Physical control

Think about some of the actions that you could have done today, such as:

- cleaning your teeth
- getting dressed
- making a telephone call
- writing a list
- bending down and picking up a child.

For each action decide what aspect of physical development you used, for example getting dressed involves co-ordination, fine manipulative skills, not to mention decision-making, which is a whole new area to consider!

What is intellectual and sensory development?

Some theorists refer to this area of development as **cognitive**, but it means the same as intellectual development. Intellectual development is about how our minds develop and how we learn. It includes:

- **Memory** skills, both long and short term.

- **Attention and concentration** skills.

- **Perception** skills about how children use information around them.

- **Sensory** development of sight, hearing, touch, taste and smell, but these are also linked to physical development.

What is language and communication development?

This aspect of development is not just about talking. It is about all of the ways that a child can communicate, from the different cries of a baby, such as 'I'm hungry' or 'I'm wet', to waving bye bye, writing a message and having a conversation with someone.

Many theorists believe that there are very close links between language and intellectual development. There are also close links with physical development; as mentioned before, children need to be able to control the muscles of the face, tongue and throat in order to make sounds.

What is emotional development?

Emotional development is about how children learn to deal with their feelings. It is also about how children learn to bond with their carers, or make strong relationships with one or two adults. This area of development also includes the development of self-confidence, self-control, self-image and self-esteem. It is often quite difficult to separate emotional development from social development as aspects of one affect the other. Sometimes problems with emotional development can be far-reaching and have a long-lasting effect; unfortunately, in some people, into adulthood.

What is social development?

Social development is about learning how to be with other people, how to build relationships and make friends. It is also about knowing how to look after yourself, such as using a toilet independently or getting dressed. These skills are often referred to as *self-help skills* and often involve aspects of physical development. Often children who have difficulty with language and communication have problems developing relationships with others.

Other approaches to development and growth

Piles and spice

In the study of children's growth and development different terms may be used to identify different aspects. One way is **p**hysical, **i**ntellectual, **l**anguage, **e**motional and **s**ocial (**piles**). Another way is **s**ocial, **p**hysical, **i**ntellectual, **c**ommunication and **e**motional (**spice**). Some people refer to the 'C' in SPICE as cultural development. In this way of looking at growth and development language and communication is included in intellectual and the area of cultural development is added.

Cultural development

This looks at how cultures, society, customs and traditions affect a child's growth. Many cultures have different but very acceptable views on bringing up children, behaviour and social rules, for example. It is very important that every childminder creates an environment in which all children are welcome and given opportunities to develop and grow regardless of their racial origins, gender, family background or disability. However cultural development is also very closely linked to intellectual, emotional and social development.

The seven Cs

Another way of looking at growth and development is often referred to the '**Seven Cs**'. These are:

1 confidence

2 co-ordination

3 competence

4 creativity

5 communication

6 concentration

7 co-operation

Learning Outcome Activity 25 (ECP)

The Seven Cs

Look at the chart of the 'Seven Cs' below. Try to match each one to another area of development, or when one area of development affects another; for example creativity can be matched to intellectual development and is also affected by cultural development.

Seven Cs	Other areas of development
Confidence	
Co-ordination	
Competence	
Creativity	
Communication	
Concentration	
Co-operation	

Looking at the whole child

When you have completed the chart above, you will hopefully see that many areas of growth and development affect or can be matched with others. For this reason it is often quite difficult to just look at one area of a child's development in isolation. It is often better to look at children's growth and development overall. This is usually referred to as a **holistic approach**. By using a holistic approach you look at the whole child and may be able to work out a variety of reasons for some of the things a child does; for example, a child ignores you when you talk to them. Are they deliberately doing this to get a reaction from you (attention-seeking which is part of emotional and social development), or have they really not heard you (possibly temporary deafness as a result of a cold – an aspect of physical development), or is the child concentrating so much on the activity that they are not aware that you have spoken (concentration is part of intellectual development)?

Stages in a child's growth and development

The following section is divided up into ages, but these are only *very rough* guides to the stages of development and you must remember that each child will develop at different rates even though they will all pass through the same stages. You must remember that there are many factors that can affect a child's growth and development and you must take these into account before deciding that a child has a problem or special need. Some of these factors are looked at in more detail later on in this chapter. There will be some suggestions for activities that you could use in your childminding setting to help the child develop, grow and learn new skills.

The first year of life

How does a baby grow and develop in the first year of life?

It is not very likely that as a childminder you will be caring for a very new baby, but it could happen. However it is important that you understand about children's growth and development right from the start so that you can build up a complete picture.

A baby grows and develops very quickly in the first year. Within a year a tiny helpless being, that is totally dependent on adults for everything, probably will triple its birth weight, grow about twenty centimetres in length and become an active, energetic person. It is essential that you understand what happens in that exciting first year.

At birth – growth and development

All newborn babies are conscious of the world around them, although they are not able to make sense of it. A baby is conscious of and will respond to changes in temperature, some sounds, bright lights and contact with another human. A new baby will be startled by loud and sudden noises, the arms and legs can jerk and the baby may start to cry. However the baby's nervous system is not developed enough for any response to be controlled.

All new babies are born with some reactions and responses, which gradually disappear. These reactions are often referred to as **reflexes**. After a baby has been born a doctor will check to see if the baby has these reflexes and as the baby grows the health visitor, or other health professional, will check to see if these reflexes have disappeared or changed. There are seven basic reflexes:

1 **Rooting** – if a baby's cheek is stroked he or she will turn their head to seek out food.

2 **Sucking** – anything that is put into the mouth will be sucked.

3 **Grasping** – a baby will grasp tightly to anything that is placed in his or her hand. This reflex is very strong and experiments have shown that a baby can support its own weight if lifted.

4 **Moro** – if, whilst being held, a baby's head is dropped a little, he or she will throw their arms out with open hands before bringing them back over their bodies.

5 **Startle** – when a baby is disturbed by a sudden noise he or she will fling their arms back and then bring them back over the body.

6 **Placing –** if the top of a baby's feet touch the underneath of a flat surface, such as a table, he or she will lift their feet up and place them on the top of the surface.

7 **Walking** – if a baby is held so that his or her feet touch the ground or a flat surface, they will start to make walking movement.

Emotional and social development is dependent on the new baby's needs being met. A baby will cry when he or she needs to be fed and the sound of the cry will change if the baby is left unattended for too long, or startled and so feels insecure. The first few days of life are very important for the baby to learn to make attachments and bond with familiar adults. At the start the baby begins to recognise the familiar voice sound and skin smell of the mother. This recognition helps the baby to learn that this person will meet their needs and so they begin to form an attachment and bond with that person. The baby is not aware that this relationship is being developed. If for some reason the baby is not able to make attachments and bonds, their future social development is put at risk. As a child they could have difficulty forming relationships with other children and adults.

Needs

The newborn baby is entirely dependent on an adult for all his or her needs. These needs are to be kept clean, warm and to be fed. A new baby needs to hear the sound of voices so that he or she can start to distinguish between familiar and strange voices. New babies also need lots of close contact with adults; this helps them to distinguish smells and to 'bond' with a familiar person.

Activities to promote development

- It is important that the adult talks to the new baby and also looks directly at them.
- Musical mobiles and bright objects that catch the light can be hung over the cot and babies will respond to light and sounds. This will help their sensory development.

One month – growth and development

By the end of the first month a baby will respond to the sound of his or her main carer. This can be stopping crying when hearing the familiar voice, or lying still. The baby's eyes will follow an object when moved in front of their face and he or she will stare intently at a face or other things that they can see, especially when being fed. He or she may well try to lift their head and will move and stretch fingers, toes, hands, arms and legs. Much of the time the baby will hopefully be asleep or dozing, unless feeding.

Needs

The needs of a month-old baby are still very much the same as for a newborn baby. The need to feel loved and cared for, if possible by one person, is very important. It is still important that the baby has lots of sensory stimulation, such as hearing voices, looking at mobiles and around the room.

Activities to promote development

- Lots of opportunities for close contact, such as cuddles and stroking or massage of arms and legs.
- Young babies will respond to quiet singing and music.
- Babies need to be around other people and so placing a baby in a chair and carrier in a safe place in a room where there are other people will help stimulate their growth and development.

Three months – growth and development

A three-month-old baby is more alert and interested in what is going on around them. Babies of three months have gained more control of the muscles of their arms and legs and will kick and push against firm surfaces. When placed on the tummy, babies will push themselves up with their arms and so give themselves a better view of their world. Many babies of this age will try to roll over from their backs to the side. They play with their own fingers and hands and are developing a limited amount of muscle control. Babies of three months are quite sociable and enjoy being with other people. They will smile at familiar faces and will respond to voices by making sounds, other than crying.

Needs

Quite often at around three months a working mother will have finished her maternity leave and will be considering child care for her baby. It is very important that if you start to care for a baby at this time, you and the mother work together as much as possible to make sure that all the baby's needs can be met and that the experiences with the parents and you are as similar as possible. This does not just mean food, warmth and being kept clean. A three-month-old baby needs company, love and attention as well. They also need opportunities to kick, exercise and stretch their muscles.

Activities to promote development

- When you are changing the baby's nappy, allow a little extra time for them to kick and move their legs without the restrictions of a nappy.
- Bath time provides excellent opportunities for stretching and exercising arms and legs. Don't forget to add a few toys that the baby can kick.
- Put the baby on his or her tummy on a clean floor, or baby mat. This gives good opportunities for them to develop the back and neck muscles that are needed for crawling.
- Play finger games and sing rhymes, you will surprised at how quickly the baby will learn the sequence of the games and anticipate things such as a tickle!
- Put the baby on a baby activity mat that has different textures and colours. This will help sensory development.
- Lying under a 'baby gym' will help a baby develop hand/eye co-ordination as they reach and try to pat and grasp the objects. Toys that make a noise and are attractive can also be attached to prams, buggies and carriers.
- Have conversations with the baby, talk to him or her, then stop and wait for them to respond, then start talking again. Not only does this help develop relationships, but the baby will begin to understand that 'turn-taking' is part of having a conversation with someone.

Six months – growth and development

By six months a baby will usually have more than doubled their birth weight. Many six-month-old babies can roll over from their tummies to their backs and can sit propped up with pillows and cushions for a little while. Feet and toes as well as hands and fingers become playthings, and the baby now realises that their feet and fingers belong to them. They have developed a level of hand/eye co-ordination so that they can hold objects in one hand and pass them to the other without dropping them. They use a 'whole hand grasp' and cannot yet consciously open the grasp to give an object or toys to someone else. If a baby drops a toy they will watch it fall, which shows that they are beginning to understand 'cause and effect'. Babies of six months will laugh and chuckle; they are also beginning to make some short sounds deliberately such as 'ma ma ma' or 'da da da'. Babies enjoy looking at books with a familiar adult and try to repeat some sounds, blending vowels and constants together to make strings of sounds.

They are now interested in, and an interesting member of, the family. They are not quite as sociable as they were when three months old and they can distinguish between strangers and familiar people.

Babies of six months have quite distinct mood swings, going from a happy, contented baby to a cross, angry person in a very short space of time. At around this time parents and childminders will decide to start to introduce foods other than milk; however some mothers may want to start earlier. This is a good time to introduce different foods as the mouth is very sensitive and babies will put everything into their mouths. This is not because they are hungry, but it is a way of finding out about objects through taste and feel. A baby's gums are beginning to harden as the first teeth are nearly ready to come through. Babies get pleasure from biting hard rusks as well as toys, but make sure that small toys and objects are kept well out of reach to prevent choking.

Needs

As babies put everything in their mouths you must make sure that you have very high standards of hygiene and cleanliness in your home to prevent the spread of infection and illnesses. They need to be able to find out about their world in a safe, hygienic and clean environment.

Babies of this age need to be with people who will play with them, talk to them and stimulate all areas of development.

Activities to promote development

- Put some toys and familiar objects slightly out of reach to encourage the baby to stretch and try to move and crawl.
- Put cushions or pillows around a baby so that they can sit supported and will not hurt themselves if they fall or topple.
- Play and sing nursery rhymes that involve movements or actions so that babies can bounce whilst you sing.
- Point to familiar objects around the house and in books and name them at the same time.
- Talk to the baby as you go about your daily routines and tell them what you are doing; this will help all aspects of language and communication development.

Nine months – growth and development

At this age many babies are becoming mobile; they have started to crawl or shuffle, and some make attempts to pull themselves up using any available piece of furniture or object that is at the right height. As well as becoming more mobile and active babies of this age can sit unsupported and can reach out and grasp objects. Their fine motor skills and hand/eye co-ordination have developed to the point where they will use a 'pincer grasp', that is the finger and thumb, to pick up small objects. They will also clap and point at objects. By nine months many babies have teeth and can feed themselves with finger foods. Most nine-month-old babies are having three meals a day and their routine for feeding usually will fit in with older children and other family members.

A baby of this age will babble and make a wide range of noises to communicate. He or she will probably understand some words and respond accordingly, such as to 'bye, bye', 'dinner time' and 'no'. Babies start to use gestures and sounds to attract the attention of others when playing, such as copying sounds that others make, shouting and laughing out loud. They will clap hands together to show pleasure and other emotions are often expressed by large body movements, moving the whole body when excited, or throwing themselves backwards or stiffening the whole body when angry or frustrated. By now babies have become increasingly suspicious of strangers and can become quite anxious and distressed when separated from their mother or main carer. Some babies become very clingy at this stage, which can be distressing for parents, baby and the childminder.

Needs

The baby's most important need at this age is to be safe. The active baby needs to be able to move and play without fear of hurting themselves. Clothes should be comfortable and appropriate for crawling. There should be no ties or straps that could get caught or parts of the clothes that could get stuck under the body and so restrict movement. A baby of this age still needs the love and attention of familiar adults, with whom he or she can play games and learn from.

Activities to promote development

- Introduce the treasure basket as described in Chapter 3.
- Continue to talk and sing to the baby.
- Play clapping and activity games, such as peek-a-boo.
- Look at books together and with the other children, introducing new words. Children who have not handled books from a very early age may find reading more difficult later on.
- Be consistent with your routines, especially for sleep and nap times. A baby who shows concern at being left can be sometimes difficult to settle. Talk to the parents and decide on a settling routine that you both can use.

- Make sure that furniture and objects that a baby might use to pull themselves up on are firm and stable. Door and stair gates are absolutely essential if you have a baby of this age in your care.
- Ask parents to provide a soft toothbrush for their baby and start to introduce a routine for caring for the teeth.

Learning Outcome Activity 26 (DCP, ECP)

Using songs or rhymes to stimulate a baby

In the section on growth and development it is suggested that singing rhymes are good activities for stimulating a baby.

First of all make a list of all the rhymes that you know, especially ones that have simple actions, such as 'Round and round the garden like a teddy bear' or 'This little piggy'.

When you have made your list, ask another childminder, or someone on your course, to do the same.

Compare the two lists and see if there are any new rhymes on the other person's list.

You might want to suggest to your tutor that a fun and light-hearted way to end each session is for one person to teach the others a song or rhyme. You could be surprised how many new ideas you can get.

12 months – growth and development

At one year old a baby is a friendly sociable person, who is becoming increasingly independent. Most one-year-olds spend about thirteen hours asleep, with often just a short nap in the day. Many babies have achieved the major milestone of walking independently by the time that they are one, some still need the assistance of either furniture or a friendly adult. This added mobility opens up a whole new world to the baby; new things are now within sight and reach, such as doors and cupboards that need to be opened and investigated. The inside of the washing machine can be a fascinating place and possibly just the right place to put a book or toy! If not walking, babies can crawl or shuffle, and get from one place to another quite quickly. One-year-old babies are able to hold a cup by themselves to drink from and will make good attempts to feed themselves with a spoon as well as fingers. Their grasp is well developed and not only can they pick things up using a pincer grasp, they can also choose to release their grip and drop things.

Babies at this age can let adults know what they want by pointing at objects and can often say one or two familiar words. They can understand and obey simple instructions, such as 'Give it to me please', and 'Wave bye bye to Mummy'. One-year-old babies know their own name and often those of other family members or adults and children with whom they spend a lot of time.

They delight in copying adult actions and sounds and obviously thrive on the reaction that this will get from adults. Babies of this age are still wary of strangers and like to have either their mother or a familiar adult within sight. Dressing a baby of this age becomes somewhat easier as usually they will start to co-operate and respond to requests such as 'Put your arm up please'. Often as babies become more active, the need to restrain and restrict some of their explorations becomes greater. This leads to frustration for the baby and outbursts of anger or rage. On the whole the mood swings are less dramatic than when younger, and the baby is much more curious and shows little fear.

Needs

As before, safety is a vital need at this age. The curious baby, with little fear, does not understand danger and you will need to be constantly on your guard. Babies need to be allowed freedom to explore and you have to decide when exploration becomes risky and respond. Babies need other children to watch and play alongside. They need the reassurance and love of a familiar adult within sight at all times. Many babies at this age need a comfort object, which can be almost anything depending on the child. Some children have a favourite cuddly toy, some like a piece of soft material such as a blanket.

Activities to promote development

- Babies of this age like to put things in and out of other things, so toys such as posting boxes and stacking toys are good. You could provide different-sized, clean, smooth-edged tins and containers with pegs and small bricks to put inside.
- Taking a baby to new and different places expands his or her world and also provides good opportunities when you are talking to introduce new words.
- Co-ordination and control can be developed by giving a baby things to bang together, such as a drum, or a wooden spoon and tin lid.
- Push-along toys on wheels help to develop walking skills and balance.
- Babies can be introduced to sand, water and other messy play activities, such as finger painting, playing with shaving foam on a flat surface and bubbles; but you will need to watch them very carefully. Some children can have an allergic reaction to some messy play materials, such as shaving foam, so you may need to consider other things such as corn flour and water.

CASE STUDY

Angie is working towards Unit 2 of the Certificate in Childminding Practice. Her tutor has suggested that everyone tries to make a resource that will help the sensory development of a young baby between six and nine months old.

The resource has to:

- be made from or use things that are normally found in the home
- be cheap and easy to make
- be suitable for older babies and young children.

Angie is immediately worried, she feels that she cannot do this. She was no good at art or craft at school and feels that whatever she makes will be very inferior to what other course members have made. Also, at the moment Angie is only caring for two children, one of whom is two, the other nearly four. Angie's first idea was to make a mobile, then she thought about a 'feely' mat. However when Angie looked around her home, she couldn't find anything that she thought she could use.

The nearer it got to the evening when everyone would show their resource, the more inadequate Angie felt. One afternoon she was making play dough with the children when the younger child started to play with the wooden mixing spoon, turning it round and round and feeling the shape. Angie remembered reading something about 'Heuristic play and treasure baskets'. This gave her the idea of trying to put together a collection of wooden objects that babies could safely feel with both their hands and mouths. Later that evening, when the children had left, Angie and her eight-year-old son went round the house and found twelve wooden things that were safe for a baby. There were wooden spoons, wooden bricks, a brush, pegs, curtain rings, far more things than Angie could have imagined. Her son carefully washed a bread basket that was not used very much and put everything in it. Angie went off to the course hoping that she had done the 'right thing'.

Angie realised that her resource was a success, not only did it meet all the criteria, it used things from around the home, it hadn't cost anything and it could be used by older babies and young children, as Angie found out when her son was helping her. It was also very simple. Angie could really see and understand how her resource would help to develop a baby's senses, and, as her tutor pointed out, this resource could be used for one of the activities for assignment 1.

The second year, active toddlers

The best way to describe this year is one of discovery and exploration. Physically, all the skills that have been practised during the first year come together to allow the toddler to walk and balance successfully. This means that the opportunities to explore and discover the world around them are vastly increased and by doing this the toddler also gains some control over his or her immediate environment. They can decide what they can do and where they want to go.

During the first year the baby has been practising and mastering all the sounds and physical movements that are needed for speech. The baby has also been listening to all the sounds around and storing these in his or her memory. During this second year language development is rapid. However, if a baby or toddler is cared for by someone who does not have time to talk to them, or is very quiet, there is the possibility that the child's language development could be seriously deprived.

Toddlers tend to be very active and want to explore and investigate the world around them

15 months – growth and development

One characteristic of a fifteen-month-old child is that they are often restless. They want and need to be active. This need can often lead to conflict and frustration as adults thwart the toddler's explorations for safety reasons. Toddlers of this age change rapidly from wanting to be independent and do things on their own, to wanting an adult very close. They often show jealousy when an adult gives attention to another child and can get very angry and cross.

Most children of this age can stand and walk reasonably steadily, but cannot yet steer a path away from objects. When something is in their way they will quite often sit down and crawl around it, then stand up again and carry on walking. Stairs are now achievable and toddlers can often walk upstairs by holding onto either an adult or a rail. Coming down is a different matter, and you should teach a toddler to come down backwards by crawling, for safety reasons.

By now up to twelve teeth may have come through with the first molars erupting during this time. Toddlers do not put as many objects and toys in their mouths now as they have learnt and remembered the shape, feel, taste and smell. However if a new toy or something strange is discovered, toddlers will use their mouth as well as their hands and fingers to explore it. They can usually hold a crayon and will try to make marks with it. They try to turn pages of books and will become excited when recognising familiar pictures.

The toddler at this age can understand far more words than they can actually say, but are quite skilful at getting other people to understand what they want. They use gestures, body language and single words to make themselves understood, for example a toddler could point at their cup and say 'Me', which means 'Please can I have a drink?'

Although fifteen-month-olds want to be independent, they show interest in other children and will watch them closely. However they have not yet developed enough social understanding to realise that biting and hitting other children is not the way to make friends. They will co-operate with adults more, especially at times such as getting dressed.

Needs

Toddlers need to be active. They need safe opportunities to explore and investigate their world. They need to be allowed to developed their independence in a safe way, so should be allowed to feed themselves and try to put on articles of clothing. Fifteen-month-olds need lots of praise and encouragement of their achievements. This will give them confidence to do more and so learn more. Adults will need to have lots of patience with children of this age as they can be very demanding and tiring.

Activities to promote development

- Use meal times as opportunities for the child to learn independence and grow in confidence and they successfully feed themselves.
- Independence and self-help skills can also be encouraged by allowing the child to respond to simple instructions such as 'Please pass me your shoes'.
- Provide big chunky crayons and large pieces of paper, such as wallpaper, and let the toddler make marks. This will help develop their fine manipulative skills.
- Spend time together looking at books. Point to and name things in the pictures to help the child to learn more words. Talk about the pictures and tell the story. This will make the child aware of sentence construction and word patterns, especially if there is lots of repetition of sounds and words.
- Develop the idea of the 'treasure basket' as described in Chapter 3. Introduce bigger containers, tins and boxes with lots of things that can be put inside, such as corks, wooden blocks, pegs, lengths of chain, small tins and boxes, lengths of tube, baking tins, wooden and metal utensils. Make sure that the toddler helps you to tidy these things away. It can be part of play, as tidying away is just an extension of putting things inside a bigger container.

18 months – growth and development

By now the toddler can usually walk well, placing their feet closer together but it is not necessarily cause for concern if they do not. Discuss with the parents if you think that there may be a problem. They can now avoid things in their way and

watching. Many children of this age are now toilet trained and will take themselves off to use a potty or the toilet independently. Often they can cope with getting pants down, but may still need help in organising themselves when they have finished. Usually children of this age have all of their milk teeth. Many children now give up their daytime nap between two and two-and-a-half; although some may have given it up much earlier, others still need a quiet time, if not a sleep or nap, at some point during the day. Many children of this age will show a clear preference for using their right or left hand when holding writing materials for example, or left or right foot when kicking a ball.

It is important for a child of this age that adults approve of what he or she is doing. This is an important part of their social development and their development of self-confidence, self-esteem and self-image. Although they can have dramatic mood swings, they are usually becoming calmer, especially towards their third birthday. Being independent is very important and this can lead to unco-operative behaviour at times. However many children of this age will allow themselves to become part of older children's play and will co-operate, such as 'being the baby' when pretend playing. The children however still do not really play with other children, and will play either alongside or in parallel or just watch (spectator play).

'What's that?' is still a very popular question as the active toddler explores and investigates. They will now refer to themselves as 'I' and 'me' when talking, another aspect of understanding who they are and social development.

Needs

Children of this age need patience and firmness from their childminders and parents. It is very important that both the childminder and the parents deal with tantrums, for example, and other behaviours consistently. The child will become very confused, insecure and often fearful if they have to cope with inconsistencies from adults. They need to have all of their questions answered no matter how numerous. They need adults and other children to take an interest in and join in their play and activities. In this way they will learn how to share, be co-operative and learn associative play.

Activities to promote development

- If you care for several children between two and three years old you will need to make sure that whatever toys or play materials you provide, there are lots of them. Children of this age are still not able to share and so by providing plenty of things to play with you will avoid unnecessary disputes between the children. You may need several dolls or cuddly toys to pretend to feed, for example.
- Provide lots of things to sort into piles or to put into other containers, such as cards, small boxes and containers, and small-scale toys such as cars, animals, bricks and blocks. This will help develop ideas about colour, size and shape.

- Let the children experiment and play with paint and different media such as chalks, crayons and various writing materials. Let them paint with their fingers, chalk on your patio outside (it does wash off!) and make marks on different types of paper, such as newspaper or off-cuts of wallpaper. Don't expect an end product, just allow the children to experiment and play for the joy and fun of it.
- When looking at books together, get into the habit of running your finger along the words as you read them. This will introduce the idea that words and print carry a meaning and also develop the idea that print is read in a particular direction.

Learning Outcome Activity 28 (ECP)

Observing children playing

As part of your course on Unit 3 Extending Childminding Practice, you will look at ways to observe and assess children's development. This helps you to make decisions about the children's stage of growth and development and their needs. This is discussed in much more detail in Chapter 6. If you are childminding a child between three months and three years you will be able to do this activity. If not, ask another course member or childminder if you can share their observation.

What to do

Choose a child within the age range of three months to three years.

Spend about six or seven minutes watching them play. Write down everything that they do. Then try to answer the following questions:

1 What do they play with?
2 How long does the child play with one toy or object or part of the body such as fingers or toes?
3 What can they do well?
4 What do they find difficult?

Think of some things that you could do to extend their development and learning, especially physical skills.

The fourth year

By the time that most children reach their third birthday they usually have had contact with other children in a variety of settings. Many will have been attending pre-school or toddler groups for several months. The opportunity to be with other children of their own age soon lets children learn that play and their games can be more fun if they let others join in. However you must remember that along with the bonuses associated with mixing with other children, some three-year-olds find the adjustment to another routine unsettling and it will be part of your job, as their childminder, to help them settle and adjust to any new routine and situation.

Three years – growth and development

Children of three are usually well co-ordinated and have good control of their movements. They enjoy 'rough and tumble play', or vigorous play, and you will need to make sure that you can provide safe opportunities for this very natural form of play, either in your own home or further afield. Many three-year-olds make determined efforts to use scissors and cut out things. They will now draw recognisable 'pictures'; for example they will draw a picture of a person, but will only draw the head and face and not the body, or have arms and legs coming from what is in effect the

Three-year-olds are experiencing more of the world

head. They will make good attempts to dress themselves and want to do things for themselves, such as fasten buttons and shoes.

Three-year-olds can be very skilful at mimicking adults, not just their actions but their mannerisms, gestures and attitudes. Children of this age are usually less likely to throw a temper tantrum and have better control of their emotions. They will often describe experiences that have happened to themselves through play, for example a doll may have 'tummy ache and feel unwell' or 'Teddy broke the toy'.

Depending on their previous experiences some three-year-olds will at times still be egocentric, but are able to understand more about the consequences of their actions. Three-year-olds are able to understand that they must adapt the way they act in certain situations and places, for example, they learn that at nursery they have to sit quietly and listen at story time and that a bell might indicate 'tidy-up time'; in your home they understand that they are not allowed to jump and climb on your furniture, whereas at nursery they can climb and jump.

Some three-year-olds appear to never stop talking! They can be constantly asking questions, or providing a commentary on what is going on around them and who and what they are playing with. However some three-year-olds can become nervous, shy or self-conscious, especially in new or unfamiliar situations, and this can affect how they communicate with others.

Needs

Three-year-olds need other children of a similar age to play with. They also need the approval and encouragement of adults. Children will test and try out new ideas and ways of behaving and it is important that all adults have consistent standards of behaviour. This does not mean that you have to change your routine to that of the nursery. Children of this age need as much independence as possible and as much variety of activity as possible. They need positive role models so that they can learn positive and acceptable ways to behave and act.

Activities to promote development

- Three-year-olds will copy not only your actions but also your attitudes. It is very important that you are a positive role model for them. If you are pleasant, helpful and loving towards other children and adults, children will learn these attitudes from you. If you are cross and shout, the chances are that the children in your care will also shout and appear to be cross.
- Provide opportunities for safe vigorous play, with times to extend and stretch themselves physically. Remember that children will never climb higher on a climbing frame, for example, than the height at which they feel secure, so do not push them to go on 'one step more' if they do not want to.
- Suggest to parents that their child mixes with other children in different situations, if not already doing so.
- Provide lots of opportunities for imaginative play with dressing-up clothes, safe hiding places (even under the table can be a very exciting place) and things to play in, such as big cardboard boxes
- As their world and experiences increase, introduce the idea of 'stranger danger' and other aspects of their safety, such as stop, look and listen when crossing a road'. Make sure that you do not frighten the naturally friendly and curious three-year-old.

CASE STUDY

Surinder is three years and three months old. He has been cared for by Jenni, a childminder, since he was eighteen months old, along with Jenni's own school-aged children and two others both older than him. His parents both work full-time. Surinder has been described by Jenni as confident and very talkative. He has just started to attend the local nursery school each morning. Jenni takes him, together with an older child that she cares for, to the school and collects him at the end of the morning session.

Surinder has suddenly become very shy and reluctant to let Jenni leave him at nursery. One morning Jenni felt that he was going to start to cry. He has told his parents that he doesn't want to leave Jenni and they are concerned about this apparent change in his behaviour. Jenni makes arrangements with his parents to talk together when they come to pick him up at the end of the day. Jenni does her best to reassure Surinder's parents that this is 'normal' behaviour for three-year-olds when in unfamiliar situations, and that they and Jenni need to be reassuring towards Surinder. Jenni explains that he will become confident at nursery, provided that both she and his parents say the same things. They agree to talk again about this in two weeks time.

1   Was Jenni's explanation of Surinder's behaviour right?
2   What would you have done?

The fifth year, starting school and the wider world

Generally speaking the child of four is more boisterous and energetic than the three-year-old. He or she is much more aware of others and not egocentric. The world is now a place to explore with confidence and with children of his or her own age rather than with adults. Many children of this age are in full-time education, in reception classes. It is important that children have good, positive role models.

Four years old – growth and development

Children of four have often developed co-ordination skills to the point that they can pedal a tricycle, steer a course around obstacles, talk and play imaginatively with friends all at the same time. They are often more prepared to test their physical skills, for example they may try to go a little bit higher on a climbing frame or hang by their knees from a bar. By now it is usually very clear whether he or she is left-handed or right-handed and they use the most preferred hand to paint and draw. Many children are also making good attempts to write recognisable letters. They use

Four-year-olds are more energetic and more aware of others than three-year-olds

a combination of physical, intellectual and creative skills to make complicated models. Four-year-olds will often have a more logical approach to life and are beginning to understand how to reason and work things out for themselves.

Four-year-olds have a vast vocabulary which is growing all the time, as they continue to ask many questions, to which they expect reasonable answers. They will tell long involved stories, often mixing fact and fantasy. Four-year-olds experiment and play with language and sounds, and delight in making up 'silly' words which they find hilariously funny. They may also start to use bad language and swear words, partly to challenge adults and see what reaction they get, and partly as a form of imitating older children and adults. By now they will have adopted and copied the standards of behaviour of their parents or other familiar, close adults.

It is quite usual for children at this age to develop a friendship with one particular child, although they play well in groups and will be co-operative. They can take turns and share but are often not consistent, and sometimes find games with rules, that they have not decided upon, confusing. Four-year-olds are developing an understanding of the needs of others and will show concern for another child who is hurt or distressed, often offering comfort and telling a familiar adult. They are usually confident children who show some control over their behaviour and emotions. However when tired, anxious or unwell they will seek comfort and reassurance from a familiar adult.

Needs

Although they are confident and self-assured individuals, four-year-olds still seek the approval of adults. They need to have a secure and consistent framework of standards and behaviour that they can follow. They will often check the actions of others against their known framework, for example a four-year-old will say to another child 'You haven't washed your hands' before they sit down to eat. They need to have their numerous questions answered in a truthful and reasonable way. If the child does not feel that you have given them a reasonable answer, they will persist in questioning you until satisfied. They need to be treated by adults as sensible and reasonable individuals and they will respond positively, if given small jobs and areas of responsibility. They need more advanced books, stories, songs and games to 'feed' their increasing thirst for knowledge.

Activities to promote development

- You will need to make sure that you have a good range of books and reading material. If you have not joined the local library this is a very good time for you to do so. Trips to the library can become good learning experiences, you can talk about the numbers on the car registration plates or house doors, you can play simple 'I-spy' games, based on colours or shape as well as initial sounds.
- Allow the four-year-old to help you with 'proper' jobs, for example, pouring drinks for other children, sorting clean laundry or putting away shopping.
- Don't laugh at a child if he or she uses words in the wrong order or context. They need to be able to experiment with language, and not only will it be hurtful and damaging, you could give the child the impression that to experiment is wrong. It is better to repeat what the child has said, but use the correct order of words and add a word of praise; for example if the child says 'I've doned it', you could reply, 'That's great, I'm pleased that you have done it.'
- Make sure that you answer questions in a truthful and reasonable way. Four-year-olds often only want the answer to the immediate question that they have asked and so it is not always necessary to go off into long involved explanations. Four-year-olds will get bored and either wander off or ask you another completely different question. If they want to know more than you have given in your answer they will ask another question.

The sixth year and beyond

In this country, many children of this age will have been in school for at least a year, either in pre-school groups, nursery or reception classes. By now they are self-confident and sociable. Friendship become increasingly important and the child becomes less dependent on adults and more in control of their own lives.

Five years old – growth and development

In terms of physical growth and development, many children of this age have lost the body shape associated with pre-school children. Although they still have the same body proportions from babyhood, in that they have a large head and relatively short legs, the proportions begin to change between the ages of five and eight. Children's legs grow longer and they gradually take on the body proportions of adults. They tend to lose the baby pads of fat around the face. This makes their facial features more pronounced and family likenesses are more obvious. Body movements are controlled and co-ordinated and can be adapted to suit different learning situations, such as holding a pencil to write or holding or successfully doing small fastenings on clothes.

What are some of the changes a five-year-old goes though?

Five-year-olds often 'show-off', but this is a natural outcome of their increased self-confidence. They still tend to mix fact and fantasy and will sometimes embellish facts about themselves and their family members, such as when talking to another child they will often say things like 'My mummy's car is bigger than yours'. They will even do this when they know very well that mummy doesn't actually have a car! Five-year-olds are usually friendly children, and they expect to be liked by others. They are eager to learn and want to please adults. They trust adults and seek their help to sort out arguments with friends. Five-year-olds usually prefer games of rivalry to team games. They play well together in groups, but at the same time will often choose to play alone quite happily. Mixing with other children and adults gives the five-year-old many role models and he or she can decide for themselves which ones they want to follow and copy.

Children of this age have little or few fears. Some don't like the dark and have a fear of being lost. They have little or no understanding of dangers on the road; this is because they do not understand how to control a vehicle or how to judge speed. Five-year-olds often act on impulse and so will run across a road to talk to a friend, with no regard for danger.

They can use language skilfully to explain want they want, learn new things and extend their play. Many five-year-olds are beginning to read which will open up a whole new world to them. They can have an understanding and use up to 3000 words, and this is increasing all the time as they ask questions and learn more about their world.

Needs

The needs of a five-year-old are not that much different from the needs of a four-year-old. They still need positive role models. They need calm and consistent adults whom they can trust to deal with their problems reasonably. They need accurate answers to their questions. They need the company and stimulation of other children and adults. As with a child of any age they need to be cared for in a safe and secure environment where they can grow and develop in a healthy way.

Activities to promote development

- At the end of a busy school day some children are often tired and can be cross. You will need to adjust your routine to cope with this. The child may want to be on their own for a while; they could be hungry and need a snack. On the other hand, some children come out of school bursting to tell someone about the exciting things that they have been doing. Whatever the case, take your cues from the child and respond to their individual needs.
- Read stories to five-year-olds with positive, strong and powerful characters. This helps the children to learn about other role models and develop their own standards.
- Provide opportunities for the children to develop new skills and to concentrate for longer periods of time. If you are caring for five-year-olds during school holidays for example, when they could be with you all day, share with them some of your routine jobs around the garden or house. Get the children to help you rake up and bag fallen leaves, or wash and clean toys and play things.

Six years old – growth and development

Children of six are growing steadily, although not as fast as in the first years of life. Around this age they start to lose their milk teeth, which can be viewed with excitement as a sign of 'growing up', or with some apprehension, fear of the unknown and embarrassment and shyness. For example, a gap between teeth can affect the way a child speaks or eats. Many six-year-olds will respond to music and match their movements to the type of music with confidence and skill. Many can confidently repeat a complete dance routine of a popular group, and enjoy doing it tremendously.

Emotionally six-year-olds are often not as stable as five-year-olds. They swing between loving and hating something or someone rapidly. They can be rebellious and self-centred, but at the next moment will be co-operative and loving. Many six-year-olds find failure and frustrations very difficult to accept and can then become aggressive and irritable. Although they can often quarrel with their friends they will play co-operatively and many have one particular friend. They are now beginning to understand fair play and games with rules, often making up the rules of such games, or changing them, as they go along.

Six-year-olds place a great deal of weight on the views and opinions of their teacher at school and this can sometimes be a source of disputes with childminders, parents and the child. Six-year-olds can be quite defiant and unhelpful out of school, but willing to work and do tasks at school. School is a special place for many six-year-olds and it is therefore very important that parents and childminders develop good relationships with the children's teachers.

Needs

Six-year-olds need much patience from childminders, parents and teachers. They also need firm guidelines and boundaries as to how far they can explore and experiment. Although a lot less dependent on adults, six-year-olds need praise and encouragement of their efforts and achievements. They need opportunities to rest at the end of a busy school day.

> **Activities to promote development**
> - Provide more complex construction sets or materials that stretch the skills and concentration levels.
> - Introduce new skills such as electronic games and equipment or musical instruments.
> - Many six-year-olds enjoy playing with small-scale toys. They will devise complex play situations and play imaginatively with other children for comparatively long periods of time.

Seven years old – growth and development

Seven-year-old children are usually active and energetic, but there is a tendency for them not to understand their own energy levels and so become overtired. Children of this age are often more stable emotionally than, say, a six-year-old, but they can be very self-critical. This can lead to moodiness and dissatisfaction. They can now distinguish between fact and fantasy, and although they still play in an imaginative way, the inspiration for the play is familiar practical situations. They will play games with peers and friends that involve rules being consistent and not changing the rules to suit themselves. Some seven-year-olds become aware of what is or isn't fair and will complain to adults about what they see as unfair treatment, especially in a home environment involving brothers and sisters. Many children have a 'best friend' who is often of the same sex, but it is not unusual to find a boy and girl as 'best friends'. These children enjoy planning things to do together and have the ability to carry out their plans within reason.

Needs

Seven-year-olds still need adults to set firm boundaries and show understanding and patience. They need to be encouraged to take short rests, or quiet times, and not get overtired. They still need adult help to arbitrate in disputes with friends or to give specific help with school or home work.

Activities to promote development

- Provide lots of different materials for children to make things. You may need to extend your collection of recycled materials to satisfy the needs of the seven-year-old as they have now usually got good fine motor skills, dexterity and co-ordination. They can build models and make pictures with small pieces, such as used match sticks, grains of rice, seeds and small pieces of paper. Children of this age respond well to suggestions that they make pictures or models following a theme or specific idea.
- During holiday times, keep a look out for special activities at sports centres, museums and libraries that, with the parents' permission, the seven-year old could attend.
- Provide a quiet place where they can complete homework after school, or have some privacy from younger children.

Eight years old and over – growth and development

These are usually regarded as the years of stability and vitality, before the onset of puberty. Emotionally, children of this age are independent of adults, and the company of children of their own age is more important to them than that of adults. They are no longer as self-centred and want to do things with other children. Long-lasting group friendships form as well as 'best friends'. Quite often the groups will be a mix of both boys and girls, but as they get older it is usual for children to seek group friendships of the same sex. Conforming to group standards is very important. They like to wear the same clothes, listen to the same music and own the same things. Children who do not or cannot conform, are often rejected or ignored by the group. This can lead to acute distress and needs very sensitive handling by adults. Sometimes children will behave and act very differently in groups than when on their own.

Needs

Children need to be trusted and loved. They need to be able to do things independently, whilst at the same time maintaining their safety. They need acceptance by their peers and want to 'belong'. They need adults to manage their environment, but the adults must appear to the children to be consistent, reliable and 'good managers'. Children will respect such adults, but will reject the authority of adults who they regard as incompetent or weak.

Activities to promote development

- Adjust your routine so that children of this age can take part in after-school activities with groups of children of their own age.
- Although children like to organise and structure their activities independently, allow them time to play freely, as a contrast from the organised school day, and express their feelings.

Learning Outcome Activity 29 (ICP, DCP, ECP)

Your daily routine and children's needs

Think about your daily routine and the children that you are caring for at the home.

1 What could you do to give new tasks to encourage independence and responsibility in school-aged children? Why is this important?
2 How would you need to change your routine to accommodate meeting children from after-school activities?

Think about why children need to belong to groups.

1 How would you explain to the parents of a child of eight as to why their child wants to wear only some types of clothes, especially if the parents don't think the child needs them?

Factors that can affect children's growth and development

There are many factors that can affect a child's growth and development. Some can be temporary, such as being temporarily hard of hearing after having a cold, some can be more long-lasting, such as food allergies, and in some cases they are permanent. It is almost impossible to list and consider all the factors that can affect a child. In most cases a factor that affects, for example, physical growth and development will affect other areas of a child's development and it is difficult to separate them into 'developmental areas'.

Some experts who study child development divide the factors that can affect growth and development into three areas:

- **Antenatal** – from conception to birth.

- **Perinatal** – the actual birth.

- **Postnatal** – after birth.

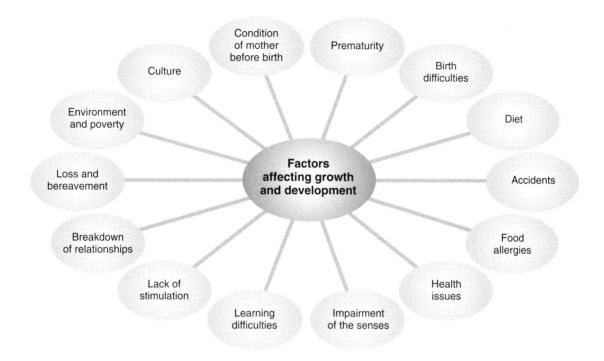

Figure 5.3 *A child's growth and development can be affected by a number of factors*

Condition of mother before birth

This is an antenatal factor and includes such things as smoking, diet and how much alcohol the mother has had whilst pregnant. Scientific studies have shown that the lifestyle of a pregnant woman affects the unborn baby. It has been proved that mothers who smoke and drink whilst pregnant give birth to smaller babies. Recent studies in America have shown that children with low birth weights have lower intelligence scores than those children who are heavier at birth.

Prematurity

Premature babies are those who are born early, and have not fully developed. They are usually born between 24 and 37 weeks of pregnancy, whereas a full-term baby is born between 38 and 40 weeks. Premature babies have low birth weight, are small and can have developmental delays. Also, babies who have low birth weights are often more susceptible to infection, feeding difficulties and problems with breathing.

Birth difficulties

There can be many varied factors that will affect the birth of a baby. Significant medical developments in recent years have reduced the risk to both the baby and the mother and in many cases increased care of the mother before birth can anticipate and sometime avoid difficulties at birth. However one of the most common birth difficulties is when the baby is deprived of oxygen during the birthing process. This is called **anoxia** and can cause a wide range of problems such as learning difficulties and cerebal palsy.

Diet

The quality of a child's diet is crucial at all times during their life. Children who are undernourished, that is, those who do not get enough to eat, and those who do not have a balanced diet and are malnourished can show many signs of developmental delay. Food provides children with energy, which helps them to grow and develop.

It is very important that before you start to plan food and meals for the children in your care, you talk to the parents. There could be cultural, medical and religious reasons why children do not eat some foods and you must respect the wishes of the parents. The chart on page 305 shows you some of the customs and religious practices associated with food.

In order for the body to grow and develop it requires nutrients of which there are five types:

1 **Fats** are found in dairy products, meat and fish, vegetable oils. They help to provide the body with energy.

2 **Proteins** are found in meat, fish, dairy products, soya and vegetables. These help the body to grow and help with healing.

3 **Vitamins** are found in many different forms and most fresh food products will have some type of vitamin in them. It is well known, for example, that vitamin C is found in fruit. Vitamins are essential to all types of growth and development. In Victorian England, many children had limited diets and developed a bone disease called rickets. It was found that vitamin D, which is present in dairy products and fish, helped the body to develop strong bones and teeth, so by giving children milk to drink doctors were able to eliminate rickets.

4 **Carbohydrates** provide energy and are found in bread, potatoes, bananas and vegetables. Often when adults want to lose weight they cut out or reduce the amount of carbohydrate in their diet, which could explain why many dieters complain of feeling tired.

5 **Mineral elements**, like vitamins, are present in many foods and in many different forms; for example, calcium is needed for healthy teeth and is found in dairy products. Lack of iron can lead to anaemia, where people lack energy and are pale. Iron can be found in red meat and some green vegetables.

There is much debate over the safety of some foods, such as beef products, genetically modified products and chemical additives. Many food products contain added salt or sugar, so it is always a good practice to read the nutritional information on food labels as you shop. You will clearly have your own opinion as to those matters and what you feed members of your own family, but you should discuss these issues with the parents and respect their views.

You want the children in your care to develop and grow in a healthy way. You also want to help them understand which foods are good for them and which are not. A good starting point is to think about your own eating habits. What sort of role model are you and what are your attitudes towards food? If you are always eating as you rush about, never sitting down to eat a meal in a calm and relaxed way, the children in your care will learn that as an acceptable way to eat, which you know is not the case.

Some experts in children's care believe that young children should be offered small meals and snacks throughout the day rather than just three large meals a day. Snacks can be as good for children as 'normal' meals provided that what you give the children is good for them. Pieces of fresh fruit, raw vegetables and some crackers are healthy snacks.

Learning Outcome Activity 30 (ICP, DCP, ECP)

Working out a menu

Below is the start of a week's menu for two children aged three and four being cared for each day from 9 am to 6 pm by a childminder. The children have breakfast with their parents at home.

Mid-morning snack	Milk
	Fruit
Mid-day meal	Pasta shapes with cheese sauce
	Green vegetables
	Water
Mid-afternoon snack	Diluted fruit juice
	Yoghurt
Late afternoon meal	Fish fingers
	Chips
	Salad
	Fruit
	Water

Try to add meals and snacks for the rest of the week, using foods that you would normally buy and give to the children, but also making sure that the children have a balance of all the necessary nutrients throughout the week.

Food allergies

Many children suffer from food allergies or intolerances, either all of their lives or only when young. Some food allergies can be potentially fatal, such as an intolerance to nuts and/or shellfish which can cause the body to go into anaphylactic shock. This means that breathing becomes difficult, and as the airways swell up it is often impossible to breathe, and children can die.

Diabetes is another condition that can be potentially life-threatening. Most diabetic children have to avoid sugar in their diet, so it is very important that they have regular and well-balanced diets. If the sugar levels in the blood of diabetic children get too low a child can go into a diabetic coma or seizure, and will need glucose to raise the blood sugar levels. On the other hand, too much sugar in the blood can lead to excessive thirst, a need to pass urine frequently and weight loss.

Both asthma and eczema can be aggravated by some foods, especially dairy products. Some children are intolerant of gluten, which is found in cereal products. This intolerance is usually referred to as coeliac disease. Studies have shown that some hyperactive children and sometimes those with behaviour problems, are intolerant of yellow food colouring – tartrazine. This additive can be found in many food products, such as the crunchy coating on chicken pieces, sweets, soft drinks and butter-type spreads. It cannot be emphasised enough that you must talk to the parents and find out if their child has a food allergy or intolerance before you start to care for them.

Accidents

Accidents, emergencies and keeping children safe are the main part of the first chapter in this book. Accidents can affect a child's growth and development, sometimes permanently. It should be obvious that a child who has been involved in a serious accident that has affected the way that they move or walk about, will suffer some form of developmental delay in that area. In such a case their social skills could also be affected as they may not be able to get out and about to meet other children. Their language skills will be affected as they could have limited opportunities to communicate with others and emotionally they could become frightened, clingy and unsure when previously they were confident. In some cases developmental delay as a result of an accident is exactly that – a delay – but provided the child has sensitive and understanding carers they will eventually make up the delay.

Health issues

The range of health issues that could affect children's growth and development is vast. They could range from infections such as childhood illnesses, colds and ear infections to a serious illness that could be life-threatening. You also need to think about the children's general health, diet and energy levels. A child who is always tired, for whatever reason, will not be able to concentrate and so their learning will be affected.

Impairment of the senses

Children who have a sensory impairment may show some delay in their intellectual or cognitive development. When very young they rely on their senses to give them information about the world and they build on this information later on. Today severe sensory impairment, such as lack of hearing or sight, are usually identified by the normal health checks. Sometimes however a child can suffer from a temporary sensory impairment, for example the after-effects of a bad cold can affect hearing and this could temporarily delay their development, especially of language skills.

Learning difficulties

There are many reasons why a child may have learning difficulties which can affect all areas of growth and development. If you think that a child in your care has a learning difficulty, discuss the difficulty with the parents and suggest that they seek expert advice and help.

Lack of stimulation

In order for all children to develop and grow they need to be active and involved. Activity or stimulation appropriate to their stage of development is essential if children are to progress and learn. Lack of activity and stimulation means that they simply do not progress.

CASE STUDY

In Romania, which was ruled by a Communist dictatorship for many years, many orphaned and abandoned children were put into orphanages and more or less forgotten. In the early 1990s following the overthrow of the Communist government, the aid agencies of the West discovered the appalling conditions in which these children were existing. Many of the staff in the orphanages believed that the children were mentally impaired from birth. In fact many children had been completely 'normal' at birth, but due to lack of stimulation, and other factors such as diet and quality of care, they had not been able to develop. There were documented cases of children of six and seven years with the behaviour and development of babies of six or seven months. Eventually, with much sensitive care, stimulation and attention some of the children began to show signs of development in all areas, and so were not intellectually impaired as thought by their former carers.

Breakdown of relationships

Children's social and emotional development can be affected by the breakdown of relationships between their parents, or their friends. Children can become anxious, unsure and sometimes frightened that their parents will not come back for them. Confident, happy children can become withdrawn, tearful and lack trust in adults or other children. If their parents are in conflict the child could become drawn into the arguments. However not all children are affected by breakdowns of relationships and some cope well with little, if any, effect on their development, so do not always assume that children in such situations will have problems or difficulties. You need to talk to the parents and take your cues from the child.

Loss and bereavement

Loss and bereavement for children can be as traumatic as it is for adults. However, to a child losing a favourite cuddly toy, moving house and losing a well-loved childminder can be just as traumatic as the death of a parent, brother or sister, or other close family relative. Sometimes children will try to hide their feelings about loss and death, especially if they think that it will upset other people. This can lead to children showing their emotions in other ways, such as aggression or withdrawal.

CASE STUDY

Mick is a childminder for Tom aged five. Tom was collected each day by his grandfather, with whom he had a very close and loving relationship. Tom is confident, very sociable and friendly. Sadly, Tom's grandfather had a fatal heart attack. Tom is now collected much later in the day by his mother after work. She is also grieving for the loss of her father and often looks tired. Tom has become withdrawn and does not want to play with the other children after school. He has started running away and hiding when his mother comes to collect him, shouting that he wants his grandad. Naturally his mother finds this very upsetting and has asked Mick to help.

Mick goes to the local library and finds some books on loss and grief. He also is given the number of a voluntary organisation for help. Mick and Tom find a quiet time to read the books together. Mick encourages Tom to draw pictures of his grandfather and talk about how he is feeling. He answers Tom's numerous questions honestly and simply. He tries to explain to Tom that his mother is also upset, but wants to talk about grandad too. Gradually Tom is able to show and share with his mother the pictures that he has drawn and Mick gives them the books to read together. Tom starts to watch the other children playing and gradually asks if he can join in with their games. He stops running away when his mother comes to collect him. It takes time, but by doing things together and with Mick's sensitive support, both Tom and his mother cope with their loss.

Environment and poverty

Poverty can have a detrimental effect on all aspects of a child's growth and development. Poor housing can affect a child's health; lack of money can affect the amount of food that is bought and therefore also affects the child's health.

The environment in which a child is cared for can also have very positive effects. A loving, secure environment will help a child develop good relationships and social skills. A stimulating environment will enable them to explore and investigate the world around them, developing good language and cognitive skills.

Culture

A child's cultural background must always be respected, even if the traditions of that culture are not yours. We live in a multicultural society, with many parenting styles, languages and religions. Children should be encouraged to learn about cultures other than their own in a positive way. They need to feel confident about themselves and be sure that they are valued. You should be a very positive role model in encouraging this aspect of a child's development.

Some theorists and theories that have influenced views of how children grow and develop

Child development is a relatively new area of study and is now recognised as a part of psychology. While it is not necessary for you to study psychology, unless you really want to, it can be useful to have some understanding about how the work of some psychologists has affected the way we care for and educate children. Some psychologists who have studied children will produce a theory as to why the child is developing in a certain way. Quite often when a psychologist or another expert has come up with a theory, they are usually referred to as a theorist.

In this book it would be impossible to write about every theorist who has ever come up with a theory on some aspect of children's growth and development. Indeed entire books have been written on just one theory or a small part of the work of one theorist. So the following is a very brief outline of the main ideas of some theorists. They are not placed in order of importance but by the date of their birth.

Friedrich Froebel (1782–1852)

Froebel's work and beliefs are possibly some of the earliest influences on how young children are cared for today. He believed that parents, especially mothers, were very important for healthy growth and development. He believed in both indoor and outdoor play and that children needed to play imaginatively in order for them to learn and develop. Froebel set up his first kindergarten (which literally means children's garden) so that he could try out his ideas. Today you probably provide opportunities for indoor and outdoor play without really thinking about it, but this has not always been the case.

Sigmund Freud (1856–1939) and later Erik Erikson (1902–1994)

Freud and Erikson both developed theories about emotional and social development which had stages of development through which all children pass. Erikson believed that for a child to go successfully through each stage, they had to have enough confidence to do so. This means that childminders and other adults working with children should make sure that they offer lots of praise and encouragement to help the child become confident. How many times when reading the earlier section of this chapter on how children develop and learn did you notice that a child needed lots of praise and encouragement?

Maria Montessori (1870–1952)

Montessori was a doctor working in Italy and was able to study how children developed. Montessori created an environment that was purposefully designed for young children and did not include many opportunities for play. Children were encouraged to work on their own, at their own level of development and in a structured way on activities that were based on life-skills, using real-life equipment and tools. Montessori's ideas are still popular today, throughout the world. Many Montessori establishments are called 'Children's Houses', to reflect the idea that children are working in a specially designed place. You may not have a specially designed building or room in your childminding business, but you may have child-sized chairs, low tables and cups and plates that the children use – evidence of the influence of Maria Montessori's theory on your business.

Rudolph Steiner (1861–1925)

Steiner believed that children's development was continuous from one stage to the next and that in order to meet the child's needs, in all ways, it was necessary to understand the sequence of development. He placed a lot of importance on the quality of a child's diet and the amount of rest they had. A section of this chapter looked at providing a healthy and balanced diet for the children in your care. You probably regard this as a natural aspect of your childminding practice and not part of Rudolph Steiner's theory!

Lev Vygotsky (1896–1934)

Vygotsky placed a lot of importance on the adults that a child came into contact with. He believed that adults led children on to the next stage of their development, by showing them how to do things. He thought that play was important and based much of his theory on the idea that we should concentrate more on what a child can do rather than on what they cannot do. Several times in this chapter and the book, the importance of being a positive role model for the children in your care has been stressed. This is reinforcing Vygotsky's theory.

Jean Piaget (1896–1980)

Piaget has been the inspiration for many students studying children's intellectual or cognitive development. Although some aspects of his theory have been challenged and debated, much of what he said is still relevant today. Piaget believed that children's thinking passes through four clearly defined stages, for example babies up to the age of about eighteen months or two years are in the 'sensori-motor' stage. In this stage they learn about their world through the senses and see everything from their point of view (which he called egocentric). The other stages identified are pre-operational from about 2 years to 6 or 7; concrete operation, from about 7 to 11; and finally formal operations from 11 up to adulthood. Each stage has its own distinct characteristics and stages. Piaget also considered the effect of both nature and nurture in children's growth and development.

Play with a treasure basket is based on sensory experiences for a baby or young child. One of the suggested activities is that you set up a treasure basket, especially for children who in Piaget's view were in the sensori-motor stage of development.

John Bowlby (1907–1990)

Bowlby is recognised as developing what is known today as 'the theory of attachment'. He was able to identify the emotional damage that can be caused to babies and young children when separated from their main carer with whom they have already developed a strong relationship. His work was developed by **James** and **Joyce Robertson** who produced some very distressing films of children in hospital and in residential day-care. These films showed very clearly the effects of separating children from their main carers. The work of both Bowlby and the Robertsons has had a tremendous influence on how children and their parents are treated in hospital. In the 1950s a child who went into hospital had to cope with an unfamiliar place with unfamiliar people around them. Visiting was strictly restricted and parents were not encouraged to be involved. Today, children's wards in hospitals involve parents as much as possible and provide places for parents to stay with their child. Also the theory of attachment emphasises the importance of having a settling-in routine for young children and babies when being separated from their parents for the first time. This is especially important for childminders.

Other theorists that you may come across in other books or course materials are:

Johann Pestalozzi	Albert Bandura	Ivan Pavlov
Burrhus Frank Skinner	Lawrence Kohlberg	Mary Ainsworth

Donald Winnicott   Mia Kellmer Pringle   Elizabeth Newsom
Fredric Truby King   Benjamin Spock

The list could go on and on.

Look in your college or local library and also on the internet if you want to find out more.

CHECK YOUR KNOWLEDGE

True or False or Maybe?

Read the following statements and then decide if they are true, false or maybe. The answers are given on page 291.

1   Childminders need to know about children's growth and development so that they can show that they know more than the parents.

2   Holistic mean looking at parts of things.

3   Areas of children's growth and development are all inter-linked.

4   **Spice** stands for social, physical, intellectual, cognitive and emotional areas of development.

5   All children pass through the same stages of development and growth at the same time.

6   Co-ordination is a physical skill.

7   All children need positive role models.

8   Temper tantrums are more common in three-year-olds than children of two.

9   Two-year-olds are usually toilet trained.

10 Three-year-olds draw people with heads and faces but no body.

11 By about two-and-a-half a child will have cut all their milk teeth.

12 Children of two will play co-operatively with other children and share their toys.

13 Young children can sometimes regress in their growth and development when tired, anxious or unwell.

14 Four-year-olds are not interested in the feelings of others.

You must remember that all children are different and that there can be huge differences in the growth and development of children of the same age, but both would be considered to be developing 'normally'. The answers given are ones that you could 'normally' expect.

CHAPTER 6
Planning and supporting children's learning and development

Some childminders think that if they are planning and supporting children's learning, they have to write lots of things down in a formal way and 'teach' children in the same way that teachers would do in schools. This is not the case.

As professional childcare practitioners, childminders plan activities and support children's learning in many valuable ways. Many experienced childminders do this almost instinctively and do not always appreciate the full extent of their work in this area. They can and often do provide children with an excellent start to their formal years at school and also support all aspects of a child's growth and development in ways that could not be achieved in schools. This is one of the many benefits for parents choosing a childminder to care for their child.

Learning is an individual process for everyone. You may remember being in school, in a class with others of the same age and all being taught the same thing. Some of the class will learn what was being taught the first time, others will need to go away and think about it, others will have to ask questions and some may need to be taught the same thing again in a different way. Some will never really learn what was being taught. The way that the teacher will find out if any learning has taken place will be to test the class in some way.

Learning does not just take place in schools. Learning can happen in any situation, at any age and everyone can learn something. Learning is not only about cognitive or intellectual growth and development. These areas are a fundamental part of learning, but not all of it. Physical development, that is, controlling and co-ordinating movements, is a form of learning. Knowing how to act and behave in certain places and situations is part of social development, but is also learning. Understanding how to talk and communicate with others is a form of learning.

How do children learn?

There are many theories and points of view on how children learn. In general they fall into three categories:

1 **Behaviourist** theories. This suggests that children learn by making links between their actions and what happens next. This is also known as **association.** An example of this is a young child who in playing with a toy learns that by pressing a certain button something will happen, such as a sound being heard, or something popping up. In the same way a child will learn that by doing certain things they will get a good reaction, such as praise and smiles from the adult, so they will do it again. In contrast, this way of learning can also have negative associations, for example if a young child has had an unpleasant or hurtful experience with a doctor wearing a white coat, they might associate being upset and hurt with anyone who wears a white coat.

It is interesting how advertisers and retailers use association to entice us to buy things. For example, the smell of freshly baked bread in a supermarket may make you think of something pleasant or feel hungry, so you go and buy bread.

Learning Outcome Activity 31 (ECP)

Learning through association

I can remember as a child walking home from school past a house where the dogs ran out and barked at me, very loudly. I was frightened of these two dogs and so learnt that all dogs were frightening animals and I avoided them. It was not until many, many years later when I owned a dog that I eventually overcame this fear, although sometimes if a much bigger dog approaches me when out walking, I still feel fearful.

Can you think of anything that you have learnt through association?

2 **Constructivist theories**. These theories take the idea that rather than children learning because of things happening to them, they learn from exploring, doing things for themselves and then building on those experiences. This is often referred to as learning from first-hand experiences. The theorist Jean Piaget, who was mentioned in Chapter 5, developed this theory. He suggested that children explore, play and collect information about the world around them. When presented with new experiences they use what they already know to build and develop new ideas and so learn. This works in the following way:

- Assume that you always give a toddler in your care milk to drink in a yellow cup.

- The child learns that all yellow cups have milk in them. This happens every day so the idea is firmly established.

- One day you put water in the yellow cup, so the idea that all yellow cups have milk in them does not work.

- The child now learns that yellow cups can have both milk and water in them.

Eventually the child will learn that there are many different drinks and many different colours and sizes of cups.

The main point of this theory is that the child has learnt new ideas for themselves, through first-hand experience, and not as a result of something happening to them. If you are a driver, you learnt to drive by first-hand experience. You learnt how to get clutch control, for example, by doing it for yourself; you learnt to reverse round a corner by doing it yourself, not by watching someone else doing it.

3 **Social learning theories**. These ideas build on the ideas of association and behaviourist theories, but also consider that children learn from watching other people. This explains why children copy and learn from adults. If you are playing alongside a child and start making a tower with a construction set, the child will often copy you and make a tower as well. Often children will copy adult mannerisms, such as the way they walk, or their gestures. Children also learn negative things from others, such as bad language, prejudiced attitudes and unacceptable behaviour. This makes you realise how important it is for children to have good role models.

Learning Outcome Activity 32 (ECP)

Learning from others

Take time to watch the children in your care playing. It does not really matter if they are playing together or alongside each other.

See if you can identify and make a note of when younger children copy the actions, words or play of older children.

Whatever theory or theorist you feel fits in with your views, there is another way of looking at how children learn, grow and develop. There are three main things that we all want children to be able to do, or learn.

These are to:

1 develop and extend their **knowledge and understanding of the world around them and in which they play and live**.

2 develop and extend their own **skills and the way they act, or behave**.

3 develop their own **attitudes and principles and standards**.

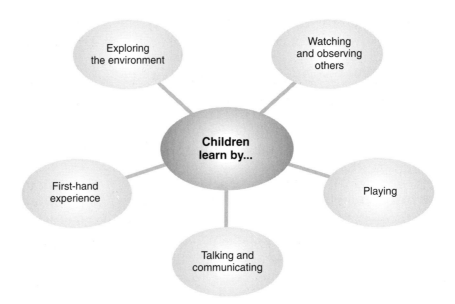

Figure 6.1 *There are certain ways that children learn*

Exploring the environment

Children, of all ages, are naturally curious and this leads them into wanting to find out and learn more. As well as creating a safe and hygienic environment for the child that you care for (as covered in Chapter 1) you need to create a stimulating and positive environment in which the children can safely explore.

There are certain ways that you can create a stimulating and positive environment.

- For children, **you** are a very important part of their environment. You need to talk to and play with the children. You need to ask questions that will encourage the children to find out more, such as 'What do you think will happen to the sand if we add some water?' You need to be a positive role model. The children will watch and copy what you do. They will learn attitudes and opinions that you show: for example, if you say to a four-year-old boy who is crying, 'Come on now, big boys don't cry', what message are you giving to that child and the others?

  - He isn't a 'big boy' because he is crying.
  - It is wrong to cry even when hurt or upset.

  or

  - You can't be bothered with children who cry.

- You need to provide opportunities for the children to do the same things over and over again so that they can learn to do things well. This is called **mastery play**. You probably do this almost without thinking about it, for example, you give young children finger foods so that they can feed themselves. You don't do this once, you do it every mealtime and so the child learns the self-help skill of feeding themselves.

- In your childminding setting, which is the environment in which the children learn, you will need to provide things to play with that suit all ages and stages of the children. Have you got a range a books, such as picture books with no print, big books, small books, story books, books of rhymes and poems, and books that provide information? Possibly not, but your local library will have and you can borrow them.

Babies explore their environment through their senses. When awake they are constantly looking, smelling, hearing, seeing and tasting. With a small baby the amount that they can explore is limited by adults. Adults move babies into different places as they cannot do this for themselves. It is very important that you think about where you place a baby when it is awake. Apart from thinking about his or her safety, think about what they can see, hear or feel from the place that you have put them. If you want to stimulate the baby's learning more, don't always put them in the same place. A room can look quite different when sitting in a different position.

Learning Outcome Activity 33 (ECP)

Seeing things from different positions

Sit on the floor in the room where you normally play with the children. Look around you. Make a mental note of what things you can see clearly and what things you can only partially see.

Now move to a different part of the room where you would not normally sit. Notice what things in the room look different, what you can see now that you couldn't see before and vice-versa.

This should make you appreciate that babies can become bored with always 'seeing' the same view, so remember to move them into different positions.

Although toddlers and young children rely less on their senses when they discover and investigate, they still need to be able to safely explore their world. Apart from finding out about things around them, exploring their environment helps children understand how they fit into the world and what part they can play. This is part of their social and emotional development, understanding about themselves and their self-image.

Watching and observing others

Watching and listening are sensory experiences just as touching and tasting are. Playing alongside and watching other children is a normal stage of development for children (spectator play). Children are able to absorb small details about how other children are behaving and playing, and what they are saying to each other. This information is 'stored' in the watching child's brain and then used later. Young children will often watch an insect, for example, with much concentration. This is because they need to focus on one thing so that they can find out as much as possible. As mentioned before, children will also watch and observe you. They will watch how you react in certain situations, how you speak to some people and what gestures you use.

Children learn a lot from watching others play

Learning Outcome Activity 34 (ECP)

Learning by watching others

What is your reaction to spiders?

Do you

- jump up and run out of the room
- get someone to remove the spider

or

- ignore it, it doesn't bother you at all?

What are the children learning from you, from each of these reactions?

Play and other activities

What is play? This question was looked at in Chapter 3, along with different types and stages of play. Play is a vital part of childhood, and even into adulthood. We all like to play in some form or other. Play supports and extends all areas of a child's growth and development and therefore help children to learn. Children do not make the artificial divisions between play and 'other activities', they are all opportunities for exploration and learning.

First-hand experiences

First-hand experiences are any activities that you do for yourself. As a child is doing something they learn through trial and error and will remember and use the information the next time they are in that situation. If a jigsaw puzzle piece will not fit one way, they will turn it around until it does fit. Sensory activities and experiences, such as tasting something different, are also first-hand experiences that help us learn about the world.

Talking and communication

Do not underestimate the power of talking and communicating with children. Sometimes you may feel that all you have done all day is answer questions, which can be very demanding and tiring for any childminder. However this is a very important way that children learn and you must answer all questions honestly.

How to observe children's development and learning

To observe means to watch, study, examine or scrutinise. These are things that you will do every day as part of your childminding practice. You will watch children to make sure that they are safe. You will watch them so that you can tell their parents what they have been doing with you. You will do this almost automatically, because you are a professional and care about children. There are however more reasons why you need to observe children.

Many childminders carry a small notebook and pencil in their pocket and jot down interesting things that they notice about the children. This is a form of observing and often provides the information for more formal ways of observing children.

However to formally observe someone is not always as easy as it sounds and does take practice.

Learning Outcome Activity 35 (ECP)

Try observing someone

Find a willing adult, perhaps a family member or friend, and ask them to mime a short sequence of actions. It does not have to last very long. You need to decide what you want them to mime, so suggest something like:

- Pouring a cup of tea
- Putting on a pair of trousers
- Opening an envelope
- Making a phone call.

While they are miming write down everything that you see them do. Make a particular note of:

- which hand they used most
- what were their facial expressions like

- whether they sat or stood
- whether their movements were smooth and co-ordinated, or fast, or slow.

When you have finished share what you have written with the other person and see if you missed anything out.

Observing children in a more formal way can last for ten minutes, or can be in the form of a series of short periods over a length of time; it varies according to what you want to observe. You cannot possibly write down everything that a child does or says for ten minutes. It is inevitable that you will get distracted, and the safety of the children is always your most important consideration. As you are writing you will miss something. The way around this is to decide on something specific to write about, in other words decide on an **aim**. This makes you focus on one thing and get as much information as possible about it; for example you might decide to focus on how well a child does or does not manage to build a tower with a construction set, or your aim might be to make a special note of how many times a young child shows aggressive behaviour towards other children.

Why does a childminder need to observe children?

Figure 6.2 *The different reasons why a childminder has to observe children*

To learn more about children's needs

Making time to specifically observe one child will help you identify their particular strengths and weaknesses, or perhaps confirm what you may have suspected. Sometimes the evidence that you produce can be used to help the child have appropriate specialist help. If you know what the needs of the children are you will be able to provide specific activities for them and so meet their needs.

To provide information for parents and other professionals

The information that you pass on to parents must be accurate. Parents need to know how their child is progressing. If you keep records of observations that you have made you will show the parents that you are not only a professional childcare practitioner, but that you see their child as an individual that you really know and understand. Sometimes a child may already be receiving help and support from other professionals for a specific problem. These professionals may ask you to provide them with information about the child, and again it must be accurate and helpful.

To check to see if a child is developing and growing

Doctors and health visitors regularly check babies and children to see if there are any growth or developmental problems. Although these checks are regular, you spend a lot of time with the children in your care and you are in a very good position to check the children more often than doctors or health visitors. You can make a game of measuring children to see how much they have grown; you can check to see if a baby is progressing to the next 'milestone' in an informal way.

To help plan activities

The more information that you have about the children in your care, the better you will be in providing appropriate things for them to do. You should not, for example, plan to make a collage of pictures cut from a catalogue if the child involved in the activity cannot use scissors. Let the child use scissors and practice cutting, but make your collage of both cut and torn out pictures.

To check that planned activities are appropriate for the children

Sometimes you may plan a particular activity that has a specific purpose, such as using scissors. It is very useful to observe the child while they are doing the cutting to see if what you have planned is effective in helping that child develop scissor control. The idea of checking the effectiveness of activities is often referred to as **evaluation**.

To help sort out a particular problem

Sometimes a parent may tell you about a concern that they have about their child and ask for your help in solving the problem. If you carry out observations of the child you will have more information that could reassure the parent that there is no reason for concern, or that could identify a problem. You will then have the information to act upon and if necessary seek professional help.

What do childminders want to learn from observation?

You are very busy throughout your working day and naturally you do not want to do anything that takes you away from the main point of your work – looking after the children. Because you are so busy, it is possible that you only give your attention to a particular child when they need it. As a result you could miss something that could be important. Not only do you need to be aware of things that the children can do, you should be aware of things that they need help with, and what they can almost do on their own.

Some childminders think that writing down observations adds to their workload and therefore takes them away from caring from the children. It is very important that you do not see observing children as an additional workload, but as a central and fundamental part of providing the best possible care for the children. The more accurate information you have about the children, the more able you are to provide appropriate activities for the children and therefore improve the quality of the service you offer. You need to include in your daily routine times when you can watch and listen to the children and so get information about their progress, development and evaluate the activities that you have provided. Doing observations has the added advantage of giving children time and space to play as they choose and guide their own activities, while still being supervised by you.

Learning Outcome Activity 36 (ECP)

Observing the children

Look at your daily routine. (You may have already written this down as part of one of the suggested activities in Chapter 4).

Identify specific times in your routine when you can watch and listen to the children.

These times do not have to be very long, between five and ten minutes is usually enough.

Get into the habit of:

- having a small notebook and something to write with handy
- identifying one specific thing to observe, in other words have an aim
- making a note of both the date and the time that you start and finish watching the children
- quietly watch and listen to the children.

What do you intend to do with the information?

Whilst it is very important that you get accurate information about the children in your care, it also very important to remember that there are limits that you must be aware of. You should never attempt to 'diagnose' the reasons for a problem or area of concern. That is the responsibility of other professionals such as psychologists and doctors. It is your responsibility to provide accurate information for such professionals and parents should they need it.

Confidentiality

It is extremely important that any records you keep on the children in your childminding setting are completely confidential. You need to think very carefully about where you keep records and observations. Some childminders put aside a section of one of their cupboards, which is not accessible to children, for keeping confidential material. It is a matter of personal preference and practicalities. You should never record anything about a child that you are not willing to share with the parents.

Data Protection Act 2000

More and more childminders are keeping information and personal details abut children and their families on personal computers. Many are also keeping their financial records for their business on computer. The Data Protection Act, which came into force in March 2000, requires anyone who is processing personal information, both in written form and on a computer, to register with the Data Protection Commission. Your local government office should be able to give you more information on this, as will the National Childminding Association.

Bias and judgmental issues when observing children

You should make sure that any observation that you make is objective, or impartial. This means that you need to consider your own attitudes and values towards the children in your care. If you have preconceived ideas about what a child can or cannot do, what they are like and how they may behave, you are more likely to write down what you expect rather than what actually happened. This will be looked at in more detail in Chapter 8.

Different methods of observation

There will be times when you want to record something that a child has done very informally and quickly. On the other hand, there will be times when you will want to

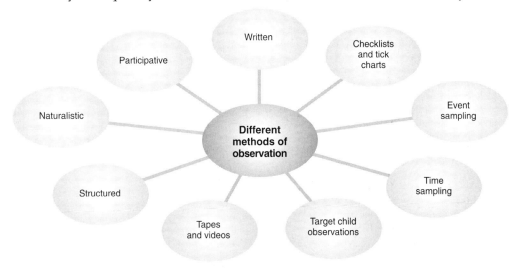

Figure 6.3 *There are different ways to observe children in order to gather information about them*

record something in a more formal, organised way. There are several different ways, or methods, that you can use to record information about children.

Written

Written observations are ways of recording information about a child's growth and development or behaviour over a short period of time. They provide a description of what happened at the time of the observation. Written records are usually written in the present tense, for example 'She sits and looks at the book, holding the book with her right hand and turning the pages with her left'.

Plus and minus points

Written observations require little preparation, just something to write on and with, and can be done quickly. However this type of observation can only be used to record for short periods of time and it is difficult to make a note of everything that is happening.

Below is an example of a written observation that a childminder could make.

> Ahmed Hameed   17 August 2001
>
> Age 2yrs 4 months   10:15 am
>
> In the childminder's home, with two other children in the room
>
> Ahmed is sitting, with his legs folded underneath him, on the carpet of the playroom. Two other children are also sitting with him. There is a box of Duplo in front of Ahmed. He reaches into the box with his right hand and takes out two pieces. Ahmed looks at one of the other children and smiles at her. He then looks very closely at the Duplo in his hands and tries to put the two pieces together. When he has fixed them together he reaches into the box again and takes out two more bits. Concentrating, he tries to fix one piece to the other two, but as he pushes all the pieces separate. Ahmed sighs loudly and tries to put them together again. The girl sitting next to him says 'Let me do it'. Ahmed says 'No, me do it' in a loud voice. He tries again to put all the pieces together, but can't do it. Ahmed stands up and throws the Duplo pieces across the room. I stop writing at this point.
>
> <u>Concerns</u> - Ahmed throwing the Duplo around
>
> <u>What to do next</u> - Help Ahmed to join Duplo pieces and
> Make sure he knows not to throw toys

Checklists and tick charts

There are many checklists and tick charts that are published to record different aspects of development, such as whether the child recognises all the letters of the alphabet or different colours. Health visitors and other medical professionals use a form of checklist and tick charts to record a child's height and weight at a given age. These charts are usually referred to as **centile** charts and can be a very useful way of comparing children's growth and development with other children of the same age and sex. You can produce your own checklists to record specific information about how a child is behaving or how they complete a task that you have given them.

Plus and minus points

Checklists and tick charts are quick and simple to use and can be used again at a later date to see if there has been any change. You can also use checklists and tick charts for more than one child, if, for example, you are evaluating children's responses to a particular activity. The main disadvantage of checklists and tick charts is that their design limits the amount of information you record and what you observe. Also, what exactly do you tick? Do you tick something off the first time a child does something, and then find that the next day they can't do it? Or do you tick when they have done something consistently and well?

Event sampling

Event sampling is a formal way of observing and recording patterns of behaviour. This is used especially if there is something that a child is doing that both and you and the parents want to change, such as sucking a thumb. Using this method of recording, you only make a note of something when you observe it happening, so the actual observation can carry on over quite long period of time, such as several days. You make a note of what actually happened and how long the child did the behaviour or action.

Below is an example of an event sample, which has been partly completed.

Susie   17 August 2001

Age: 4yrs, 2 months

Aim: to make a note of when Susie sucks her thumb

Event	Time	Situation	Comment
1	8:30 am	Has just been dropped off by Mum. Susie is a bit upset.	Susie finds saying goodbye to mum difficult. Sucked thumb for about 5 mins.
2	9:00 am	Another child has just been dropped off by their Mum.	Maybe this has reminded Susie of her Mum? Again sucked thumb for about 5 mins.

Event	Time	Situation	Comment
3	10:15 am	Listening to me read a story.	Susie was sitting very close to me, we were both relaxed and comfortable. She was listening to the story and asking questions. She sucked her thumb throughout the story, about 15 mins.
4	11:45 am	Sitting at the table with other children, waiting for me to put lunch on the table.	Sucked for about 3 mins.
5	12:20 pm	Sitting at the table waiting for one other child to finish his yoghurt.	Sucked about 3 mins.

Plus and minus points

Event samples build up a picture over a period of time of a particular behaviour or action that you, or the parents, or another professional, want information on. Event samplings are quick and easy to use. However you need to carefully prepare the form that you use and you may have to ask other adults, such as the parent, to help you record each event. Parental involvement is not included here as a minus point, merely something for you to think about.

Time sampling

Time sampling is a different form of event sampling in that you make notes of what the child is doing at fixed times and intervals throughout the day, such as every fifteen minutes throughout a morning or for two minutes every half an hour. As with all observations you will need to decide exactly what it is that you want to find out more about. You will need to prepare a sheet beforehand as with event sampling, but will not need the column headed 'Event'.

Plus and minus points

Time samplings, once you have prepared the recording sheet, are simple and quick to do. You can record specific behaviour and things that a child does, as well as more general activities. However you will need to keep an eye on the time throughout the period of the observations. It is so easy in a busy day to get involved in something with the children and forget that it is time to make an observation. As with event sampling, you may have to involve the parents if the observation is to go beyond one day.

Target child observations

Although this type of observation is not really an appropriate method for childminders to use it is useful for you to know about it. It is inappropriate because it needs an adult to focus on one child for quite a while, and that is just not possible for childminders to do and is less necessary because the child spends so much time in your care and with fewer children. Target child observations are used in day nurseries, nursery classes and pre-school groups. This method of observation requires codes, as it would be impossible to write everything down; for example, TC means target child (the one you are focusing on), A means adult, C is another child, Sol means solitary play.

Plus and minus points

Several specific activities can be observed at the same time. However, whoever is doing the observation has to be able to understand and use the codes and has to concentrate very hard.

Tapes and videos

You will need the written permission of the parents to make any form of recording of their child. You may also need to consider the quality of the equipment that you are using, as some recording equipment used in the home also picks up all the background noises.

Plus and minus points

If the child is not aware of the equipment you can often get some very good spontaneous reactions and behaviour. However some children will 'act' to the camera or tape recorder and you will not end up with a natural observation. If you are using a normal tape recorder you may find that all the background noises have been recorded as well, and it may be difficult for you to hear what you wanted.

Participative

Participative observations are those where you participate or get involved with the activity, such as cooking, playing with a construction set or reading a story. If you are part of the activity it will be a lot more difficult for you to write notes and you will have to rely on your memory to help you record what happened.

Plus and minus points

You can set up an activity and as you are involved you can to a certain extent have control over such things as how long it will last and the learning that will take place. On the other hand, if you haven't got a very good memory, or will not have the chance to write down what happened immediately after the activity is over, this may not be a very successful method of observing for you.

Structured

Structured observations are so called because you set up a situation so that you can observe the child or children. You are likely to set up an activity to observe one specific skill, such as pencil control, recognising colours, or putting on a coat or jacket. It is important that you choose an activity that the child enjoys, so that you will get a true picture of their abilities. You will need to decide how you are going to organise this observation, for example, are you going to show the child what you want them to do, or are you going to ask them questions?

Plus and minus points

You can set up this observation to suit your routines and at a time to suit you and the other children. You are more or less in control of what is going on. However the child may become distracted and not complete what you wanted to observe. This does not mean that you have to abandon the observation, as you can carry on with it later.

Naturalistic

Naturalistic observations are the opposite of structured ones. You simply observe the children or child in the normal routine of the day. You make notes on what they are doing, who they are doing it with and what they are saying.

Plus and minus points

This observation takes place in a normal situation. You should therefore get children behaving and doing things spontaneously. The downside of this method is that you do not really have any control over the situation and it may be difficult to 'stick' to your aim.

Longitudinal records

If you are regularly observing the children in your care and keeping records of their growth and development, you will build up a set of observations which will show progress and changes over a long period of time. Each set of records and observations for each child is a longitudinal record. These will enable you and the parents to identify important milestones in the child's development and learning.

Learning Outcome Activity 37 (DCP)

Using methods of observation

Assignment 1 for Unit 2, Developing Childminding Practice, asks you to reflect on the play and activities that you provide for the children in your care and explain why development and learning take place. This activity, and the next one, should help you with that explanation.

Using one of the activities that you plan to use for the assignment, identify one aspect of a child's growth and development that this activity will promote. This will become the aim of your observation.

For example, you could choose to provide a finger-painting activity for an eighteen-month-old to help sensory and intellectual development, or you could choose threading pieces of macaroni on to string for a three-year-old to help develop physical skills such as hand/eye co-ordination.

Now select a method of observing; for example, both activities could be observed by the following methods:

- written
- structured
- naturalistic
- participative.

Carry out an observation of the activity. Remember to make a note of the date, time that you started and the exact (years and months) age of the child.

It is not expected that childminders who are studying Unit 2 of the CCP will necessarily be expert at doing observations, as this unit covers a general approach rather than specifics. However, using the information in this chapter, your own experiences and professionalism, you should be able to do an observation that will help you reflect on the activities you have provided.

How to use observations to assess children's development and learning

The information, or evidence, that you collect when you do an observation can be invaluable for several reasons:

1 It can **show that you understand how children learn, grow and develop** and that the activities you provide take this into consideration.

2   Observations will give you information so that you can check if the activities are at the right level and if the children have learnt or progressed in any way. This is called **assessment**.

3   The information that you have, plus your own knowledge and experience, will help you to plan appropriate activities. Your observations may have made you more aware of a particular need of a child. You will then be able to plan a suitable activity to help that child.

4   As a professional childminder you have a busy workload and you want to make sure that everything that you do for the children is for their benefit. Sometimes, when you are working very closely with children, it can be difficult to decide if the activities you are providing are really meeting all the children's needs. In other words, you need to be able to reflect on and evaluate what you are doing. One way that you can reflect on and evaluate the activities is to make observations of the children whilst they are playing. This will then provide you with evidence that in a quieter moment you can look at and decide if the activity really did what you intended it to do.

Learning Outcome Activity 38 (DCP)

What you can learn from observation

You will need to use the observation that you did for the last activity.

Read through the information that you have recorded.

Ask yourself the following questions:

1   What learning did I expect to take place, in other words what was my aim?
2   Does the observation show me that some learning took place? In other words:
3   Could the child do the activity?
4   If not why not?
5   What were his or her reactions?
6   Did he or she talk about what they were doing?
7   What were his or her facial expressions like?
8   How did I know at what developmental stage the child was at?
9   How could I change this activity if I were to do it again so that the child continued to learn?

Write down your answers to these questions and include them as part of your observation and record of the child's growth and development.

Planning

Everybody makes plans at some point in their lives. They can be short-term plans, such as what you will wear that day, or longer-term plans such as booking a holiday three months in advance and putting £50 a month aside to help with spending money. Writing a shopping list is a form of planning, so is making a 'Things to do today' list.

Planning is really about preparing, making certain arrangements and checking that those arrangements will work. For example, you plan to wear a certain top one day so,

- you need to check that it is clean, and

- if it isn't, make arrangements to wash it.

But you may need to ask yourself,

- have I got time to wash the top and get it dry?

- if not, should I plan to wear a different top?

This is where you started, thinking about which top to wear, so you have in effect gone round in a circle. However it is not a meaningless circle. You did the following:

You **planned** – Which top to wear?

You **assessed** – Is it clean?

You **evaluated** – Have I got time to wash and dry the top?
Do I need to choose a different top?

You **implemented** your plan – either by wearing the top or by choosing another one.

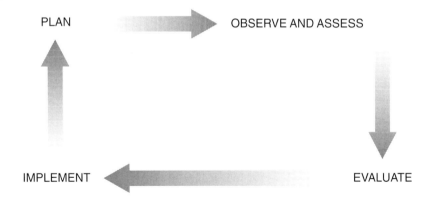

Figure 6.4 *The planning process*

Why do childminders need to plan?

In order to work effectively and efficiently you need to plan your day and your working week. How you do that will be a matter of individual choice, and you may not write down much of what you plan. However if you are prepared to take a planned approach to your work with the children and make records of what you do, not only will you build up a collection of activities and things to do with children that you can refer to in the future, but you will become more professional.

If you intend in the future to claim nursery education funding and become an accredited childminder who provides education for children, you will need to keep written plans. Standard 3 of the National Standards for Under-Eights Day Care and Childminding, which took effect in September 2001 (in England), clearly says that the registered person (you the childminder) plans and provides activities and play opportunities that will develop a child holistically. The inspectors from the Early Years Directorate of OfSTED (in England) can ask to see how you plan play and other activities for the children.

All childminders are registered in accordance with the Children Act 1989, which does actually require anyone who is providing group care to observe children, assess their learning and development, report and record it. In order to meet with this requirement you do have to do some form of planning.

How to plan

It is very important to remember that there is no right or wrong way to plan. The way that you plan is up to you. Your methods of planning will, and should be, different to the way that your friends or other course members plan. That is because you are unique person and childminder, and the children that you care for are also unique. Your plans have to meet the needs of the children you care for and your own needs. Therefore, your plans cannot be the same as anyone else's. You do not have to write down your plans in any particular way, or fill in any special sheets or forms. The important thing to remember is that your plans must work for you and your children. If they don't, then change them.

Before you start to write anything down, you need to decide what you and the parents of the child you are caring for want him or her to achieve. What are the 'goals', the new skills you want the child to develop and, perhaps, the new ways of behaving? Decide a time frame for achieving these goals. This will then help you see the difference between long, medium and short-term plans. Share your plans, in whatever form, written or in your head, with the parents and the children. They should be involved, if possible and if appropriate, in deciding what activities you plan to provide.

Some childminders like to plan to themes or topics or areas of development. This will very much depend on the age and number of children that you care for. Some childminders find following a theme, for example, restricts them and does not allow for spontaneous activities and some forms of free play. Again it is very much up to you what you want to do.

CASE STUDY

Kate is studying Unit 3 Extending Childminding Practice. She cares for Jessica who is 20 months old and intends to write a curriculum plan of learning experiences for Jessica for a two-week period. Kate decides to make a chart covering the ten days that Jessica is with her, with each day broken down into approximate time slots. In each time slot Kate intends to write in an activity that will cover one area of Jessica's growth and development. By doing it this way Kate feels sure that she will be able to check if she has covered all areas of learning.

When talking to other course members Kate realises that some childminders are writing spider plans, some are making lists, some are writing their two-week plan like a diary; in fact no one seems to be doing the plan the same way. Kate mentions this to the tutor and the group spend a few moments after the coffee break discussing 'the best' way to write a curriculum plan. There is little or no agreement amongst the group. Kate is concerned, but the tutor points out that they are all caring for different children with different and individual needs and so their plans cannot be the same.

Long-term plans

These are for goals and skills that you want to develop over a length of time. Here are some examples of long-term plans:

- You might decide on a long-term plan of eight weeks for a seven-year-old to help them to remember to bring their library book back from school on a Wednesday and all of his or her sports kit back from school on a Friday afternoon.

- You could decide on a long-term plan of a month to help a three-year-old learn the colours red, blue, green and yellow.

- You could decide to have a long-term plan of a whole year that covers all areas of growth and development for a two-year-old.

Figure 6.5 on page 172 is one way to write a long-term plan.

This example of one method of long-term planning is often called a **spider plan**. This long-term plan could last a month. The goal would be to help a child learn four colours.

Medium-term plans

Each 'leg' of the spider plan on page 172, that is, each box relating to one colour, could become a medium-term plan that would last a week and the goal would be to help the child identify red, or blue, or green, or yellow through a range of different activities.

Medium-term plans can focus on one particular aspect of learning, growth and development, such as one colour for the three-year-old, fine motor skills for the two-

171

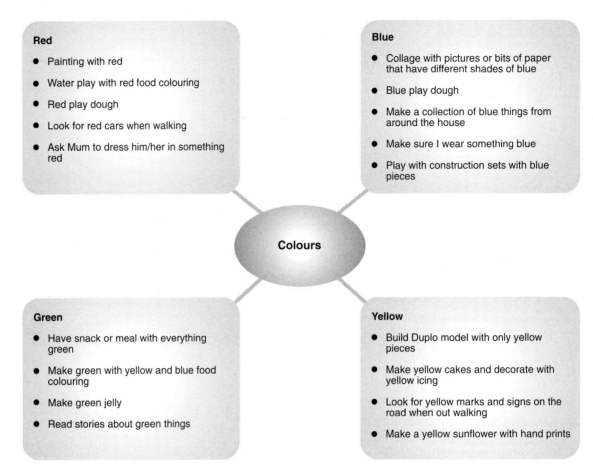

Figure 6.5 *A spider plan*

year-old and reading skills for the eight-year-old. It is at this point in the planning process that you decide what your role will be, if the play, or activity, will be very structured and led by you, or if the child will take the lead.

Short-term plans

Short-term plans can be either for one day, or one specific activity. You could have a short-term plan to do some cooking, which is part of a medium-term plan to develop physical skills, which is part of the long-term plan to make sure that the activities that you provide for the children cover all areas of their growth and development.

Each activity in each of the boxes, or legs of the spider plan, could be a separate short-term plan, with the aim or goal, for example, to help the child recognise blue by collecting only blue things from around the house.

Learning Outcome Activity 39 (ECP)

Making plans

Matthew is three years and two months old. He loves anything to do with trains. He doesn't yet know the numbers 1, 2 and 3. He has been coming to his childminder every day from 8:30 am to 4:00 pm, for a year.

- Can you identify a long-term goal for Matthew?
- What could be part of a medium-term plan for Matthew?
- Think of one play activity that you could do together (short-term plan) to help you achieve some of the medium and long-term plan goals.
- Using what you have learnt earlier in this chapter, think of an aim for an observation that you carry out on Matthew to see if your short-term plan has been successful.
- What would you use the information from the observation to help you to do next?

Planning appropriate activities for babies and toddlers in your home

In Chapter 3 play activities for babies were looked at in detail, including making up a treasure basket and extending your collection of rhymes and songs.

When you start to consider how to plan, or take a planned approach to children's learning, it is good practice to remember that babies and toddlers are learning through their senses and explorations. Therefore, if you are thinking about an overall framework for a long-term plan for children of this age, you should relate your plan to the areas of growth and development.

A **long-term** plan should include:

- Sensory and intellectual development
- Physical skills
- Language and communications
- Social development
- Emotional development.

The **goal** would be to provide activities that will stimulate and promote all areas of growth and development.

A **medium-term** plan for babies and toddlers could focus on physical skills, such as co-ordination. The **goal** could be to develop co-ordination skills.

A **short-term** plan could include play and activities such as:

- playing with a baby gym for a small baby
- doing a large puzzle with few pieces with a toddler
- feeding themselves with finger foods.

You could do a **written observation** of a baby playing under a baby gym for about ten minutes, with the aim of observing hand and eye co-ordination, or an **event sampling** to see how many times the baby's hand manages to pat or connect with the objects on the baby gym.

You could use the information from your observation to decide, or **assess**, if the baby needs to have more opportunities to play with the baby gym, possibly because they did not manage to connect with the objects often; or **evaluate** if the baby needs to be introduced to a different play activity, such as a toy that when touched or patted makes a noise, to develop their skills.

Whatever you decide as a result of your observation, you will provide or **implement** another play opportunity, and the planning cycle will go around again.

You could carry all this information around in your head. You could write it down. You could transfer your written notes on to your personal computer, where you have stored all the children's records, or you could do something else to suit you.

CASE STUDY

Mick is hoping to become a registered childminder as he has recently been made redundant from his job in an office. He has started to do Unit 1 Introducing Childminding Practice. For task 2 of the assignment he decides to describe his plans for providing basic play and other activities. His long-term plan is to provide play and activities that will help children grow and develop in all areas. His medium- and short-term plans are based on the age and needs of the children that he is hoping to care for and includes ways that he will assess them if the play and activities meet the children's needs. He also intends to describe what he plans to do if he thinks that some needs are not being met, and how he can extend and develop other needs if appropriate.

Planning appropriate activities for the Foundation Stage – The Early Learning Goals in your home (or Desirable Outcomes in Wales, or Curricular Guidance for Pre-school Education in Northern Ireland)

Much research has been done on early years education and appropriate learning experiences for children aged between three and five years. In 1990 the Rumbold

Report was published and as a result the Desirable Learning Outcomes for Children's Learning on Entering Compulsory Education were published.

In 1998 all four-year-olds, in England, were able to receive free nursery education, if their parents wanted it. So that all children were offered the same standard of education, all settings that received the nursery funding had to be inspected by OfSTED and agree to follow a curriculum, or set of goals. Initially, in England this curriculum was called the Desirable Learning Outcomes on Entering Compulsory Education. The funding for nursery education was later extended to three-year-olds. In 1999 the Qualification and Curriculum Authority (QCA) published the Early Learning Goals for the Foundation Stage for use with children receiving funding in England. During the following year QCA published detailed guidance on how to implement the Early Learning Goals.

In 2000 Awdurdod Cymysterau, Cwricwlwm ac Asesu Cymru (ACCAC), the Qualifications, Curriculum and Assessment Authority for Wales published the Desirable Outcomes for Children's Learning.

All of these documents are available from QCA Publications or ACCAC whose details are given at the end of the book.

At the present time the nursery education grant in England and Wales is made available through local Early Years Development and Childcare Partnerships (EYDCPs). The EYDCPs will allocate the funding to settings that can show that what they plan and provide for the children helps them to make progress towards achieving the Early Learning Goals.

A childminder who meets specific requirements will be able to gain accreditation and offer early years education to the children that they care for. This means that they will be able to receive funding for three-year-olds and four-year-olds in their care, but must plan and implement activities that follow the Early Learning Goals or the Desirable Learning Outcomes for two and a half hours a day for five sessions each week. The EYDCPs will only pay the nursery education grant to accredited childminders who are members of the National Childminding Association approved 'Children Come First' networks.

What are the Early Learning Goals?

By the time that most children reach their fifth birthday they are in a reception class. The period of time from the age of three to the end of the reception year is described as the Foundation Stage. The Early Learning Goals describe what it is expected most children should be able to do *by the end* of the Foundation Stage, in other words when they are approaching their sixth birthday. The Early Learning Goals are divided into six areas. These are:

1 Personal, social and emotional development

2 Communication, language and literacy

3 Mathematical development

4 Knowledge and understanding of the world

5 Physical development

6 Creative development.

Each of these areas is divided into smaller goals called **stepping stones**. It is intended that a three-year-old would start on the first stepping stone in any area and progress along until they reached the last stepping stone at the age of about six. This is a very planned approach to children's learning, with clear goals and stepping stones. The planning of play activities comes from the goals and stepping stones. As the child develops, grows and learns the stepping stones and the goals change to match the development of the child.

What are the Desirable Learning Outcomes?

The Desirable Learning Outcomes differ from the Early Learning Goals in that they cover play and activities that most children are expected to be able to do before compulsory school age. The Early Learning Goals are what children are expected to have achieved after they have started compulsory school and have been in school at least a year.

Like the Early Learning Goals, the Desirable Learning Outcomes are also divided into six areas of learning. These are:

1 Personal and social development

2 Language and literacy

3 Mathematical development

4 Knowledge and understanding of the world

5 Physical development

6 Creative development.

Curricular Guidance for Pre-school Education in Northern Ireland

Parents of children in Northern Ireland are also able to receive nursery funding if they wish their child to have pre-school or nursery education. The curriculum, or set of goals, is very similar to both the Early Learning Goals for the Foundation Stage and the Desirable Outcomes.

Unless you intend to become an accredited childminder in a network, it is not expected that the play and activities that you provide for children between three and six years will follow the Early Learning Goals or Desirable Learning Outcomes, or that you will have to show how you plan. You will not be inspected on the education you offer unless you are accredited. However, OfSTED (in England) or CSIW (in Wales) will still inspect your home to check that it provides a safe and caring environment and that you are providing suitable play for the children.

Your role is to support the children's learning and help the children grow and develop. However in order for you to do this, you will need to have an understanding of these curricula. Many of the activities that are suggested in the QCA guidance are things that you will be doing in your home all of the time, such as:

- cooking
- dressing-up
- looking at books
- counting
- talking about what the children did at the weekend with their parents
- putting aprons on before painting
- singing rhymes.

Each one of these suggested activities covers one or more of the areas of learning. Cooking, for example, involves:

- personal, social and emotional development, as the children share and take turns
- mathematics, as they count, weigh and measure the ingredients
- communication, language and literacy – have you ever cooked in silence with children!
- knowledge and understanding of the world, as they see the ingredients change as they are mixed together and possibly cooked
- physical development, as the children handle the cooking utensils and probably put on their own aprons
- creative development, as they make something and perhaps decorate the tops of cakes, or pizzas.

Learning Outcome Activity 40 (ECP)

The six areas of learning

The cooking activity above covers all six areas of learning in some way.

1 Choose an activity that you do often with three-year-olds and four-year-olds. If you are not caring for children of this age, choose an activity that you think you would do.

2 Using the headings of the six areas of learning try to think of how your activity would cover some part of each area. If you are working in Wales, use the headings of the Desirable Learning Outcomes.

You may find it helpful to write down your ideas in the table below.

Activity	What the children and I do
Personal, social and emotional development	
Communication, language and literacy	
Mathematical development	
Knowledge and understanding of the world	
Physical development	
Creative development	

Teaching methods

In both of the publications for the Early Learning Goals and the Desirable Learning Outcomes there is educational jargon, which can be very off-putting. The term 'practitioners' is used throughout, which means anyone who is supporting children's growth, development and learning at this stage. A practitioner could therefore be a childminder, a supervisor and assistants in a pre-school group, an early years worker in a day nursery, a nursery teacher in a nursery class, or a teacher in a reception class.

Another common phrase that many people who work with young children find off-putting is 'teaching methods'. Many people associate teaching methods with schools and qualified teachers.

As a professional childminder you will be 'educating' the children that you care for all the time. You will be helping them to learn, to grow and to develop in every way. You will not set aside times of the day when you make a conscious decision to 'educate' the children, but you may include in your daily routine time to play with them. You do not have to provide work sheets and special educational toys to 'teach' the children. You will talk to the children and play with them, help them to do things that they couldn't do before, such as feed themselves or fasten up their own coat.

All of the things that you do as part of your childminding service are your teaching methods. If you wanted to list your methods you might include:

- **Talking**, as young children learn through talking and communication.
- **Providing a safe environment** and equipment for the children to play, as young children learn through play and first-hand experiences.
- **Offering a wide range of activities and experiences**, as young children learn through exploring the world around them.
- **Playing with** the children and guiding them.
- **Joining in** and supporting their play.

Learning Outcome Activity 41 (ECP)

Your teaching methods

Choose an activity that you provide for children between three and four years old.

If you do not look after children of this age, think of something that you might do.

Make a list of your 'teaching methods', the things that you do to help make the activity a meaningful learning experience for the children.

CASE STUDY

Val is a very experienced childminder, having looked after children for almost twenty years. At the moment she cares for a baby and two other children who are three and four. The four-year-old goes to the local nursery class each morning. The nursery uses topics to plan the Early Learning Goals, and their current topic is 'shapes'. Val wants to support what the nursery is doing and as it always puts a copy of its medium-term (topic) plan on the parents' notice board, Val can see what activities it is planning to do. One fine afternoon she takes all three children out on a shape hunt to look for squares, triangles, circles and rectangles that are all around them.

Have you ever noticed that some road signs are circles, some are triangular and some are rectangular?

Supporting the development and learning of school-aged children

Childminders are often employed to care for children before and after school and during school holidays. Quite often these will be children that you cared for before they started full-time schooling and you will know them well. So that you can support the development, growth and learning of school-aged children it is important that you have some understanding of what they will be doing in school.

The National Curriculum

Children between the ages of five and eleven years attending state schools all study the same nine subjects. These nine subjects, in England and Wales, are referred to as the National Curriculum. Scotland and Northern Ireland have their own, similar versions. The National Curriculum also cover subjects studied by children in state secondary schools, but they do not all study the same nine subjects. The nine subjects are:

- English
- Mathematics
- Science
- Physical education
- Technology
- History
- Geography
- Art
- Music.

Children in Wales also study Welsh.

The National Curriculum was first introduced into schools in 1988 to ensure that all schools would provide a consistent standard of education. Each subject is divided into attainment targets, or levels, so that children can be assessed against the targets. All state schools must offer all nine subjects (plus Welsh in Wales) to all the children. The only exception to this is for children who have a statement of special educational needs.

Like any other form of educational provision the National Curriculum is constantly being assessed and examined. The most recent changes have been to introduce the Literacy Hour in September 1998 and the Numeracy Hour in September 1999. Both were intended to help raise the standards in English and Maths, so that all children, by the time they left primary school at eleven, could read and have a good understanding of mathematics.

How you can support school-aged children

Links with school, the teachers and the parents

Your role in supporting school-aged children is different from what you did with pre-schoolers. Many childminders will be the main contact with the school and it is therefore very important that you establish very good lines of communication with the child's teachers so that you can support not only the child, but also their parents. It is very helpful if you can ask the parents to explain to the child's teacher who you are and what your job is. This is sometimes useful if some teachers feel that they could be breaching confidentiality if they speak to another person, other than the parent, about a child.

You can also support both the child and their parents by finding out about the school time table; for example which day does the child go swimming and so need the appropriate kit, or when do they need to return their library book. Helping the child to have the things they need for school on a particular day will make their day at school much easier.

Many schools rely on letters and bulletins to communicate with parents. School-aged children may neglect to pass these on. It is a good idea to make it part of your routine when you meet the child after school to ask if they have a letter or note that their parents need to see. It's a good idea to make this as light-hearted as possible. You will have to remember to remind the child to hand it over to the parents!

Starting full-time school is a significant milestone in children's lives, and their parents'. It marks a phase of growing independence. The opinions and values of his or her friends, usually called the peer group, become very important to the child. Sometimes the need to be independent and fit in with the peer group can cause conflict between the child and the adults who care for him or her. You will want to avoid all unnecessary conflict; at the same time your first consideration is the safety and well-being of the children.

Helping children gain independence

If you have cared for the child before they started school you will know whether they can use the toilet independently and that they can dress and undress themselves. If you have just started to care for the child, it is worth mentioning to the parents at the first visit how important self-help skills are in a school situation. If you feel that the child's self-help skills could be developed, use the time after school to help the child become more independent, perhaps by playing games to see who can fasten up a jacket the quickest, for example.

Road safety is a very important part of being independent. If you walk children to school you will have lots of opportunities to teach children to stop, look and listen and make them aware of traffic and some of the dangers, even when crossing a road at a 'safe' place (see Chapter 1). It is also important to remind children often about 'stranger danger', especially as the children become more independent and perhaps walk to and from school on their own.

Dealing with peer group pressures

Some peer group pressure can become too much for some children to handle; in the worst cases it can turn into bullying. Bullying will be discussed in more detail in Chapter 7. It is important that you are aware that children can face difficult situations at school, and it is especially important that you support the child as much as you can. You should work with the parents and the school to help the child, and hopefully sort out their problems.

Supporting school-aged children before and after school

Chapter 3 considered some of the activities that you might provide for school-aged children. It is important that you support their growth and development in every way you can. When a child starts school, and even in the first few days after a holiday, they may become less confident and unsure of themselves. What did not worry them before, could become concerns. It is very important that the child can trust you. Always be on time if you are meeting children at the end of the school day, or at the end of an after-school activity. Being a couple of minutes late can distress some children. It is important that the children get to school on time. Some people say that learning to be punctual is an important social skill. Remember, being late to school can be distressing for the child and disruptive for the teacher.

You can also support the growth and development of school-aged children by listening to them read, and possibly providing a quiet place for them to do homework. You could find out about the school's policy on home reading and homework. By doing this you will ensure that both the parents and yourself have a consistent approach.

Supporting school-aged children during the school holidays

School holidays should be fun for everyone. Your routines may have to change during school holidays, and you could have more children to care for, or sometimes fewer. Many childminders find that caring for school-aged children during the holidays can be demanding. You can cope with this by planning ahead; you know when the holidays are and you can be well-prepared. It can be quite a challenge to provide activities for mixed-age groups of children and to be realistic about coping – just how many children can you cope with and still enjoy your work? As mentioned in Chapter 3, take advantage of the local facilities in your area, such as swimming pool, sport centres and talk to the parents about their school-aged children enrolling on play schemes.

Whenever you care for school-aged children, remember that your role is to support their growth, development and learning in all areas. Your role is not to provide activities that are best done in the classroom although you might listen to children reading, as agreed with their parents. Remember, all children learn through:

- Play
- First-hand experiences
- Talking and communicating.

So these three things should be at the heart of the activities that you plan.

How childminding networks can support children's development and learning

The National Childminding Association (NCMA) 'Children Come First' networks are rapidly developing. Each network has a co-ordinator whose role is to recruit childminders, who are already registered by the local authority to join together to form the network. Each childminder has to agree to meet the standards that NCMA has set out in its Quality Childminding Charter. The co-ordinator arranges appropriate training for the childminders, gives practical support, such as putting childminders in touch with toy libraries, and can help match families and childminders.

The benefits to individual childminders are enormous. They are no longer 'working on their own' as they have the support of others. Childminders can keep well informed of new developments and get good quality training to further their own careers. Being a member of a network will raise the professional status of childminders.

Childminding networks are very flexible and can offer a professional service which will meet a variety of needs. The provision falls into roughly four categories; some networks will specialise in one type of provision, some in a mixture or combination of all.

1 **Early years education** – accredited childminders who are part of a network can claim the 'nursery education grant' for three-year-olds and four-year-olds, which is paid from the Early Years Development and Childcare Partnerships. This means that the activities the childminders plan for children of this age must promote the Early Learning Goals (in England) or the Desirable Learning Outcomes (in Wales). Accredited childminders also have to agree to be inspected by the Early Years Directorate of OfSTED in England or CSI in Wales.

2 **Out-of-school provision** – childminders provide almost four times as many out-of-school places in England and Wales compared to the places available in clubs for school-aged children.

3 **Community childminding** – this is especially the case for children and families 'in need', some disabled children, families and children with specific health problems, and many other areas of social need.

4 **Employee support** – some employers may provide childcare for their employees at the workplace, or the employer can fund a childminding network, such as by paying the salary of the co-coordinator. This provides parents with the advantage of having their children cared for in the area in which they live, and for the employee it is a cost-effective method of providing a childcare service.

It is important to remember that the information about networks and accredited childminders could change, to reflect new legislation or current development. If you are interested in networks, it is always advisable to speak to your tutor, or contact NCMA at the address given at the end of the book.

CHECK YOUR KNOWLEDGE

True or False?

Read the following statements and decide if they are true or false. The answers are given on pages 291–292.

1 Teaching methods means getting children to work from books and work sheets.

2 There are eight subjects in the National Curriculum.

3 There are six areas of learning in the Foundation Stage

4 Peer groups are very important for school-aged children.

5 In order to support the growth, development and learning of children it is necessary to set aside time each day to teach them.

6 You do not need the permission of parents to observe children and keep records about their growth and development.

7 Parents, teachers and childminders should work together.

8 Children learn through play, first-hand experiences and talking.

9 Babies learn through their senses.

10 Observations should be secret.

CHAPTER 7
Managing children's behaviour

Children are not born with an understanding of what is acceptable behaviour. This is something they learn as they grow and develop. Adults play a very important part in helping children to learn acceptable forms of behaviour that will help them become useful members of our society.

What is behaviour?

Behaviour is the way in which an individual acts or responds to a certain situation. Every society has its own rules and social boundaries, with behaviour that is considered to be acceptable or not acceptable. Each family can also have its own rules and boundaries, for example some families always expect children to ask before they leave the table after a meal, in other families this would be unnecessary.

You will have your own views on what is acceptable behaviour and what is not. These views will have been formed by your upbringing and culture. Your views on acceptable behaviour may have changed over the years, or may have been altered by where you live and who you live with.

Learning Outcome Activity 42 (ICP, DCP, ECP)

What are my views about behaviour?

Read the following statements and then decide if you agree with each one or not.

- Children should not eat or drink in the street.
- Children should not hit each other.
- Children should be taught to chew with their mouths closed.
- Children should be allowed to play with what they want, when they want.
- Children who swear, or use 'rude' words, should be ignored as it is only a 'phase' that they are going through.

You may find it difficult to agree or disagree with some of these statements, and maybe you are thinking, 'well, it depends on...'.

Discuss some of these statements with other childminders and compare your views and opinions.

Are there any statements that you all agree with?

There is a danger when thinking about behaviour that it is always bad, negative or unacceptable, and that we want to change it or stop it. However we must remember many children are very well behaved and most children are well behaved most of the time. They need and deserve praise and encouragement as much as any other child. Never forget to praise and encourage the children who play happily with others, who are helpful, thoughtful and considerate. Remember, not only to praise these children, but tell their parents too. This helps boost the child's self-confidence and self-esteem.

Establishing boundaries for behaviour – a framework

It is important to establish a framework for what you consider to be acceptable behaviour in your home very early on in your childminding career. You will probably base your framework or house rules on things that are important and matter to you, for example, most people believe that keeping children safe is very important, so your framework or house rules could focus on preventing children hurting or injuring themselves. House rule number 1 could be:

No children are allowed in the kitchen unless I am in there as well.

House rule number 2 could be:

No children are allowed to open the gate.

You may not have rules like this written down, but they will become part of the everyday things that the children learn whilst in your care.

Other things that you could base your framework for behaviour on are:

- Preventing children from doing anything that is dangerous, offensive or hurtful to other adults and children.

- Doing things that will not make them welcome in other people's homes or things that other people would find unacceptable.

- Doing something that would cause damage to other people's possessions.

You could write down a few short simple sentences about your framework for behaviour. This will be your **behaviour policy**, which you could give to parents and discuss it with them at your first meeting.

An example of a framework for behaviour, or behaviour policy, is shown opposite.

Hayley Smith – Registered Childminder

I have very few 'rules' in my childminding business, but I do expect all children that I care for in my home to learn to accept my rules.

My rules are:

- Nobody will do anything that is hurtful, offensive or dangerous to another person.
- Nobody will damage another person's things.
- We will all care for each other.

I believe that if children know what the boundaries are for their behaviour, they feel more secure and are less likely to misbehave.

I will be firm when establishing my rules, or framework, for behaviour and I will expect all children to do as I ask at all times.

If children do not do as I request, I will not use any form of physical punishment. I will not humiliate, restrain or isolate a child. I will be firm and will not give in. I will tell you straight away if I have a problem with the way your child behaves.

I will praise children when they behave as I expect and will teach them how to behave by my own example.

If you would like to talk to me about any part of my framework for behaviour then please do so.

Tel: 01234 567890
September 2001

Children need to know and understand that your 'rules' and boundaries will not keep changing. It is very important that you are consistent and firm in applying your boundaries for all children. If a child is not dealt with in a consistent way this can lead to difficulties in behaviour. Knowing what the rules are and that boundaries are set, helps to make children feel secure.

It is inevitable that the rules, boundaries or framework that you establish in your home may be different to the accepted rules in the child's own house. For example, you may not allow any child to go into the kitchen unless you are also in there; at home they may have no restrictions on going into the kitchen. It is therefore very important that you explain to children clearly and simply why you have that 'rule'. You might say something along these lines:

'I want to make sure that you, and all of the other children, are safe and not in any danger . There are things in the kitchen that could hurt you, or other children, such as the electric kettle, the oven and the cupboard doors. I do not want any child to be hurt so we all go into the kitchen together, then we can make sure that we are all safe.'

Learning Outcome Activity 43 (ICP, DCP, ECP)

Creating a behaviour policy

Try writing a framework, or behaviour policy, for your home.

If you already have a behaviour policy, have another look at it. You may have written it some time ago.

Ask yourself:

- Does it really say simply what I believe?
- Does it work?

If you answer no to either of these questions, you need to review your framework or policy.

It is good practice to review *all* your policies at least once a year. Some childminders review their policies every three months.

Establishing your behaviour framework

Establishing your personal behaviour framework as early as possible is very important for you, the children, the parents and other members of your family. It will mean that everyone will know what is expected of them and will lead to a consistent approach.

Your framework will consists of boundaries which set limits on behaviour and are simple rules that children will learn must not be broken, for example 'You must not go into the kitchen on your own'. When you start to establish your boundaries there are things that you can do:

- Help children to learn the rules by reminding them of these whenever appropriate, for example, in response to a request for a drink you may say 'Yes, you can have a drink when I go into the kitchen.'

- Explain why you have rules; children are much more likely to remember your rules if they know why you have them.

- Use simple clear language when managing children, for example 'It is time to come in now.'

- Explain in clear simple language what will happen if your rules are broken. You could say, 'I may have to put that game away.'

- Some rules or boundaries can be written down. This is especially appropriate for school-age children who often quite enjoy doing such an activity. You could get the children to produce a poster or chart of 'the rules of the house'.

- Always praise and encourage children when they do follow your boundaries and rules.

CASE STUDY

Jane has recently started to mind three-year-old twin boys. They often jump on the chairs and sofa. Jane explains to the boys that they could fall and hurt themselves and that she does not let other children behave in this way. Jane explains to the boys that she does not want them to do this and that they can climb and jump outside in the garden. The boys tell Jane that their mummy lets them do it at home. Jane arranges to talk to the mother and explains that she fears that the boys could fall and hurt themselves if they jump on the furniture. She also explains that she does not let other children behave in this way. Jane reminds the mother about her framework of behaviour that was discussed at their first meeting. The mother agrees with Jane that the boys should do as Jane asks when they are in Jane's home. She agrees to talk to the boys and explain that they must do what Jane asks them when she is caring for them.

1   Do you agree with what Jane did?
2   Are there any other ways of handling this situation?
3   What would be your reaction if the boys' mother felt that Jane was making a fuss over nothing and that it didn't matter?

Influences on a child's behaviour

Overall development

There are so many things that can affect a child's behaviour. One of the main ones is their overall development. A child could behave in a certain way because they have emotional difficulties, or because some aspect of their development is delayed. It is often the case that children with some form of developmental delay will show behaviour that is not normally associated with a child of a certain age.

Self-image

The way a child feels about themselves can affect the way they behave. Their self-image is in turn affected by many things such as:

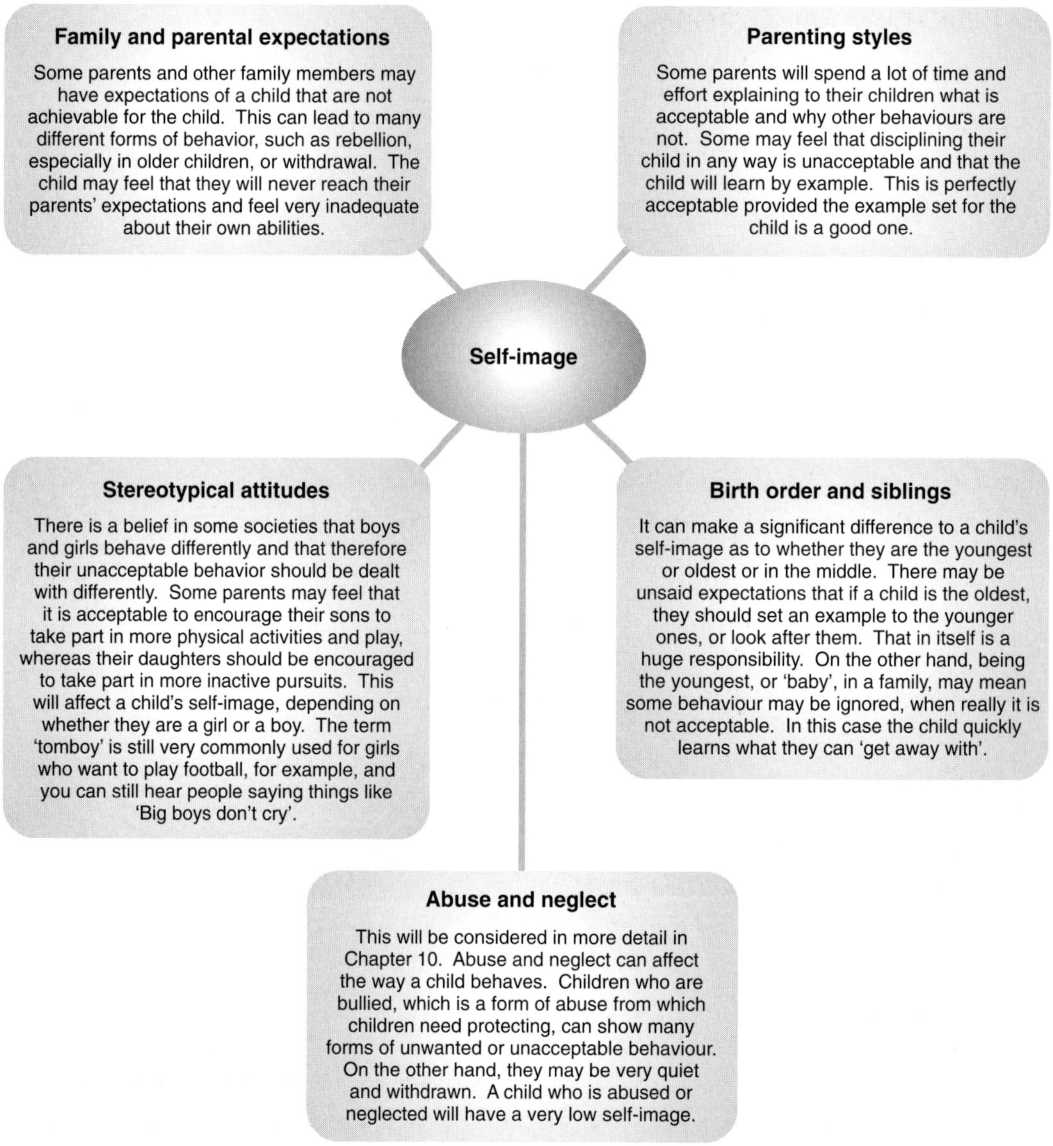

Family and parental expectations

Some parents and other family members may have expectations of a child that are not achievable for the child. This can lead to many different forms of behavior, such as rebellion, especially in older children, or withdrawal. The child may feel that they will never reach their parents' expectations and feel very inadequate about their own abilities.

Parenting styles

Some parents will spend a lot of time and effort explaining to their children what is acceptable and why other behaviours are not. Some may feel that disciplining their child in any way is unacceptable and that the child will learn by example. This is perfectly acceptable provided the example set for the child is a good one.

Self-image

Stereotypical attitudes

There is a belief in some societies that boys and girls behave differently and that therefore their unacceptable behavior should be dealt with differently. Some parents may feel that it is acceptable to encourage their sons to take part in more physical activities and play, whereas their daughters should be encouraged to take part in more inactive pursuits. This will affect a child's self-image, depending on whether they are a girl or a boy. The term 'tomboy' is still very commonly used for girls who want to play football, for example, and you can still hear people saying things like 'Big boys don't cry'.

Birth order and siblings

It can make a significant difference to a child's self-image as to whether they are the youngest or oldest or in the middle. There may be unsaid expectations that if a child is the oldest, they should set an example to the younger ones, or look after them. That in itself is a huge responsibility. On the other hand, being the youngest, or 'baby', in a family, may mean some behaviour may be ignored, when really it is not acceptable. In this case the child quickly learns what they can 'get away with'.

Abuse and neglect

This will be considered in more detail in Chapter 10. Abuse and neglect can affect the way a child behaves. Children who are bullied, which is a form of abuse from which children need protecting, can show many forms of unwanted or unacceptable behaviour. On the other hand, they may be very quiet and withdrawn. A child who is abused or neglected will have a very low self-image.

Figure 7.1 *The ways in which a child's self-image is affected*

Changes in a child's life

A change in a child's circumstances is often shown by a change in their behaviour. These changes can immediately affect the child or have an effect on their family.

The changes can be:

- The birth of a baby
- The death of a family member, close friends or pets
- Moving house
- Illness within the family

- Divorce or separation of parents
- Work pattern of parents or unemployment
- Adapting to a step family following the re-marriage of one parent.

A child's personality

Think about how a child's personality develops. See nature/nurture debate in Chapter 5 and the following activity.

Learning Outcome Activity 44 (ICP, DCP, ECP)

How do you get your personality?

- Do you believe that the child of 'well-behaved' parents is also 'well-behaved'?
- Does it follow that if a parent of a child is always breaking the law, the child will 'follow in their footsteps'?
- Will shy quiet parents have a shy quiet child?
- Think about your personality!
- How many of your personal traits or behaviours have your children inherited from you?
- Think about your mother's or father's personality!
- How many of her or his personal traits or behaviours have you inherited?

A child's school

School, nursery or pre-school group will have its own behaviour expectations that the child will have to adapt to. This can affect how they behave before or after attending the school. Children who have been inactive and quiet for a period of time in school, will obviously need to 'let off steam' and use up surplus energy when they get to your house.

Peer group

Some peer groups will set their own rules for behaviour, which can have both positive and negative effects on an individual child. The influence of the peer group, and the need to belong, is very strong in older children. The desire to fit into the group can bring a child into conflict with his or her carers at times.

The influence of the media

If a child sees a person on video or television behaving in a certain way they may think that because the person is famous that the way they behave is a good way.

Children may copy the behaviour of people they see on television. Examples are the way famous footballers spit during the games, or argue with the decisions of the referee. A child who sees the way these 'stars' behave, may believe it acceptable and so copies them.

Some common causes of unwanted behaviour

Unwanted behaviour can be loosely grouped into four categories:

1 Inappropriate spoken comments

2 Destructive behaviour

3 Comfort behaviour

4 Attention-seeking behaviour.

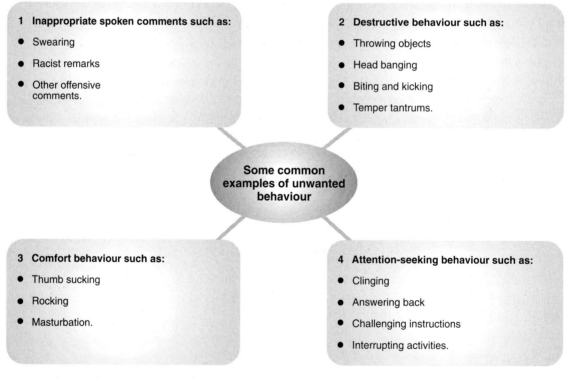

Figure 7.2 *Four categories of unwanted behaviour in children*

1 Inappropriate spoken comments

One of most common causes of this type of behaviour is insecurity. Sometimes older children will deliberately say something to another child that they know will hurt. By doing this the child who made the remark gains 'power' over the other child. It is a form a bullying. Sometimes children may behave like this because their own self-esteem is poor.

It is natural for young children to repeat words and phrases that they have heard. This is one very important way that a child develops their language skills. Often they will overhear and repeat words that they do not understand.

2 Destructive behaviour

Destructive behaviour is often a sign that a child is frustrated, possibly by developmental delay, or inappropriate activities. If you have given a child a book that is too difficult for his or her reading ability, they could become frustrated by their lack of achievement and throw the book down in anger. Sometimes destructive behaviour and anger can be a sign of deep emotional disturbance and that the child is temporarily not in control of the situation. Children who are being bullied sometimes show destructive behaviour.

3 Comfort behaviour

Very often when children are tired or bored they will show some form of comfort behaviour, such as thumb-sucking before falling asleep. Children who are feeling unwell may also show comfort behaviour. Sometimes when children are unwell aspects of their development will regress, for example, a child who no longer sucks his or her thumb may start again when they are feeling ill. Sometimes fear or anxiety over something can cause children to show forms of comfort behaviour. It should be remembered that masturbation is common in very young children, especially boys. Most children will have stopped masturbating in public by the time they are five years old. Very occasionally comfort behaviour can be a sign of serious emotional distress and you will need to advise the parents to seek specialist help.

4 Attention-seeking behaviour

As with other forms of unwanted behaviour, attention seeking can be a sign of insecurity and sometimes indicates that a child has low self-esteem. Sometimes children use attention-seeking behaviour out of habit, as they have learnt that they can get a response from an adult if they behave in this way. Children may feel the need to seek attention because they are not being given sufficient adult attention.

Using observations and assessments to help understand underlying reasons for unwanted behaviour

Observations and assessments give you detailed information about the children in your care. They can be used for very specific reasons, such as recording changes in a child's behaviour. In a busy childminding day it is very easy to forget how often or when exactly something happened. You may have noticed that a child is, for example, crying for what seems to be no apparent reason. When you are talking to the parents you should be able to give precise information rather than only say, 'He cried a lot today'. Observations will help you to obtain this information.

Observations may also help you determine some of the underlying reasons and causes for changes in a child's behaviour. You will have detailed and factual information about what exactly happened. At a quiet moment you will be able to look at your observations and possibly see a pattern to the unwanted behaviour. It might be that the behaviour only occurs at a certain time, in which case you might want to look at your routines and consider other ways that you could manage this unwanted behaviour. Your observations might help you see if there are any specific antecedents to the behaviour and again decide what you can do. Observations will also give you information about what the child did after the unwanted behaviour happened, and again you can decide if there are any underlying reasons for the behaviour, such as attention seeking.

Chapter 6 looked at different methods of making observations. Some of the methods are more suitable than others for recording changes in behaviour or how often behaviour occurs. Event sampling is a very good method to record how often the behaviour happened. You should also record on the event sample what happened, who the child was with and make a brief note of what you did. An example of part of an event sampling observation is given below.

Event	Time	Children and adults involved	What happened	What I did
1	8:40 am	Amy, Amir Me, baby in buggy	Amy hit Amir when he went to hold my hand on the way to school. Amy tried to push him away.	Explained to Amy that is was not friendly to hit Amir and that everyone had to hold onto either the buggy or me when walking to school. Moved Amy to the other side of the buggy
2	9:05 am	Amy, Me, baby in buggy	Amy refused to hold my hand on the way back from school and started to kick the buggy. The baby started to cry, Amy laughed at him.	Explained to Amy again about my rule of holding onto each other when outside. Explained that kicking the buggy upset the baby. Persuaded Amy to help me push the buggy home.

Event	Time	Children and adults involved	What happened	What I did
3	10:00 am	Amy, Sam, Laura	Amy broke Sam's Duplo model and then threw the pieces at Laura. Both Sam and Laura started to cry. Amy ran over to the other side of the room shouting 'cry baby, cry baby'.	Asked Amy to help pick up the pieces of Duplo, she refused at first, but then began to help. Explained to all that it is wrong to spoil other children's play, and that it is dangerous to throw toys as others can get hurt. Gave Amy another construction set to play with.

A diary may be a good way of recording what a child does, over a day or longer period of time. It is an informal way of getting information and can include lots of details, such as the child's mood, things that they say, as well as their behaviour. Many childminders keep individual diaries of a child's activities as a matter of course so that they can share good quality information with parents at the end of the day. This is especially useful when minding babies, for example, as you can record how long they have slept, what they have eaten and anything special that might have happened.

Collecting specific information

One form of managing children's behaviour requires childminders to collect specific information. This involves looking at what the child was doing before the behaviour happened – the **antecedents** – the **behaviour** itself – and what happened after the behaviour – the **consequences**. This is usually known as the **ABC** method of managing behaviour. Childminders usually find it easier to write down this information in brief notes. What the notes should contain:

- **Antecedents** are the details of what the child was doing immediately before the behaviour happened.

- **Behaviour** should be described factually, for example 'Amy hit Amir on the chest when they were playing with the Duplo before lunch.' You should not say, for example, 'Amy is driving me nuts this morning. She is causing so many problems.'

- **Consequences** should also be described factually, for example, 'Amir started to cry and Amy ran over to the other side of the room shouting "cry baby, cry baby"'. You should not say, for example, 'Amy is so naughty today, she is causing everyone to get cross, must speak to her Mum about it.'

Learning Outcome Activity 45 (ICP, DCP, ECP)

Observing unwanted behaviour

Look at the example of an event sampling observation for Amy. Assume Amy is three and has recently started at your childminding setting as her mother has got a full-time job, following a separation from Amy's father. Assume also that between 8.30 am and 5:30 pm there were 10 similar events of unwanted behaviour (not shown on the example).

Now try to answer the following questions.

1 Is this type of behaviour unusual for a child of Amy's age?
2 Why might Amy be behaving in this way?
3 Are there any triggers or clear antecedents to this behaviour?
4 How does Amy behave immediately after the events?
5 What can you do to help Amy understand why her behaviour is not acceptable?
6 Would it be helpful to do more observations? If so why?
7 What have you learnt from looking at this observation?

Managing children with behavioural and emotional difficulties

Behavioural difficulties

It is important to remember that no child will behave perfectly all the time. Occasionally you will care for a child whose behaviour constantly causes you concern. You may be aware of this before you start to mind the child, for example if you are a member of a community childminding network and have been requested to mind a particular child because they have difficulties. On the other hand, a child may start to have behavioural difficulties, such as destructive behaviour or aggressive actions towards others, whilst you are minding them. You must always talk to the parents about your concerns. You must decide if the child's behaviour is significant and affecting their development. If you are unsure what to do and how to talk to the parents, seek professional help.

Emotional difficulties

One of the main causes of emotional difficulties is low self-esteem and poor self-image. Children need to be reassured that they are loved and cared for, unconditionally. So much emotional damage can be caused to a child who is constantly told negative things, such as 'Your sister is so pretty/clever and slim', that the child will believe that they are not pretty or attractive, that they are not clever or that they are fat. Poor self-image and lack of self-esteem leads to lack of self-confidence. This in turn can lead to developmental delay and poor self-control. This in itself is a form of behavioural difficulty.

Taking a positive approach to managing unwanted behaviour

Very often our response to a child's behaviour, whether unwanted or not, will send a message to the child. All childminders should aim to send positive messages to children at all times. Sometimes it can be very difficult to be positive when managing children with behavioural and emotional difficulties. However you should always try to turn around what you are going to say so that instead of always saying 'No' or 'Don't', you say 'Let's do this'. Rather than saying 'Don't leave those toys there,' try saying, 'Let's tidy up those toys together, so we won't fall over them.' Another disadvantage of saying 'Don't', is that it sounds like an order. There will obviously be times when you will say 'Don't' to protect a child from a potential hazard or danger. In that case you will want them to respond immediately; so if you are always saying 'Don't', there is the possibility that they will not respond quickly and may even ignore you.

Learning Outcome Activity 46 (ICP, DCP, ECP)

Be positive

Try putting these negative statements in a more positive way:

- Don't spill your drink
- Don't make a mess
- Don't walk so slowly
- Don't do that
- Don't make so much noise.

Your influence on a child's behaviour

The theorist Albert Bandura carried out a very famous experiment in 1965 which showed that children learn from watching and copying others. This theory is known as the **social learning theory.** Bandura showed three groups of children a film. In this film the children saw an adult hitting an inflatable doll. The first group only saw the adult hit the doll. The middle group saw the adult being praised and rewarded for hitting the doll and the last group saw the adult being punished for hitting the doll. After the children had seen the film they were given a similar doll to play with. The first two groups copied the aggressive behaviour that they had seen and the last group were less aggressive. This theory suggests that children model their behaviour on the behaviour of adults around them.

If you believe that Bandura's theory is right, it follows that you also believe that if you are kind, gentle and are a good role model in your management of the children, they will copy you and model their behaviour on your positive example.

Practical ways to manage unwanted behaviour

1   Once you have identified the problem through observations and assessment you must **discuss with the parents** what your observations show.

2   **Decide what is the most important thing to tackle first**. For example, you may have a child who is biting other children and cannot share. It may be they are too young to understand what 'sharing' means, but you can decide to try to stop the child biting.

3   Use a **positive approach** to guide the child, to **distract** them and so avoid situations where the chances of the unwanted behaviour happening are increased.

4   Be **firm** and **consistent**. If you say 'No', mean it, and make sure that your framework, goals and boundaries are firm and not altered.

5   **Avoid confrontation**. Distract the child, or gently remove from the situation. Offer an alternative play activity or toy, with a positive statement.

6   **Show your disapproval**. Children naturally want to please adults, so showing your disapproval of their unwanted behaviour can be a powerful reason for some children not to behave in that way again. However do not show your disapproval by humiliating or embarrassing the child.

7   **Explain** why the behaviour is not acceptable, and if the child is old enough explain also the possible consequences of their behaviour.

Learning Outcome Activity 47 (ICP, DCP, ECP)

Managing a difficult child

Imagine that you are caring for a three-year-old girl whose behaviour you are finding increasingly difficult to manage. The girl often refuses to do as you ask, frequently doing the opposite; for example, when you ask the children to help you tidy away toys before lunch, she will deliberately get something else out of the toy cupboard and tip it over the floor. This child can also be very disruptive, especially at mealtimes, and sometimes upsets the other children.

Using the list of suggested practical ways to manage children's behaviour:

- decide what you could do first
- what would be your next step?
- how could you record such incidences of behaviour, or do you need to?
- have you ever been in a similar situation?
- what did you do?
- could you have handled the situation differently?

Other ways to manage unwanted behaviour

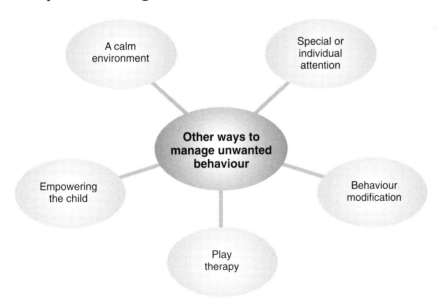

Figure 7.3 *How to manage unwanted behaviour*

- **A calm environment**. It is generally acknowledged that our lives today are more stressful and pressurised than those of our parents. Parents under pressure can sometimes, unwittingly, transfer their stressful feelings to their children. In such cases the childminder's home can be one of the few places that a child can relax and unwind. Your childminding business may be busy, with children coming and going, but it can still be a place of calm. You can deal with minor arguments and disagreements calmly and without raised voices. You can make a corner of one room a quiet area where children can be quiet, especially after a stimulating day at school. Children who are living in a stressful home may feel insecure, especially if there is inconsistency in their lives. Your rules and boundaries for behaviour can help make the child feel more secure.

- **Special or individual attention**. In Chapter 4 'Routines', it was suggested that you should try to include in your routine a 'special time' that you set aside to spend with a difficult child, if possible. It is suggested that children who show attention-seeking behaviour are less likely to behave this way if they are given adult attention, as they will not need to seek attention. Children who have difficulty maintaining attention or concentration can sometimes be helped by quiet conversations with good eye contact.

- **Behaviour modification**. The way a child behaves can be changed through encouraging positive behaviour with rewards, and discouraging unwanted behaviour by either ignoring it or by using restrictions. Sometimes it can be difficult to find something to praise with some children, but very small amounts of acceptable behaviour should be acknowledged. For example, a child who is constantly interrupting, should be praised when sitting quietly at the table, even if it is only for a minute. The childminder can say something positive such as, 'I am really pleased to see you sitting so well, that is great.' It is hoped that eventually the child will learn that acceptable behaviour will be praised and unacceptable behaviour will not be. From learning this, it is hope that the child's behaviour will also change.

Ignoring unacceptable behaviour can be extremely difficult to do. You should never ignore unacceptable behaviour if there is a danger to the child or other children. It is believed that if children do not get attention with unacceptable behaviour and are praised when behaving in an acceptable way, they will learn that it is better to behave in an acceptable way.

Some children respond well to rewards in the form of stickers or star charts. The aim is that if a child behaves well, they are given a star or sticker. If they achieve a certain number of stars they are rewarded with a 'treat'.

Some childminders do not like this form of behaviour modification as they think that children who are not able to get a star, for whatever reason, will feel bad and their self-esteem will not be helped. It also can encourage competition between children, and whilst some childminders feel that a competitive spirit between older children can be healthy, others do not agree. It is very much a matter of personal opinion as to whether you agree with this form of behaviour modification.

Using sanctions or restrictions is another area of debate. In no way should the use of sanctions involve smacking or humiliating a child. Restriction can be placed on, for example, what toys a child is allowed to play with or how long they are allowed to play on the computer. Giving a child 'time out' is a form of sanction that can allow the child time to calm down if they are very cross or angry, but as with any form of sanctions or restriction they should be used with care and caution.

- **Play therapy**. Play can be used as a form of relaxation for children and adults. There are many adults who, after a hard day's work, go to a gym or fitness centre and 'work-out' their tensions and stresses. This work-out is really an adult form of play. Play can take the unknown fear out of a situation and so act as therapy.

  For children play can and does provide very good opportunities to act out situations that could cause anxiety and so lead to problems with their behaviour. It can provide a child with a way to release strong emotions in a safe and non-threatening way. If a child is angry or cross about something it is better to let them take out their anger on play dough, clay or a football, rather than on another child. Sometimes children cannot find the words to express how they feel, but are able to put across their feeling in paintings and drawings. Giving children play activities where they can dress-up and pretend to take on other roles can help them express their fears or worries. A 'classic' dressing up activity is 'hospitals', when a child, or family member, is due to go into hospital.

  There are a large number of books for children about situations that can cause stress and anxiety, such as starting school, loss and bereavement, visiting the dentist and a new baby arriving. Take a look in your local library if you think a child in your care could be helped by a story about a specific problem.

  Some children will play with puppets, small-scale toys and dolls in imaginary games that let the child transfer their worries and problems on to the toys. Psychologists and some therapists working with children who have been abused, use dolls and puppets to help children explain their experiences.

  Some children with behaviour problems are helped by playing musical instruments and listening to quiet, calming music. Sir Paul McCartney set up an musical establishment in Liverpool for children who were identified as 'disadvantaged'. Many of these children also have behavioural and emotional problems. The children are given opportunities to play, create and listen to music. It is widely recognised that in many cases the children have benefited tremendously from this form of play.

- **Empowering the child**. Childminders can use this way of managing older children's behaviour, in particular. The main focus is to give children opportunities where they are in control of situations. You could, for example, offer a child more choices about what they can do, or different ways of doing activities, and so give them more control over what is happening to them.

Some childminders give children specific responsibilities that are achievable. When the child carries out their tasks of responsibility they are rewarded with praise and thanks. This helps to build up self-confidence and self-esteem.

Being able to communicate well is very important and a child with poor communication skills could feel that they are not in control of situations. This leads to anxieties and sometimes problems with behaviour. Helping children to express themselves, explaining what they want and how they feel is another way of empowering children.

An organisation called Kidscape has developed excellent programmes to empower children who are being bullied or abused. The programmes are also useful means of learning for all children as they teach children ways to protect themselves in a wide range of situations. The Kidscape address is at the end of the this book.

Learning Outcome Activity 48 (ICP, DCP, ECP)

Think about this situation

Imagine that you are minding a three-year-old child every weekday from 8 am to 6 pm. Both parents work full-time. The child cries every time either parent leaves, but when being collected runs away and hides behind a chair, shouting 'I don't want to go home.' The parents find this behaviour quite distressing, especially at the end of a busy working day.

1   How could you reassure the parents?
2   Why do you think the child is behaving like this?
3   What could you do?

Bullying

You could be in the unfortunate position of caring for a child who is or who you suspect is being bullied. Bullying can take many forms, such as:

- Name-calling

- Fighting or physical attacks

- Not allowing a child to join in play activities or games with the peer group

- Racial remarks and abuse.

There are many other forms of bullying, but all usually result in distress and emotional problems for the child concerned. Often this stress is shown in changes in the ways a child normally behaves. You are very well placed to be able to spot changes in behaviour. Look for things such as:

- A child suddenly not wanting to go to nursery or school.

- A child making up 'illnesses' to avoid going to school, for example an unexpected tummy ache, or head ache.

- Crying a lot.

- Coming home with unexplained injuries or ripped clothing.

- A child who starts behaving in an aggressive way, or 'bullying' other children when in your care.

- Parents telling you about disturbed sleep and possibly bad dreams and nightmares.

You must always tell parents if you suspect that their child is being bullied. With the parents' permission you should also pass on your concerns to the school.

Together with the parents, you need to ensure that help is given to the child. It is important that the true facts are established in a calm way and that the child is given comfort and reassurance. However you should not take 'matters into your own hands' in such situations. Always work with the parents and the school.

The smacking debate

If you are a member of the National Childminding Association you will have signed up to the Quality Standards, which does not allow members to use any form of physical punishment. However, there has recently been much public debate about smacking, and about whether childminders should be able to smack children with the permission of parents. One of the problems is what constitutes a smack. What is perhaps a light smack to one person, could be a hard slap to another.

Whatever your personal views on smacking, it is worth remembering that you are registered with a local authority who will have a policy based on the Children Act (1989) which states

'Corporal punishment (smacking, slapping or shaking) should not be used.'

It is also worth remembering that you do put yourself at risk if you use physical punishments to manage children's behaviour. The parents may decide that you have smacked their child too hard, for example, and this could lead to misunderstandings and in extreme cases accusations of abuse. It is also important to remember that insurance companies will not provide cover for injuries to a child as a result of smacking.

Does smacking work?

Many parents and childminders believe that giving a child a smack is a quick, instant and effective way of stopping a child behaving in a certain way, for example smacking a child immediately after they have thrown a toy and broken something, or smacking a child who has just hit another child.

There has been a lot of research on the effects of physical punishment on children's growth and development and there are now some very good reasons why smacking does not work.

- **Children learn that being violent or aggressive is acceptable**. Smacking is a form of aggressive behaviour. An adult hits another person which gives the message to the child that it is acceptable to be aggressive. Smacking is also a form of anger, so children who are smacked may not learn how to control their own anger so that they don't behave in violent or aggressive ways.

- **Smacking does not teach children how to resolve problems** or conflicts in a peaceful way. Quite often people who smack are not consistent about when a smack is given. This confuses children and they are not able to learn boundaries of behaviour. Many young children do not understand the reasons why they have been smacked, and again because they do not understand will not be able to learn boundaries of behaviour. In some cases the fear of being smacked can make some children tell lies about what they have been doing.

There is strong political pressure to make it an offence for anyone, including parents, to smack children. Many European countries, such as Sweden, have had this legislation for several years and Britain is one of the last European countries where smacking is legal.

Children with Attention Deficit with Hyperactivity Disorder (ADHD) or Attention Deficit Disorder(ADD)

Children who have ADHD are:

- unable to concentrate
- constantly demanding attention
- unable to stay at one activity for any length of time
- constantly talking and interrupting others
- unable to share
- unable to establish friendships and maintain relationships
- very demanding of adults who care for them

Children with ADD are:

- unable to concentrate
- often don't seem to listen, and forget things

- easily distracted and lose things

- often quiet or withdrawn

- often unable to complete tasks and so their progress and learning can be affected.

Medical research into children who suffer from either of these conditions is ongoing, although the exact reasons why some children suffer in this way is not yet understood. It is generally accepted that these children make better progress when cared for in small groups, which places childminders in a very strong position to help both the parents and children in such cases. Children with ADHD and ADD can be very exhausting to care for and you should consider the implications for you, other children and your family before you agree to care for any such child. Some children with ADD and ADHD respond well to the drug Ritalin, although it can have side-effects and some parents are reluctant to let their child take it.

Sources of help and support for childminders and parents

There may be times when a child's behaviour causes both you and the parents extreme concern. These will usually be situations that are just too complex for you to deal with, so you should encourage the parents to seek support and guidance from other professionals or support groups. Conditions such as ADHD and ADD have effective support groups that can help the parents, child and you. Some of these addresses can be found at the back of the book.

Often a child with serious behaviour problems will be taken to a GP in the first instance. The family doctor can then refer the child to a range of specialists such as:

- an educational psychologist, who will carry out investigative tests on aspects of the children's development

- a child psychiatrist, who will work with the child and their family to try to find out how the child is feeling and thinking

- a play therapist who works with children through play activities which allow the child to express their feelings and fears

- family guidance clinics or centres which are usually in the child's local area and can involve a range of professionals from social services, health and education.

CHECK YOUR KNOWLEDGE

1   What changes in behaviour could make you think that a child in your care is being bullied?

2   How can play help you manage a child's unwanted behaviour?

3   What does 'taking a positive approach to managing children's behaviour' actually mean?

4   Give two reasons why observations can help you understand some underlying reasons for unwanted behaviour.

5   Explain two reasons why smacking is not an effective way of managing a child's behaviour.

6   Give four common causes of unwanted behaviour.

7   Suggest a way that you could deal with each common cause in the case of a three-year-old and a seven-year-old. Put your answers in the chart below.

Cause of unwanted behaviour	How I can deal with it	
	3-year-old	**7-year-old**
1		
2		
3		
4		

CHAPTER 8
Treating children and their families with equal concern

It is a requirement of registration for all childminders that they comply with the Children Act (1989) and its guidance. The Act has the requirement 'to treat all children as individuals and with equal concern'.

Treating children as individuals is not the same as treating all children in the same way. This is impossible to do, as all children are different. What is important is that childminders understand how to treat all children and their families with respect and in a fair way.

You may find that during your course you will start to question your own views and opinions. Some course members may challenge your views and attitudes, and some people can find this threatening and become defensive or angry. However if equal concern is about treating people fairly, it follows that everyone has the right to express their own opinion, even if it is different from yours and everyone should expect to be challenged if they make prejudicial or discriminatory remarks. You should respect the views of everyone.

What is meant by equal opportunities?

The words 'equal opportunities' are often linked and associated with anti-discriminatory and anti-bias practice. In most cases people also think of issues about race, cultural or social background, disability and gender.

There are many people in our society who have discriminatory views and prejudicial attitudes. It is fair to say that most people who work with children will come across prejudice in some shape or form, either directed at the children or at themselves. It could be argued that to say 'You're just a childminder' is a discriminatory and prejudicial remark in the same way that saying 'He wears funny clothes' is discriminatory.

If you discriminate, you are effectively treating someone unfairly, therefore if you say that you have anti-discriminatory policies this should mean that you treat all children and adults fairly, regardless of their racial origins and cultural background, their gender, their family group or the disability that they may have. You should not, for example, have different toys for girls and boys. There may be some toys that the girls may *choose* to play with more than the boys, but that is their choice. It could be argued that if you care for a left-handed child and do not have left-handed scissors, for example, you are not treating that child fairly as they cannot learn to cut and therefore cannot reach their full potential. Maybe you need to ask yourself if it is right that some childminders only want to care for children who are the same racial origins and cultural background to themselves. Following on from that question, perhaps some would argue that children with disabilities should be cared for by childminders with the same disability because they understand the 'problems'.

You can say that you have an anti-discriminatory policy, but at the same time be prejudiced. Prejudiced people make up their minds about other people or situations *before* they know anything about them. What would your reaction be if you were asked to care for a male child of a lesbian couple?

You may need to think very carefully about your own ideas about discrimination and prejudice.

Young children develop their attitudes and values from adults around them. When put into new situations children will look to adults to give clues on how they should behave and react. The child's family is probably the strongest influence on developing views and attitudes. It is not uncommon for children to express discriminatory views that they have learnt from their parents, for example, a child saying to another something along the lines of, 'My dad says your lot should go back to where you came from.' As a child grows older their friends and peer group will also influence their attitudes.

Childminders have a very important role to play in helping children learn about being non-discriminatory and fair in their dealings with other people. One way that children learn is by copying adults. How you behave and react, the things you say and the play opportunities that you provide will all send messages to the children in your care. It is therefore very important that you are a positive role model for all of the children all of the time.

Learning Outcome Activity 49 (ICP, DCP, ECP)

Do you hold stereotypical views of people?

Discrimination and prejudice can occur when people hold stereotypical views, such as the view that all football supporters are hooligans.

Below is a list of different people. Write down a few words to describe the first thing you thought about or associated with that person.

Compare your responses with other course members or friends or family members.

- Old-age pensioner
- Fifteen-year-old teenage boy
- Nurse
- Single mother
- Student
- Fashion model
- Bank manager
- Childcare worker

Obstacles to children reaching their full potential

There can be numerous obstacles to children which have the effect of not allowing them to reach their full potential. All childcare practitioners, including childminders, need to be aware of these obstacles and do everything they can to remove them. Obstacles can be put into four categories:

1 Stereotypical attitudes
2 Negative images and environments
3 Treatment of children
4 Attitudes towards individuality.

Every child has the right to develop to their full potential as much as any other child. Sadly, even though we live a multicultural and diverse society, this right is denied to some children. Often this is not done deliberately, but more usually through lack of understanding and awareness.

Stereotypical attitudes

Sometimes our ways of thinking and our ideals are not based on our past experiences, but on stereotypes. Most of us hold stereotypes in some form or other. Some of these are learnt from books, television, advertising and so forth. Other ways of thinking will have been learnt in the early years. It is possible that judgements can be made about children, without knowing anything about them. These judgements are based on stereotypes. This is prejudice. It might be that a judgement will be made that is positive, but if that judgement is made without any prior knowledge of the person it can still be prejudicial.

If you completed the earlier activity about stereotypes, you may have realised how easy it is to be prejudiced about certain types of people. It is very easy to make assumptions about what children can or cannot achieve, the way that they ought to behave or speak, basing these assumption on stereotypical attitudes. How childminders treat the children in their care will give very strong messages about what they can do and accomplish.

Ask yourself:

• Do I have different expectations of what boys and girls can achieve?
• Do I provide different activities for girls and boys?
• Do I give the impression that some activities are more suitable for boys and not girls?

It is through being aware of our own stereotypical attitudes that we can help all children to reach their full potential.

Negative images and environments

One of the most effective ways to overcome stereotypical attitudes is to provide as many positive images as you can, including yourself. Children will learn from you. How you react towards people will teach children about attitudes and will affect how they develop their own views and opinions.

You should try to provide resources and activities for the children in your care that attempt to break down stereotypes and show children positive images and role models. Materials such as books, videos and toys should include images, for example, of men in caring, domestic and creative roles. You should take time to explain and talk to the children about how men can and do take on caring roles. Some children will already have a father who perhaps gives them a bath or prepares a meal. You can use these real life experiences with other children to help them develop a wider understanding. Materials should also include images of people of different ethnic groups and with additional needs holding trustworthy, demanding and important positions.

Learning Outcome Activity 50 (ICP, DCP, ECP)

Overcoming negative images

Talk to older children about many disabled athletes who achieve international success, for example, and prominent political figures who have a disability.

Help the children to become aware of the many members of our society, of all races, who have achieved positions of influence. Don't forget to include doctors, teachers and other professionals as well as sports personalities and pop stars.

Treatment of children

Many people think that offering children equal opportunities means that children have to be treated all the same. However this is not the case. If children are treated in the same way, no account is taken of their individual needs, personality and stage of development and growth.

Childminders should make equal treatment of all of the children that they care for the heart of everything they do. This means that in order to offer each child an equal opportunity to grow, develop and learn, it is essential that children are treated differently and adaptations are made to work practices to meet individual needs.

Many things can affect the way that children are treated. You will need to take into consideration, for example, the child's state of health, if they are tired or hungry, family circumstances, both long and short term, the child's personality and any additional need or difficulty that they may have.

In treating children differently, childminders can ensure that all children have equal opportunity to develop and grow. What is important is that you treat each child with equal concern and consideration.

Attitudes towards individuality

It is essential that all childminders accept that everyone is an individual, unique person. Children from the same family will have very different and individual personalities and appearances and will react differently in some situations. It is important that children know that you respect them as individuals regardless of their weaknesses or strengths.

One very positive way of helping children understand that you respect them as an individual and not some other person's child, brother, or sister, is to use their name. Make sure that you pronounce the name correctly and when writing a child's name make sure that it is spelt correctly.

How to create a positive environment in your home

One very effective way to encourage children to develop positive attitudes and respect for other people is to create a positive learning environment in your childminding setting. This is not just about putting 'different coloured dolls' out for the children to play with. It is more about having materials, toys and resources which reflect the diversity of our society. It is about having materials in your home that reflect the background of the children that you care for. During your childminding career you will care for children from a wide variety of backgrounds. You need to show that you value and respect each family and should ask parents to help you acquire suitable resources and toys. This will not only make individual children feel welcome and valued by you, but will also extend the knowledge and understanding of other children that you care for.

Learning Outcome Activity 51 (ICP, DCP, ECP)

The books in your home

Have a look at the books that you have in your home.

Do they reflect the cultural diversity of today's society?

Do you know where you can get a wider selection of books?

Children's understanding of equal opportunities

One way that children learn is by watching the reactions and behaviour of the people around them. It therefore follows that children will learn about prejudice and stereotypes from the people around them.

Very young children and babies need to learn about themselves, to understand that they are separate beings from their parents and carers and to understand who they are. By the time most children are two they know their name, whether they are a girl or a boy and if they are big or little. By about two-and-a-half years old children will start to explore different roles and identities through role and imaginative play. By the time most children are three they are aware of differences in gender and skin colour, and by the time that they are four research shows that most children start to attach different values to different people, for example white males have a higher 'value' than anyone else.

Children need to have accurate information about every aspect of their learning and development, and an understanding of equal opportunities is no different. They need honest and truthful answers to their questions. They need to learn that differences in people are interesting. Childminders should not pretend that the differences do not exist but need to talk openly about them and encourage children to do the same.

There is a danger that childminders can fall into the 'multicultural trap'. This means providing the children in your care with materials and images that do not accurately reflect other cultures. For example, giving the idea that all Eskimos live in igloos, when in fact many live in towns and cities. In the same way having a length of material in the dressing-up box and calling it a 'sari' does not show respect or understanding for the women who do wear this form of clothing. Childminders should avoid the potential danger of teaching children a little about a culture and then presenting a stereotypical image that everyone from that culture is the same. It is like believing that the British culture is only about Big Ben and Christmas and that everyone celebrates Christmas and uses Big Ben to set the time.

Childminders should encourage all children to treat everyone they meet with respect and consideration. Children will learn from your example so you should be a positive role model at all times.

Strategies to help deal with discriminatory attitudes, behaviour and prejudice

In our society there are groups of people or individuals who are discriminated against for many reasons. Often these people receive less favourable treatment than other people. It is very important that all people who work with children do everything possible to teach children to be fair and non-discriminatory in all their dealings with other people of any age.

It is also important to remember that children and adults who are at the receiving end of discrimination and prejudice can be very distressed, and the effects of such actions can be long-lasting.

Practical things you can do

1   Make sure that within your framework for managing children's behaviour you include rules or guidelines about children playing together and not excluding another child for any reason.

2   Get immediately involved if you hear a child make a discriminatory or prejudicial remark and talk to the child who made the remark about the hurt and distress that they could have caused.

3   Comfort any child who has been on the receiving end of a discriminatory remark. Make sure that they understand that you will care for them unconditionally. Help the child to respond positively to such remarks.

4   Be aware that sometimes children repeat things that they have heard adults say. When discussing what children have said, do not devalue or undermine the child's parents or family members. It is better to explain that everyone has different views and opinions, and without being judgemental try to explain to children how you wish them to behave when they are in your care. Hopefully the good example that you set will help the child form positive attitudes themselves.

5   Be brave and protect the children in your care from prejudice and discrimination. Point out that prejudice and discrimination are hurtful and politely give accurate information to any individual who makes a prejudiced or discriminatory remark.

6   Answer all children's questions about why some people look different, wear different clothes or behave differently from them, with accuracy and honesty. Don't ignore their question or change the subject.

7   Think before you speak! Use language that is positive and does not give stereotypical impressions. For example, get into the habit of saying 'police officers' rather than policemen.

Learning Outcome Activity 52 (ICP, DCP, ECP)

The wrong attitudes

Look at the following questions that children could ask or things that you might hear them saying to each other.

Write down a possible answer for each question or statement and compare with those on page 292.

1 Why do you wear those funny glasses, Jake?
2 You talk rubbish, Fatima, it doesn't make sense to me.
3 No, you can't play football, Katy, you're a girl.
4 Why are Amir's hands a different colour to mine? Does he need a wash?
5 Why has that man got no hair?
6 Mandy is too big to still be in a buggy.

The legal position and historical background

Legislation affecting childminders

Since the 1970s there have been several Acts of Parliament that have become laws with the aim of fighting discrimination in our society and ensuring equal opportunities for everyone.

The **Equal Pay Act** of 1972 stated that wages for men and women doing the same job should be the same. This Act was followed, in 1975, by the **Sex Discrimination Act**. The aim of this piece of legislation was to protect people from discrimination because of their sex. It became illegal to discriminate against people because of their sex when they apply for a job, in the work place, when renting, buying or selling a home, in education and when buying goods and services. The Sex Discrimination Act is supported by the **Equal Opportunities Commission**, which has the responsibility to see that the law is enforced.

In 1976 the **Race Relations Act** became law. This Act protects people from racial discrimination in the same situations as the Sex Discrimination Act, but also includes education and training and when joining a club or society. The **Commission for Racial Equality (CRE)** was set up to enforce this Act and to provide advice on improving equality of opportunity with particular reference to race.

The **Children Act 1989** had far-reaching implications for all people involved with children. It is under the requirements of this Act that childminders are registered and inspected. It is accepted that this Act was a significant step forward in the law in England and Wales as it put into law things that many professionals had been advocating for years. Central to this Act is the belief that the well-being of the child is vital. Since the Act was made law there have been several publications produced to help those people working with children interpret the law – these are usually referred to as 'guidances'.

The Children Act 1989 clearly states that an individual child's race, culture, language and religion must be respected. All registered childminders are therefore legally obliged to conform with this and have a responsibility to make sure that their practices treat all children with equal concern.

An Act to protect people with disabilities was made law in 1996, the **Disability Discrimination Act**. This Act covers the same general areas as the Sex Discrimination Act and the Race Relations Act. It also includes making sure that people with a disability have access to the same services as everyone else, so public buildings, cinemas, sport centres, for example, must be accessible for people in wheelchairs. In the same way it would be illegal for a shop to refuse to sell you something because you were disabled or in the company of a disabled person.

The **Education Act 1996** covers many aspects of educational provision. One significant element in this Act was a **Code of Practice on the Identification and Assessment of Special Educational Needs**. This is usually referred to as 'The Code of Practice'. This Act also gives parents greater rights in deciding how and where their child should be educated and the right to information about their child's progress and attainment. Childminders who are accredited members of the National Childminding Association's approved childminding networks as education providers, and so can claim funding for nursery education for three- and four-year-olds, must be aware of the Code of Practice. As with the Children Act, there are several publications of guidance to help childminders and other childcare practitioners interpret this piece of legislation. The Code of Practice was revised in January 2002.

From October 2000 the **1998 Human Rights Act** became part of English Law. This Act includes the **European Convention on Human Rights** which has been in place since the 1950s. One important part of the convention was the rights that affect family and private life. Many aspects of the convention deal with the rights of the individual and attempts to limit all forms of discrimination.

The most recent piece of legislation is the **Care Standards Act 2000**. This act came into force in September 2001; its full title is the **National Standards for Under Eights Day Care and Childminding.** There are 14 standards covering all aspects of childcare in a range of settings in England. It is these standards that will be used by OfSTED (the Office for Standards in Education) and CSIW to carry out Children Act inspections. The standards cover out-of-school care, sessional care, full day-care, crèches and childminding. All registered childminders will have to comply with the 14 standards, which are:

1   'Adults providing day-care, looking after children or having unsupervised access to them are suitable to do so.' (*Suitable person*)

2   'The registered person meets adult:child ratios, ensures that training and qualifications requirements are met and organises space and resources to meet the children's needs effectively.' (*Organisation*)

3   'The registered person meets the children's individual needs and promotes their welfare. They plan and provide activities and play opportunities to develop their emotional, physical, social and intellectual capabilities.' (*Care, learning and play*)

4   'The premises are safe, secure and suitable for their purpose. They provide adequate space in an appropriate location, are welcoming to children and offer access to the necessary facilities for a range of activities which promote their development.' (*Physical environment*)

5   'Furniture, equipment and toys are provided which are appropriate for their purpose and help create an accessible and stimulating environment. They are of suitable design and condition, are well-maintained and conform to safety standards.' (*Equipment*)

6   'The registered person takes positive steps to promote safety within the setting and on outings and ensures proper precautions are taken to prevent accidents.' (*Safety*)

7   'The registered person promotes the good health of children and takes positive steps to prevent the spread of infection and appropriate measures when they are ill.' (*Health*)

8   'Children are provided with regular drinks and food in adequate quantities for their needs. Food and drink is properly prepared and nutritious and complies with dietary and religious requirements.' (*Food and drink*)

9   'The registered person and staff actively promote equality of opportunity and anti-discriminatory practice for all children.' (*Equal opportunities*)

10 'The registered person is aware that some children may have special needs and is pro-active in ensuring that appropriate action can be taken when such a child is identified or admitted to the provision. Steps are taken to promote the welfare and development of the child within the setting, in partnership with the parents and other relevant parties.' (*Special needs*)

11 'Adults caring for children in the provision are able to manage a wide range of children's behaviour in a way which promotes their welfare and development.' (*Behaviour*)

12 'The registered person and staff work in partnership with parents to meet the needs of children, both individually and as a group. Information is shared.' (*Working in partnership with parents and carers*)

13 'The registered person complies with the local child protection procedures approved by the area child protection committee and ensures that all adults working and looking after children in the provision are able to put the procedures into practice.' (*Child protection*)

14 'Records, policies and procedures which are required for the efficient and safe management of the provision, and to promote the welfare, care and learning of children are maintained. Records about individual children are shared with the parents.' (*Documentation*)

The Care Standards are far-reaching and although there are some standards that are open to interpretation, such as who is a suitable person, it is generally accepted that all childcare providers are working on an equal footing and to the same nationally agreed standards. This can only benefit children and should rule out differences in the standards of care between local authorities. However, some aspects of the Care Standards promoted furious debate amongst childminders in England, as they allow childminders to smack children, with parents' permission, and also to smoke when caring for children. No other sector of the childcare profession is allowed to do either of these. However, members of the National Childminding Association agreed to the NCMA Quality Standards, which categorically state that no member of the Association should use any form of physical punishment and that they should not smoke when caring for children.

Despite recent laws, there are still gaps in some aspects of equal opportunities. You can still be refused by a local authority to be registered as a childminder on grounds of your age. This is a form of discrimination. There are no laws to protect the rights of gay and lesbian people, and inequalities still exist with regard to the age of consent. It is also worth remembering that there are no laws to promote 'positive discrimination'. There is a view that making it a requirement for employers to employ people from a particular cultural or racial group or gender would develop equality of opportunity; however some hold the view that this requirement could be abused.

Learning Outcome Activity 53 (ICP, DCP, ECP)

Care standards for childminders

If you have not already got a free copy of the Care Standards for Childminders in England, contact the DfES – telephone: 0845 6022260, fax: 0845 6033360, email: dfes@prglog.uk.com.

Or write to them at: DfES publications, PO Box 5050, Annesley, Nottingham NG15 0DG, and quote reference number DfES 0486/2001.

For Wales go to www.gov.uk/subisocialpolicycarestandards.

Historical background

History shapes our present and future. We cannot change history but we can learn from history, from both the positive and negative events that have happened, wherever in the world. Current views and legislation on equal opportunities, especially in relation to race, disability and gender issues, have come about as a result of historical events. Even people without knowledge of past historical events are influenced in their views and attitudes by what has happened.

You do not have to go very far back into history to find examples of racism and discriminatory practices. The Second World War and Hitler's treatment of the Jews being a prime example, as was Idi Admin's ruling on people of Asian origin in Uganda the 1970s. Many women do not realise, or cannot understand, the frustration that Emily Pankhurst and other Suffragettes must have felt before women were given the right to vote; a right that we now take for granted. In the same way, women today are able to have children and still pursue their careers; this opportunity did not exist for many women until quite recently. Maternity leave and pay only came into force in 1975.

Some of the prejudice and discriminatory attitudes expressed towards non-white people are based on inaccurate information and myths, some of which are centuries old. Countries that engaged in the slave trade and colonised other countries perpetuated racist and discriminatory attitudes. Unfortunately some of those attitudes and the impact of those practices still linger and have an influence on some people's views.

The British Isles have always been occupied by a variety of races, for thousands of years. It is this diverse mix of races that makes our society rich and varied. It is the reason why some people have blond or black hair; blue, brown or green eyes; it is the reason why we are different shapes and sizes. Some of the extreme attitudes expressed by a minority of radical individuals do not take this into account and spread their propaganda based on misinformation. The CRE has many free fact sheets that give accurate information about employment, housing, education and training, and so present a different picture to the one that extremists would have us believe.

As well as thinking about the historical aspects of racism and sexism, it is important to remember that attitudes towards people with disabilities have also changed in some parts of the world, but not all. There are still institutions in some countries which house children and adults with a range of disabilities. In such places no education is provided and often minimum standards of care are exercised; the view being that the disabled are not capable of receiving an education and do not require the same standards of care as other people. It is only recently that the education and care of disabled children and adults has been seen as a responsibility of the state and not of charities and voluntary organisations. In the past, because the care of disabled people was dependent on the good will of others, attitudes engendered pity for the disabled. Many disabled people still find such attitudes prevalent today and some regard this as insulting. It was only following legislation in the 1980s and 1990s that disabled children have been integrated into mainstream schools and have been offered the same educational opportunities as other children.

Developing your own equal opportunities policy

Your policy for equal opportunities has to show that you will treat all children with equal concern – this is a basic requirement. It is also important that any policy you have takes into consideration the wishes of the parents and shows respect for different styles of parenting. This is of course much easier said than done! However if you become a member of the National Childminding Association you will have to agree to uphold its equal opportunities policy, which opposes all forms of discrimination. Even if you do not becomes a member of the NCMA, a policy which opposes all forms of discrimination is a good starting point for you to write your own policy.

Every policy that you have in your business should be regularly reviewed, and if necessary revised. An equal opportunities policy needs revision and will probably develop as your business develops. However it is essential that your policy is in place and working for you from your first day in business.

Remember that having a policy is to follow a course of action or to produce a written statement about your intentions. Bear these words in mind when putting together your policy. It is something you actively do, and not just a piece of paper that is filed away and only brought out to show your inspection officer and prospective parents. Many childminders produce a short leaflet for parents to explain their views on equal opportunities. This idea could be seen as 'more user friendly'. It does not matter how you present your ideas as long as you are clear in your own mind about how you will treat the children in your care and their families.

Your policy might include, if appropriate, how you will care for children's skin and hair. It could include details of the language that you will use and expect the children to respond to. You can also include brief details of your own feelings and acknowledge that you will not know everything, but are prepared to seek assistance and help from parents and other people if needed, in order to treat children with equal concern. As with any policy, it is your working document and it must work for you.

Learning Outcome Activity 54 (ICP, DCP, ECP)

What to cover in your equal opportunities statement

Below is a list of things to cover in an equal opportunities statement for your business:

- Issues about religion.
- Issues about race, including colour, language.
- Different cultural practices, including food and diet, clothing, hair and skin care, parenting styles.
- Language used in the childminding setting.
- Stereotypical attitudes, including issues about gender.
- Parental or marital status.
- Sexual orientation.
- Disability.
- HIV/AIDS.

This is not a complete list. You can probably think of many other things to add to it.

Write a short statement reassuring parents that you will treat all children equally.

CHECK YOUR KNOWLEDGE

True or False?

Read the following statements and decide if they are true or false. The answers are given on pages 292–293.

1   A childminder's policy for equal opportunities should oppose all forms of discrimination.

2   Using a child's name correctly is one positive way of helping the child to understand that you respect them as an individual.

3   You need to provide different activities for boys and girls.

4   Children are not aware of gender differences.

5   Equal opportunities means treating everyone the same.

6   Children learn by copying adults.

7   Stereotypical attitudes do not prevent children from reaching their full potential.

8   Providing a length of sari material in the dressing-up box will help children learn about culture.

9   Your framework for managing children's behaviour should not exclude any child.

10   The National Standards for Under Eights Day Care and Childminding is an important piece of legislation that affects all childminders.

CHAPTER 9
Working with parents and other professionals

Parents and primary carers, such as grandparents or foster carers, are the most important people in young children's lives. It is from them that children will learn about their family cultures and religious beliefs. Parents and primary carers know their children very well, probably better than anyone else. They are a child's first teachers and can powerfully influence a child's attitudes and development.

In recent years there has been a distinct shift in attitudes towards the role of parents in the education and care of their children. The Children Act 1989 gave parents definite rights, such as being able to express a preference about which school their child should go to and the right to information about their child's progress and achievements. Most educational establishments and childcare settings have established policies that aim to make parents partners in the care and education of their children. As a childminder you may not wish to have a 'parents as partners' policy, but it is essential in your business to establish positive relationships with parents, from the first time you meet. The relationship between childminders and parents is often a close one. Parents come into the childminder's home regularly and so they get to know one another very well.

Initiating relationships with parents

Chapter 2 looked at how to manage the first meeting with parents and made suggestions on how to put together welcome and information packs.

Before you initiate any professional relationship with parents it is very important that you are very sure about the type of childminding service you plan to offer. You need to think about:

- If you will offer full-time or part-time care. In other words, will you expect all the children in your care to stay for full days, or are you willing to have children coming and going at, say, lunch-time, or mid-afternoon?

- What times your childminding business will be operating. What are the earliest and the latest times that you are prepared to care for children?

- What ages you are prepared to care for. Are you willing to care for small babies and children of school age? If so, what age would be the oldest and what age the youngest child?

- What days of the week your childminding service will be available.

- Whether you are willing to care for children at the weekends, or overnight, or throughout the school holidays. (Don't forget that you will need a holiday or break as well.)

- What meals you are prepared to offer.

- Whether you are prepared to take children to and from school, nursery, pre-school group or activity groups. Which school, nurseries and pre-schools are you prepared to take and collect from?

Even when you have made your decisions about the above issues, you will need to be very clear in your own mind about why you have made these decisions. If you are clear about your decisions it will help you explain your reasons to parents.

CASE STUDY

Lindy is a registered childminder. Her own children attend the local primary school, which is a five-minute walk away. Lindy has decided that she will only care for school-age children who attend the same school as her own children. She does not feel that she can cope with collecting from more than one school and ensure the safety of all of the children, including her own. When Lindy first made this decision she was a little concerned that this would restrict her business. However, this has not been the case and parents are reassured that Lindy places such importance on the safety of the children.

Making the first meeting a success

We are all influenced by first impressions. We look at the way someone is dressed, for example, or the way they speak, and this influences our first impression about what sort of person they might be. How often have you heard someone say something like, 'I looked at those big eyes and thought that he/she must be a lovely person.' Have you ever been put off talking to someone because you did not like the way they were dressed? This makes the first meeting with parents possibly one of the most important ones you may have with them. First impressions do count.

Think about the first meeting as an exchange of information. You need to know specific information about the child and the parents need to know about the service that you provide. For some parents, you might be the first person that they have left their child with and they may not know what sort of questions to ask. This is where your welcome and information packs are invaluable.

You should avoid being judgemental about why parents wish to leave their child. Many childminders are, in actual fact, working mothers themselves. If parents think that you disapprove of their personal lifestyle, it will affect the quality of the relationship that you are trying to build.

Communication between you and the parents

The key to any successful relationship is communication. Communication can be defined as an exchange of ideas, contact between individuals, consultation and interaction.

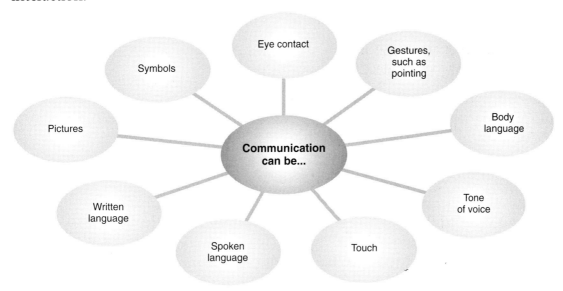

Figure 9.1 *The various ways we communicate*

Learning Outcome Activity 55 (ICP, DCP, ECP)

How you use communication

Using the above list try to think of an incident or occasions when you have used a different form of communication. For example, have you calmed a baby by gently stroking their back or used your tone of voice to manage a child's behaviour?

In the chart below record occasions when you have used different ways of communicating.

Form of communication	Incident or occasion
Eye contact	
Gestures such as pointing	
Body language	
Tone of voice	
Touch	
Spoken language	
Written language	
Pictures	
Symbols	

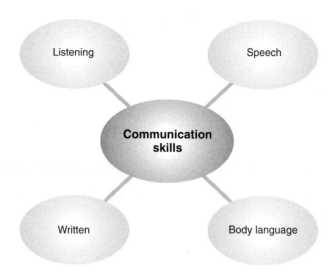

Figure 9.2 *Different forms of communication skills*

Communication in any form is a two-way process that requires a 'giver' and a 'receiver'. Communication requires time and effort from both sides. Lack of communication can lead to misunderstandings and misinformation. There are skills that you can learn that will help you become a more effective communicator, not just with parents, but also with the children that you care for and indeed all the other people that you come into contact with in both your professional and personal life.

Listening

Listening is a fundamental part of communication. It is not a passive activity, it does not just happen. To be a good listener requires time, effort and concentration. Being a good listener does not come naturally to some people. Some find that they are easily distracted, or that their feelings about a person can affect how well they listen.

There are definite things that you can do to make sure that you are an 'effective' listener.

GOOD PRACTICE *Being an effective listener*

- Give the person who is speaking your undivided attention.
- Ask questions to either show that you have listened, want more information or to clarify something that you may not have heard correctly.
- Summarise what has been said. This makes you listen carefully, lets the person who was speaking know that you have understood what they were saying and reduces the possibility of misunderstandings.
- Let the speaker know that you are listening carefully. Maintain eye contact, use appropriate gestures and body language, such as nods of the head, perhaps saying words like 'mmm' or 'yes'.

There are pitfalls that you can 'fall into' if you are not aware. Researchers at the University of Leeds came up with a list of barriers to good listening. All of these listed below, can be turned around into positive points of good practice.

- **'On-off' listening**. This is a bad habit that comes from the fact that most people think about four times as fast as the average person speaks. This means that the person who is listening has about a quarter of a minute of spare thinking time for each listening minute. Sometimes we use this 'extra' time to think about personal details, concerns, troubles or interests, instead of listening.

- **'Red-flag' listening**. Some people react negatively to certain words. When we become upset or irritated we stop listening. Think about your own 'red flag' words.

- **'Open ears–closed mind' listening**. Sometimes we make decisions that the person who is speaking, or what they are talking about, is boring, or does not make sense, so we stop listening.

- **'Glassy-eyed' listening**. Sometimes when we look intently at someone we can appear to be listening although our minds might be on other things. It is usually quite easy to see when someone is doing this.

- **'Too-deep-for me' listening**. When we are listening to something that we think is too difficult or complex for us, we 'switch off'.

- **'Matter-over-mind' listening**. We do not feel comfortable when our views and opinions are challenged. When someone does this we can stand firm as to our own opinions and in effect stop listening to the other person's point of view.

- **Being 'subject-centred' instead of 'speaker-centred'**. Sometimes we concentrate on the problem and not the person.

- **'Fact' listening**. Often when we listen we go over facts in our minds to make sure that we don't forget them. Whilst we are doing this, the speaker has moved on to something new and we have missed it.

- **'Pencil' listening**. This the classic note taker's problem, when you try to put down on paper everything that is being said. The speaker speaks faster than we can write and so we miss something. It also difficult to maintain eye contact in this situation.

- **'Hubbub' listening**. There are sometimes so many distractions around when we try to listen, that we can not concentrate fully.

Speech

You will be using some form of spoken communication every day, with your family, the children that you care for and all the other people that you come into contact with. Speaking is possibly the most effective way of communicating with other people. Spoken words help to build relationships. You can supplement your spoken words with facial expressions, gestures, body language and eye contact, in ways that you can never do with telephone conversations, emails, faxes and written messages.

However, once said, words cannot be changed. It is so easy to make a fast response to someone without really thinking about what you say. This can sometimes lead to misunderstanding, and even worse, distress. The old maxim 'engage the brain before the mouth' is good advice.

Another thing to be aware of is that spoken words are often not as exact as written words. It is common practice to have to write things down, for example when making a speech or giving a talk, to make sure that everything is covered accurately and nothing is missed out. It is good practice to make written notes beforehand if you are going to speak to a parent or another professional about a specific or important issue. In this way you can be sure that you remember everything that you want to say, and that everything you say is accurate and factual.

Speaking on the telephone is commonplace and a very important way of communicating with people. If you are using the telephone for business it is good practice to remember the following points:

- Try to speak slower than you would do if the person was standing in front of you.

- Try to speak as clearly as possible.

- Don't let your voice drop at the end of sentences. This will make it more difficult for the person on the other end to hear you clearly.

- If possible, try to use the telephone in a room or place where there is little background noise. Other noises will be distracting for you as speaker and listener and for the person at the other end.

Body language

Body language is also described as non-verbal communication. Your body is giving messages all the time you are talking and listening. Sometimes our bodies will be saying one thing and our mouths will be saying something else. Obviously, this can be detrimental to communication. You should try as much as possible to maintain positive body language when dealing with parents, children and other professionals, in fact it could be argued that you should always use positive body language!

Opposite is a chart of some of the most common forms of body language and some interpretations.

A word of warning – these are only possible interpretations and you should be careful that you do not 'read' too much into another person's mannerisms. However, it is a good idea to be aware of some of the common forms of negative body language so you can avoid them, such as rubbing your nose when telling a parent how their child has behaved that day!

Body language	Possible interpretation
Erect, brisk walk	Confidence
Standing with hands on hips	Readiness or sometimes aggression
Sitting with legs crossed, foot slightly kicking	Boredom
Arms crossed on chest	Defensiveness
Walking with hands in pockets, shoulder hunched	Dejection
Hand to cheek	Evaluation, thinking
Touching, slightly rubbing nose	Rejection, or doubt, or lying
Rubbing the eye	Disbelief, or doubt
Hands clasped behind back	Anger, frustration, apprehension
Head resting in hand, eyes downcast	Boredom
Rubbing hands	Anticipation
Sitting with hands clasped behind head, legs crossed	Confidence, superiority
Open palm	Sincerity, openness, innocence
Pinching bridge of nose, eyes closed	Negative evaluation
Tapping or drumming fingers	Impatience
Steepling fingers	Authoritative
Patting or fiddling with hair	Lack of self-confidence, insecurity
Tilted head	Interest
Stroking chin	Trying to make a decision
Looking down, face turned away	Disbelief
Biting nails	Insecurity, nervousness
Pulling or tugging at ear	Indecision

Written language

There is an assumption that every professional is able to write effectively in every possible situation, such as keeping children's records, planning documents, writing reports and messages for parents. However this is not true. Many people have problems with writing, including feeling uncertain about things like spelling, grammar, the quality of their handwriting and lack of confidence in writing something. There are many sources of help for adults who feel that they have problems with writing in any shape or form. Your college, local library and many other local amenity offices will be able to give details of the help that is available in your area.

Personal computers are a great help for people who have problems with the written word. Computer programs have built-in spelling and grammar checks. The printed word is still written, but because it comes from a printer rather than a person's own hand it will be legible.

Learning Outcome Activity 56 (DCP)

Different ways of communicating

How many different forms of communication do you use in a normal working day?

Make a list of who you have communicated with, what form that communication took and how effective was it.

For example:

Asked partner to buy milk on way home from work but they forgot. Not effective, as I got cross. Should have written it on a note and put it on the dashboard of the car.

Dealing with conflict

There may be circumstances that you find yourself in where no matter how good your communication skills are, there is conflict between you and one or both parents. It is important to remember that children will very quickly pick up on the atmosphere between you and may become distressed. Do not ignore potential conflict situations, hoping that they will go away or that they will resolve themselves. They won't.

It is good practice to deal with the situation as quickly as possible, but at the same time do not act on impulse. Take time to think about the situation in an objective and unemotional way. Be prepared to find a solution that suits you both. This could mean that both you and the parents will have to be prepared to be flexible and make compromises. Don't expect to resolve a conflict situation with one meeting, it may take several, but it is important that you keep open all lines of communication.

If in the worse possible case, though this rarely happens, you and the parents cannot resolve your difficulties after all ways have been explored, then you will have to end your contract with the parents. To continue in a situation like this would not be beneficial to the children in the long term.

Why you need a written contract between you and the parents

A contract is an agreement between two parties, in this case between you and the parents. A contract should make your responsibilities and those of the parents very clear. There should be no ambiguities, or words that could be misinterpreted. The agreement between you and the family is about the care and well-being of the child, the most important reason for having the contract.

Most childminders have written, or computer produced, contracts for each family that they are involved with. Contracts should be signed by both parties and dated. Contracts, like policies, should be reviewed regularly, and especially when circumstances change, for example you might have agreed a contract to care for a child three days a week, then the mother increases her hours of work and asks you to care for the child five days a week. In this case you will need a new contract to reflect the new circumstances. Contracts need to be agreed, signed and dated regardless of the number of days or hours you will be caring for a child and regardless of the period of time, whether it is only one day, one week, or for the foreseeable future.

Reasons why you and parents need a contract:

1 Having a written contract for parents is a professional and business-like way of conducting your childminding affairs. It should give parents a good impression of your professionalism.

2 It makes it clear exactly what you are willing to do and so prevents misunderstandings.

3 Each contract can be personal to each family, to take into account the individual needs of that family and the child. However, at the same time the contract can have standard clauses, such as details of fees, pick-up and drop-off times, that apply to all families.

4 Contracts that are signed and dated by both parties are legally binding. This could be very important if you have problems later on.

You will need to make time to discuss the contract with the parents before you agree to take on the child. Make time to go over it and explain, if needed, each part of the contract and make sure that the parents are in full agreement with all aspects of it. Don't be pressurised into agreeing to something that will have an adverse effect on either you or the other children that you care for. Be firm and use your communication skills to explain to the parents why you have written the contract in the way that you have. Make sure that both you and the parents are very clear about what will happen if the contract is broken.

Mike is a registered childminder and cares for two children, Liam and Kerry, as well as his own baby. The contract that Mike has with both sets of parents clearly states that payment will be made weekly on the first day of care. In the case of one child, Liam, this is Monday morning. For the first six weeks, Liam's father gave Mike either cash or a cheque. On the seventh week the cheque was returned by the bank and Mike had to give it back to the father, who was very apologetic and gave Mike the cash the next day. The following week, Liam's father said that he had forgotten his cheque book, the next week Liam was dropped off by his grandmother, who said that the parents were busy, and the payments were nothing to do with her.

Mike felt that he was being put in a difficult position, especially as his own partner felt that the parents were taking advantage of Mike's goodwill and his childminding was a business and not a charity. Mike recognised that he had to do something as this family had broken their contract. Mike decided to telephone the father and ask him to come a few minutes earlier as he wanted to discuss things with him. The father did not keep this appointment. Mike felt that he had no option but to write to the parents giving them a week's notice that he would not be able to care for Liam unless they paid him the outstanding fees. The result of this was that Liam's grandmother gave Mike cash for the outstanding fees and said that her son had decided that he would care for Liam himself. Although Mike was sorry that his relationship with this family had not been very good, he did acknowledge that he could not afford to offer a free childminding service, and also taking positive action meant that he had less worry and stress.

1　In your view, did Mike do the 'right' thing?
2　Was there anything else that Mike could have done?

Different patterns of parenting and different family structures

Parenting styles

Parents do not really choose their parenting styles. Most parents are influenced by the way their own parents dealt with and 'parented' them. Parenting styles are also affected by the pressure of daily living. Remember that parenting styles can be different and there is no 'correct' style.

Most parents want the best for their children and love and care for them. How they do this varies from family to family, and as a result there are many different parenting styles as well as different family structures. The family structure can affect the parenting style. Cultural variations can also affect a parenting style. Regardless of the parenting style, you must respect the way the parents choose to bring up their child. If you realise that there is likely to be serious conflict between what you expect of the child and what their parents want, you must discuss this very carefully with the parents. It may be that you will be able to reach an acceptable and professional compromise, but it may be that it would be less stressful for all concerned if the parents found alternative care arrangements for their child.

Generally there are three main styles of parenting:

1 **Permissive**. Permissive parents allow their children lots of personal choice and responsibilities. They may also not make attempts to control or manage the behaviour of their children.

2 **Authoritarian**. Authoritarian parents are more likely to be the opposite of permissive parents. They attempt to manage, limit and control the behaviour of their children, and may also spend time explaining 'rules'. Such parents often have high expectations of their children.

3 **Authoritative**. Most parents tend to be authoritative. They try to manage and control their children's behaviour. They spend time listening to their children as well as explaining the reasons for certain rules or limits. It is believed that children generally gain most from this style of parenting, because they know and understand the limits and boundaries that are set and so feel secure.

Some cultures favour a more authoritarian style of parenting, with children not expected to question their parents' views or reasons for limiting behaviour. However, children in this type of family do usually benefit because there is a consistent approach.

Family structures

There are a variety of family structures. The traditional view is of a family composed of two people of the opposite sex, being married with children. This however is no longer true. Many childminders are not married to the person with whom they live; or they can be divorced or single parents. As with different parenting styles, the family structure is not important. The important thing is that the children are loved, treated with consistency and have good physical care.

The main family structures are described in Figure 9.3 on page 232.

You need to make sure that you do not have any stereotypical views regarding a particular type of family. What is important for you as a childminder is that you and the parents agree on how you will care for the child, that the child is loved, their needs are met through consistent care and that you show respect for the family's way of life.

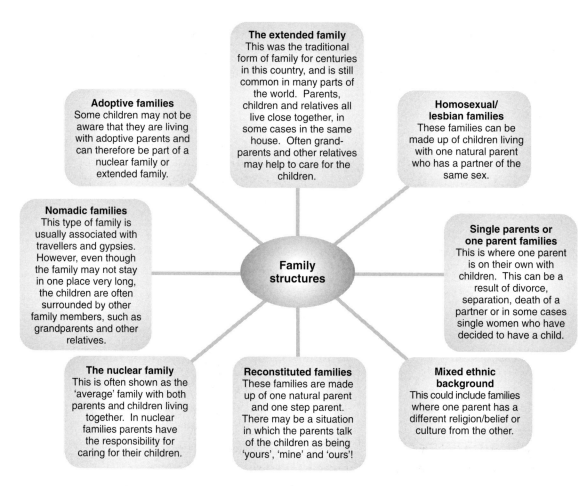

Figure 9.3 *There are a range of family structures in our society*

Learning Outcome Activity 57 (ICP, DCP, ECP)

The way I was brought up

Think about the way that your parents brought you up.

For example, did they set time limits for you to be in, or did they limit the number of nights that you were allowed out as a teenager?

How have these experiences influenced your views on parenting?

How you can support parents

Most relationships with parents will go smoothly. These will be built around frequent informal exchanges of information about the children, your contract and the business side of your childminding. Relationships become friendly and valued. Parents may share their worries and concerns about their children with you, even seeking your opinions. However, there may be times when parents are under stress and could need your support. Sometimes, childminders working in a community childminding network will have children placed with them because of family stresses. On the other hand, families and parents can come under stress unexpectedly.

Everybody reacts in different ways to stressful situations. Some people will want to talk about their problems, others will become uncommunicative. Some people become depressed and unresponsive, some refuse to accept that there is a problem. Some parents may snap or shout at their child for no apparent reason and appear impatient.

If you become aware that parents are under stress, you will need to use tact, sensitivity and professional understanding and knowledge in order to give them appropriate support.

The following are practical things you can do to help them.

Practical things to help you support parents under stress

- Stay **professional, non-judgemental and avoid stereotyping** at all times. Remember there are several different ways of parenting and also different family structures; there is not one 'correct' way to bring up children.
- Be a **positive role model** in all of your dealings with children and parents.
- Be prepared to **listen and be sympathetic**. Don't allow yourself to be 'drawn in' to possible conflicts or family arguments. Make sure you are **confident** and **assertive** enough to know when to suggest that the parent seeks specialist help. It is true that 'a problem shared is problem halved', but don't allow someone else's problem to become yours.
- Every parent will find their role difficult at some point. It is important to offer **reassurance** and help the parent understand that they are not alone in feeling the way they do.
- Stress can be caused by certain things, or circumstances, that are beyond the control of the parents. Again, you will need to offer reassurance that they are not to blame. It can be helpful in such circumstances to have a list of other support agencies, organisations or professionals that can help the parents, such as the telephone numbers of the local social services department, the local office of the DHSS, Citizens Advice Bureau, Relate, etc.
- Be **positive**. Sometimes when people are under stress they become very negative in their outlook and lack self-confidence and have low self-esteem. It can sometimes be helpful to talk to parents about the things that are going well, or things that they might enjoy.
- Stay **calm**, especially if you are dealing with an angry or distressed parent. Actively **listen** to what the parent is saying, and make sure that your response is not aggressive or threatening.

Remember you should be **working in partnership** with parents at all times, with the best interests of the child or children always put first.

Offering information and advice

It is essential that any information that you give to parents is up to date and accurate. You could make a stressful situation worse by giving out incorrect or inaccurate information. If you don't know, say so, but make sure that you can suggest an alternative source of information, such as:

- The local newspaper
- The local library
- Telephone help lines
- Citizens Advice Bureau

- Doctor's surgery, clinic or health centre
- Telephone book
- The internet
- Free leaflets from chemists, pharmacies and supermarkets

Learning Outcome Activity 58 (ICP, DCP, ECP)

How to deal with parents

What would you do in the following situations? Suggested solutions are given on page 293.

1 A parent is repeatedly late in picking up their child at the end of the day. This means that you are often late in collecting your own child from football practice.
2 You feel that the toddler that you are caring for is ready to be 'potty trained'. The parents disagree.
3 A parent confides in you that her partner is becoming increasingly violent.
4 One parent repeats personal information to you about another child.

The other professionals with whom you could work

Throughout your professional work it is inevitable that you will come into contact with other people who care for or educate children. Below is a list of some professionals that you may have had contact with:

- Teachers
- Pre-school or playgroup staff
- Nursery staff

- Other childminders
- Doctors, including GPs and those specialising in specific illnesses, ailments and disorders

- Health visitors
- Dentists
- OfSTED (OR CSIW) staff
- Nurses
- Therapists, including speech therapists and physiotherapists
- Education welfare officers

This list is not complete, and you will probably be able to add other professionals that you have worked with or could work with in the future.

Many childminders say that they feel 'in awe' of other professionals and lack confidence when dealing with such people. It is important to remember that both you and the other person that you are dealing with have the best interests of the child and his or her family at heart. This gives you common ground, a starting point on which to build your relationship.

It is also worth remembering that you are a professional person and should not feel intimidated when working with other professionals. It will be through your knowledge of the child, child development, care and your professional skills that you will gain the respect of others.

How you can develop successful working relationships with other professionals and parents

There are several things that you can do to make sure that any relationship that you develop with other professionals is good and effective.

1 Be professional yourself. Present your work with the children in a business-like way and appear confident.

2 Remember that the people with whom you are dealing will not know the child or children as well as you. You will have very valuable information to share.

3 Don't try to give the impression that you know more than you do. Be honest and say if you don't know something or are not sure. Be willing to seek advice and extra information yourself from other childminders or support groups if necessary.

4 If you are attending a meeting where you could be asked to contribute about a child, it is a good idea to make notes beforehand. Take time to think about what you are going to say, how you will say it, and use your notes to make sure that you do not leave out any important information. Remember to maintain issues of confidentiality at all times.

5 Avoid using jargon. All professions have a 'specialist vocabulary', which is perfectly acceptable with people of the same profession. However, it is not

necessary to use jargon as it may not be fully understood by others outside the profession. This can lead to ambiguities and misunderstandings. Another form of jargon can be the use of initial letters for complete words, such as ELGs for Early Learning Goals, and NCMA for National Childminding Association. Say what you want to say in clear, plain language. Similarly, if someone you are with uses jargon or initials, and you do not know what they mean, ask. It is far better to ask a sensible question to gain information than pretend that you understand when you don't.

CHECK YOUR KNOWLEDGE

1 What is meant by authoritarian parenting?

2 Give three reasons why you should have a written contract with parents.

3 What is meant by active listening?

4 Give two factors that could cause stress for parents.

5 Why should you not use jargon?

6 Suggest two ways that you could resolve conflict or disagreement between you and parents.

7 What is the common link between you and other professionals that you may work with?

8 A parent asks for advice about a financial problem. You don't know the answer. Suggest two sources of information that you could tell the parent to try.

CHAPTER 10
Child protection

Throughout this book it has been stressed that you should do everything you can to make sure that the children in your care are safe at all times. You will have looked at the possible risks and hazards in your home and garden and thought about the ways that your childminding business ensures that children are protected.

However, there could be times when, despite all your good practices, children may need protecting from harm and ill-treatment. It is important that you have a basic knowledge of types and signs of abuse and that you know what to do if you suspect that a child is in need of protection. Many childminders find dealing with any issue about child protection very difficult, so it is also important that you know where you can get support and help.

Child abuse

It is very difficult to get accurate figures about how many children are in need of protection at any time. Charities, such as the National Society for Prevention of Cruelty to Children (NSPCC), work unceasingly to protect children and raise awareness, but children are still abused. When it was suggested, by the NSPCC, that as many as one in six children may have been abused, some people felt that this was overstating the true picture. Many children who are abused, or in need of protection, do not talk about their experiences, for many reasons. The abuse may not be obvious to other people that they come into contact with and so it can be very difficult to do anything about it, sometimes until it is too late.

Every childcare professional, in whatever capacity, has a duty and responsibility to put the child's needs and welfare first. It therefore follows that if you suspect that a child is in need of protection you *must* do something about it.

Abuse can have long-term effects. Children who are subjected to repeated abuse can suffer severe psychological damage and be seriously affected for the rest of their lives. Many adults who suffered abuse as children or young people have great difficulty forming relationships and can have problems parenting their own children.

Abuse can happen in any family, whatever the family structure or parenting style. Abuse does not only happen to children in poor families, or in single-parent families. It does not discriminate; it can happen to any child. Childminders must not assume that children of 'respectable' families will not be abused and will be automatically protected.

Why adults abuse children

Children who suffer abuse are, in most cases, not abused by strangers; it is usually someone that they know, either a family member or friend. Why these people abuse is not fully understood. It has been suggested that a high proportion of adults who are abusers have themselves been abused as children and know no other way of dealing with children.

In some cases, if parents and children have been unable to form bonds from babyhood, the parents may be unable to behave in a 'normal' way with their child. It may have been that either the mother or child was seriously ill after the birth. This can lead to stress, difficulties with parenting and in some cases abuse. In most cases hospitals and medical staff make every effort to encourage the parents to become involved in the care of their child in some way and, hopefully, establish a bond and a relationship. Sometimes babies are not able to respond to their parents, children with severe mental impairment or disability, for example, may not respond to the attempts of their parents to establish a relationship and bond. Again this can lead to parenting difficulties and abuse. However, it should be remembered that many parents of disabled children have established a close and loving relationship and the children are loved and well cared for.

In some cases parents may be under extreme stress and unable to care for themselves, let alone their children. This can be related to drug and alcohol abuse, mental illness, poverty, or the breakdown of relationships, for example.

Types of abuse

It is generally accepted that there are four forms of child abuse.

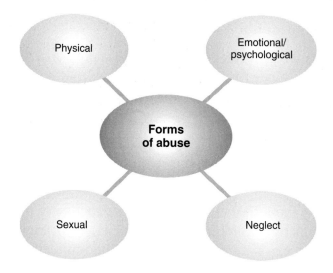

Figure 10.1 *These are the four forms of child abuse*

Neglect

Another word for neglect is 'abandon', and this sums up in a way this type of abuse. The child does not receive the appropriate care for him or her to grow and develop, they are literally abandoned to look after themselves. It can be that the child does nor receive medical care and attention when they need it, or that they are not given enough food or appropriate clothing or kept clean. Parents who leave their children unattended or on their own can be considered to be neglecting their child. They are therefore abusing that child.

Parents of neglected children often have many personal problems and this can have a negative impact on the overall well-being of the child. Many parents of neglected children will love their child, but are unable to care for them adequately.

Physical abuse

Physical abuse can occur when an adult injures a child by hitting, shaking, using excessive force, burning with cigarettes or giving a child something that could harm him or her, such as alcohol or drugs.

Smacking

There is a very fine line between smacking, in order to discipline a child, and physical abuse. A gentle smack on the hand could be considered acceptable, by some people, whereas hitting a child with an object would be regarded as a criminal offence. In recent years there has been much controversy about the rights of parents to smack in order to discipline their child. In some countries, such as Sweden, parents are not allowed to use any form of physical punishment on children. Many educationalists and childcare experts believe that smacking a child is an ineffective form of discipline. They feel that it teaches children to be violent and that it is acceptable to deliberately hurt another person.

At the present time, parents can still use 'reasonable chastisement' to discipline their child, but other people, except childminders, cannot legally do this. As the law is at the moment, childminders in England can smack children in their care, provided that they have the written permission of the child's parents to do so. However, all childminders who are members of the National Childminding Association agree, as part of the NCMA's Quality Standards, that they will not 'slap, smack, shake or humiliate' a child.

Learning Outcome Activity 59 (ICP, DCP, ECP)

What do you think about smacking?

You will have your own personal views about smacking. You may have been smacked yourself as a child. You may use or have used smacking as a form of disciplining your own children.

Talk to other course members about both sides of the smacking issue. If you don't have other course members to talk to about this, consider a family member, neighbour or a friend.

It is good practice to talk your views and opinions through with someone else. This can help you gain more knowledge and understanding and make you more aware of the issues.

Discuss:

- The view that smacking teaches children that bigger people can hurt smaller people.
- The opinion of some adults that, 'I was smacked as a child and it didn't do me any harm. I learnt what was right and wrong. If more parents smacked their children today, we would not have all the juvenile crime.'
- Smacking encourages children to be violent.

Sexual abuse

Whenever an adult uses a child for their own sexual gratification they are said to be sexually abusing that child. This can be anything from rape and full sexual intercourse, fondling the genitals and other parts of the body, such as breasts or bottom, to involving children in pornographic material, videos, internet sites, photographs or showing such material to a child. Most cases of sexual abuse of children are by people that they know. It can begin gradually and develop over a period of time. Sometimes children who are sexually abused believe that this is a way of pleasing adults and so gain their love and approval.

Emotional/psychological abuse

When an adult fails to show a child love and affection, the child will lose confidence and can become withdrawn and nervous. This is a form of emotional abuse. In the same way, continually threatening, verbally abusing or shouting at a child can have long-term damaging effects. It is very difficult to assess this form of abuse and it is only recently that emotional abuse has been considered as a form of abuse.

Common signs and symptoms of abuse

There are definite indications of each form of abuse. Sometimes childminders suspect that a child is in need of protection without having seen any physical signs of abuse. This could be through a child's behaviour, such as becoming withdrawn or distressed for no apparent reason. It is important that you are alert to changes in a child's behaviour, as well as being aware of the physical signs of abuse.

If you suspect any form of abuse, you must proceed with care, caution and be certain of your facts. It is not good practice to question a child or probe into what has happened, but is good practice to gently encourage the child to talk about how they could have been hurt or how they are feeling. Take your cues from the child. It is always good practice to make a written record of any conversation that you have with a child if you suspect that they need protection, and also make a note of any signs or symptoms. Be factual and precise, do not make assumptions; for example don't assume that because a child has a black eye that they have been hit by someone, they may well have hit their head on the edge of a cupboard.

In all cases of abuse or neglect the signs and symptoms fall roughly into two categories: **behavioural** and **physical**.

Signs and symptoms of neglect

1 **Behavioural**

- Parents can often be difficult to contact or fail to make appointments.
- Children tell you about looking after younger siblings and taking on responsibilities not normally expected of children of their age.
- Children talk about being left alone.

2 **Physical**

- A generally unkempt and uncared for appearance, perhaps dirty, unwashed clothes.
- Underweight.
- Always hungry.
- Frequently tired due to lack of sleep and regular sleeping habits.
- Lots of accidental injuries that could be caused through being unsupervised or left unattended.
- Lots of minor infections and ailments, such as colds, coughs and earaches, that are not treated.

Signs and symptoms of physical abuse

Most children will at some point in their life suffer an accidental injury. Children fall, bump their heads, become bruised and grazed or cut, in the normal rough and tumble of everyday activities and play. These are true accidents, and whilst you offer sympathy and support, you would not necessarily become concerned.

The time to become concerned is when the injuries are frequent, do not have a good and acceptable explanation, or if the part of the body that is affected is not where you would normally expect a child to have an injury, for example, bruising on the back or stomach.

The signs are:

1 **Behavioural**

- Being withdrawn and quiet, when in the past the child has been sociable.
- Aggressive play, often towards other children and in role play.
- Aggressive responses to the childminder.
- Messages from parents asking that the child is not changed or undressed for any reason.
- Unable to sit comfortably or with unusual stiffness, and reluctant to join in vigorous play.

2 **Physical**

- Unexplained bruises, cuts and grazes.
- Unusual shaped bruise marks.
- Frequent broken bones.
- Unusual scalds and burns such as cigarette burns.
- Bite marks.

Sometimes parents feel under tremendous pressure at certain times in their lives and having a small baby or child can add to their stress. At such times an adult may physically abuse a child or baby. A baby who is difficult to feed, or cries incessantly at night can put some parents under an intolerable level of stress, especially after a long day at work.

Such parents may lose control of their actions, and often feel they are also losing control of other aspects of their lives. They may lose control to the point that they violently shake their child. Shaking a young baby can cause a great deal of internal damage; for example, the damage to the brain is much the same as dropping a baby head first onto a concrete floor. The symptoms of this type of brain damage can be:

- Loss of vision
- Loss of hearing

- Fits
- Lack of response.

If you know that the parents are under stress, you should offer support and advise them to seek help from appropriate organisations and other professionals. You should be concerned if a child or baby starts to show the following signs:

- Not interested in feeding
- Unable to settle to rest or sleep
- Unusually tired and not interested in what is going on around them
- Poor muscle tone.

Remember these signs could also indicate that the child is not well, possibly in the first stages of an illness or infection. However, it could be related to physical abuse such as shaking. In either event, you should always contact the parents straight away and get medical advice.

Signs and symptoms of sexual abuse

It can be very difficult to notice any signs and symptoms of sexual abuse. Sometimes there are no visible marks, especially in the case of showing or involving children in pornographic materials. Sexual abuse in children is possibly easier to detect from changes in their behaviour rather than physical signs.

1 **Behavioural**
- Using sexual language and knowledge of sexual behaviour not normally associated with a child of that age.
- Showing insecurity.
- Clinging to trusted adults and at the same time indicating an unwillingness to be in the company of particular adults.
- Immature actions for their age, such as comfort habits like rocking, thumb sucking, wanting a comforter.
- Using imaginary play to act out sexual behaviour.
- Undressing themselves at inappropriate times or exposing the genital area.
- Drawings or paintings of a sexual nature.

2 **Physical**
- Injuries such as bruises and scratches that are non-accidental, especially around the genital area.
- Bloodstains.
- Vaginal discharge.

- Difficulty in urinating or having a bowel movement or frequent 'accidents'.

- Difficulty in sitting down or walking.

- Frequent urinary and/or genital infections.

- Showing distress or signs of fear when needing to pass urine or have a bowel movement.

Signs and symptoms of emotional/psychological abuse

It can be very difficult to see any signs or symptoms of emotional abuse, especially physical signs. Children who are subject to this form of abuse are very vulnerable. They lack self-esteem and crave attention from anyone. Any person who shows them attention, in almost any form, will get a positive response and trust from the child. Some unscrupulous individuals abuse that trust. Children who are subject to emotional abuse will have a very low opinion of themselves, very poor self-worth and very little confidence.

1 Behavioural

- Attention-seeking, such as deliberately being unco-operative, troublesome, telling lies or clinging to an adult and craving attention.

- Immature behaviour, such as tantrums at an age when normally they would not behave in that way.

- Poor social skills with children of their own age.

2 Physical

In older children the signs may be:

- Extreme eating habits and dieting caused by very low self-esteem and self-worth.

- Deliberately hurting themselves to gain attention.

Your responsibilities if you suspect that a child may have been abused

There could be numerous reasons why you suspect a child is being abused. It might be that you notice unusual injuries or marks on a child whilst helping them dress or get changed. The child may tell you, or you could have become aware of the appropriate signs and symptoms mentioned earlier in the chapter.

If your suspicions are aroused because of something the child has said, you have a responsibility to:

- Listen to what the child is saying, but do not question them or probe for further information.

- Make sure the child is sure that you believe them.

- Be reassuring. Do not be judgemental, in other words, try not to show shock, or distress, or anger, or revulsion, and do not criticise the person who is accused of abuse.

- Make sure that you record, with the date and time, details of the conversation with the child.

- Take action. Do not make promises to the child that you may not be able to keep.

- Be honest and open with the child. Do not tell the child to keep the conversation a secret. You want them to trust you and asking them to keep a secret could make the child feel that they have done something wrong and also that they cannot trust you.

At any time that you suspect that a child in your care is being abused in any way, you *must take immediate action* to protect the child from any further harm. Don't assume someone else will take action to protect the child.

The need to keep records and the correct reporting procedures

Record keeping in your childminding business is very important. Your records must be kept in a secure place and should be confidential.

Keeping factual records

Any records that you keep relating to the children in your care should be factual. You must not express opinions of your own. For example, if you were to write:

'Janine has a bruise on her leg, I think she is being hit by her Dad. He does seem to be always cross with her when he picks her up.'

You are not being factual, but expressing an opinion without any factual evidence to back up what you have written. It would be more professional to write:

'Monday 15 October 2001, 10:30am

Helping Janine to put on her wellies before playing outside. Noticed a bruise about 6 cm round just above her right knee on the outside of her leg. Asked Janine how she had got the bruise. She shook her head and went out to play. Will mention it to Dad when he picks her up today.'

Learning Outcome Activity 60 (ICP, DCP, ECP)

Keeping your records factual

Rewrite the following in a non-judgemental way. Compare these with those on pages 293–294.

1 Charlie is driving me mad. All she has done today is whinge and wee. I don't think her Mum knows how to look after her properly.

2 Went to collect Amir from school and he had a whopping lump on his head. I think he is being bullied, but I know the teacher won't do anything, so there is no point talking to her.

3 Katy threw a right wobbly again when Grandad came to pick her up. I told her not to be silly and stop making such a fuss. Grandad seems a nice enough bloke and a bit embarrassed by her behaviour.

Some childminders keep 'diary' style records, such as the examples in the previous activity. Some devise a form with standard headings, which they can complete quickly. It does not matter what format your record keeping takes. It is more important that your records are:

- Legible

- Factual

- Confidential

- Up to date – completed within 24 hours of a suspected incident.

It may be that if your suspicions are correct your records will be used by other professionals, but confidentiality will be maintained at all times. It is important to remember that the welfare of the child is vital and sharing information between professionals is essential if the child is to be protected. There is sometimes a fine line between breaching confidentiality and sharing information. You may wish to discuss with other course members what breaching confidentiality means to you and how it is different from sharing information.

Procedures to follow once you suspect abuse or neglect

You have a responsibility to report your suspicions about abuse or neglect. You may feel very hesitant about reporting your fears. It is quite natural to feel that you are being disloyal to the parents of the child, or jumping to conclusions. However you must consider the welfare and safety of the child at all times. You must remain professional and respect confidentiality *at all times*.

Outline of procedures to investigate a possible case of child abuse

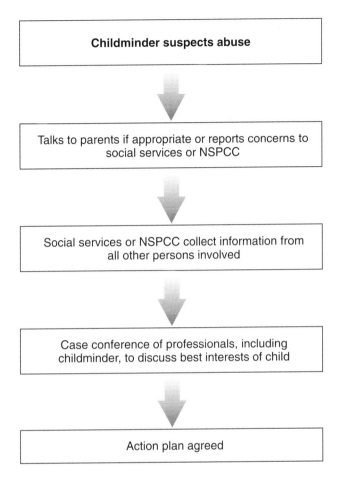

Sometimes it is appropriate to talk to the parents first about changes in behaviour or injuries, but if you feel that the child is showing obvious signs of abuse, talking to the parents may not be appropriate.

Most childminders contact their local authority to report suspected cases of child abuse. You could, if you prefer, contact the NSPCC. Both social services and the NSPCC will investigate the report.

These professionals will talk to the child, the family and yourself in order to investigate the case. This is a time when your records could be crucial. In some cases, information could be sought from the child's GP and other people involved with the care and education of the child, such as nursery teacher and pre-school group leader. Checks will also be made to see if the child is already known to social services or on the Child Protection Register.

The investigation is usually followed by a case conference. The aim of this is to decide what should be done in the best interests of the child and if they are in need of protection. It is quite possible that you could be asked to attend such a conference. Parents are also often invited to attend the case conference.

Following the case conference an action plan will be drawn up and agreed. The people involved in the case conference may also agree to meet again at a later date. It is possible that the action plan could mean that a court order is sought to protect the child. This can mean that the child is taken into the care of the local authority. Sometimes the court puts the child under the supervision of the local authority, which means that the child can remain in their own home. It also means that professionals organise medical examinations, visit the child at home and offer advice and assistance to the family.

Some local authorities have very clear procedures for child protection that they give to childminders when they are registered. If you have not got a copy of the procedures, you should contact the local authority and ask for one.

Ways you can support children who may have been abused

There are many ways that you can support children who may have been abused. Many of the things that you can do are also suitable activities for all children regardless of whether or not they are in need of protection. In addition to activities that you can do with the children, you can support them by making sure that your records are accurate and up to date.

Perhaps one of the most important things you can do is to teach children to be **confident**. They need to be confident,

- to be able to talk to you if they are unhappy
- that they will be believed
- about their own bodies and themselves
- that they will not be blamed, or accused of 'telling lies', or causing 'trouble'.

Practical things to help children become confident
- Listen to them.
- Show that you are interested in them, as individuals, not as someone's sister, brother, daughter or son.
- Give lots of verbal praise to celebrate achievements, positive feelings and success.
- Value what the children have done, perhaps by displaying drawings or paintings, or making a point of telling their parents what they have done well.
- Make sure that the activities that you provide for the children are appropriate to their stage of development; fear of failure is a common reason why children lose confidence in themselves.

Teaching children how to have control and keep themselves safe is another way that you can support children. Having control does not mean that children can get their own way, it means that they understand what to do in certain situations. You will have to use your knowledge and understanding of child development to decide if and when the child is mature enough to be able to understand what you mean by 'having control'. Personal safety becomes more important as children get older, perhaps when walking to your home from school with friends.

Practical things to help children to keep themselves safe and in control

- Teach children 'stranger danger' strategies, without frightening them. This should also include making sure that children understand that they should not leave school with anyone other than person who they expected to collect them.
- Help children to understand that nobody has the right to touch or hurt them. Their body belongs to them.
- Make sure that children understand the difference between 'comfortable and uncomfortable touches'.
- Teach children that secrets can be broken, especially if keeping that secret makes them unhappy or not safe. In many ways it is not good practice to encourage children to have secrets as it can lead to confusion and misunderstandings.
- Teach children what to do if they are lost.
- Teach children what to do if they are in danger, for example, scream and shout.
- Teach children the importance of letting an adult know where they are and what they are doing.
- Make sure that children know who they can talk to if they feel in danger, or have problems, for example, you, or perhaps a confidential telephone help line for children.

In 1984 an organisation called Kidscape was founded to help children learn about personal safety and what to do if they are being bullied. Kidscape produces information for childcare professionals to use to help teach children strategies to cope with potentially threatening situations. NSPCC and Childline provide a confidential telephone service for children to talk to someone about their difficulties and problems. Details of these organisations can be found at the back of the book.

Dealing with your own feelings

Child abuse is an emotive topic. It is likely that if you are working with children who have been abused, or suspect that a child is being abused, you will experience a range of emotions and feelings. This could be anger at the abuser, shock at what has happened to the child, a feeling of helplessness, or feeling that you have failed the child because you did not notice that something was wrong sooner. All of these feelings are perfectly normal. You may of course react in different ways.

It is important to remember that you should not expect to deal with all your emotions on your own. You should not try to pretend that you do not feel angry or frustrated or have a sense of failure. The most professional way to act is to recognise your feelings, and seek the support of another adult. It is essential to remember that you must maintain confidentiality at all times, so select your supporting adult with care.

Where to seek support for yourself

Childminders who are working in a community childminding network may be asked to care for children who are already on the 'at risk register' or subject to a protection order. In such cases there will be a range of other professionals that you could turn to for support, such as:

- Social workers
- General practitioners or local doctor
- Health visitors
- Child protection police officers.

If you are working as part of a network, your network co-ordinator could offer you support initially and put you in touch with other professionals as necessary.

If you are working on your own, you may wish to contact your local early years advisor, in the first place. If they are not able to offer you the type of support that you require, then they should be able to suggest other professionals who will support you. Organisations such as NSPCC and Kidscape will often lend a 'listening ear'. The contacts for these organisations are at the back of the book.

How to protect yourself

Childcare professionals are in positions of trust and great responsibility, given that they care for other people's children. In such positions they are vulnerable to allegations of mistreating children and accusations of abuse. In this respect, childminders are no different from other childcare professionals. In some ways you are even more vulnerable as you can be working alone and may not have the support of working with other people. Apart from behaving in a totally professional way at all times, there are things that you can do to protect yourself from false allegations.

GOOD PRACTICE *How to protect yourself from allegations of abuse*

- Maintain confidentiality at all times.
- Make sure that all your records, registers, incident report forms, accident forms and other documents relating to the children in your care are kept up to date and are stored in a safe place. You should get into the habit of completing records for each child every time that you care for them.
- Any suspicions that you have about ill-treatment or abuse of a child should be reported to social services and you must keep a written record of your conversations or contact, including the name of the person you spoke to, the date of the conversation and what was agreed.
- Make sure that you tell parents about every incident, accident or event that has happened to their child that could result in a mark or injury on the body, regardless of how insignificant it may seem. Keep a written record of such conversations and record the incidents or accident and get parents to sign that they have seen what you have recorded.
- Make sure that you tell the parents if the behaviour of their child changes, such as playing or speaking about things in way that causes you concern.
- Never leave the children unattended or in the care of unauthorised people.
- Encourage the children to be independent as soon as they are able, especially when carrying out personal tasks.
- Make sure that you do not handle a child roughly when managing unwanted behaviour.
- Make sure that you always use appropriate language when with the children.
- Take your cues from the children and do not ask for cuddles and so forth if the child is reluctant to respond.
- Be open and honest with the children and do not ask them to keep secrets.
- Attend child protection courses and keep yourself well-informed and up to date.
- Help the children to learn to protect themselves.

There have been cases of childminders and other childcare professionals being accused of abuse. This can be a most distressing time and experience for all concerned. If this happens to you, you must remain calm and professional. Keep records of all conversations that you have regarding the accusation, and keep copies of all letters that you write. It would be sensible to seek legal advice as once an accusation is made there is a legal requirement that it be investigated. Organisations such as NCMA offer legal help and advice to its members, or you can seek independent advice from the Citizens Advice Bureau.

CHECK YOUR KNOWLEDGE

1   Give two long-term effects of abuse.

2   Name the two categories of signs and symptoms of abuse.

3   Give three examples of the signs that might show a child is being physically abused.

4   Who should you contact if you suspect a child is being abused and needs protection?

5   Why is it important to teach children to be confident?

6   Give two ways that you could teach a child to become more confident.

7   Why is it important to teach children about personal safety?

8   State two things that you could do with a child to teach them about personal safety.

9   Why is it not a good idea to encourage children to keep secrets?

10   Why is it important to keep records?

11   Apart from being confidential, what else is important when keeping records?

CHAPTER 11
Working with children with additional needs

All children have the same basic needs, and at certain times in their life they may have additional needs. Additional needs can be of a temporary nature, or remain with the child for the rest of their life. The additional need may not be evident when you start to care for a child. Often childminders can be instrumental in ensuring that the child and their family get the extra help and support they require.

It is not intended that this chapter will cover every additional need that you may encounter in your childminding business. That is impossible. There are definitions of certain conditions such as hyperactivity, diabetes, cerebal palsy, asthma, but they are general definitions. Every child is unique and different regardless of whether or not they have additional needs. Not every child with a specific condition will exhibit the same signs and symptoms at the same time or to the same extent. It is more important that you understand how to meet the needs of all children in a positive and professional way, than try to have a little bit of knowledge about some conditions.

Issues that affect children with 'special educational needs', emotional and behavioural difficulties and HIV and Aids will be considered as separate sections. However the emphasis will still be on recognising the needs of the 'whole' child.

Understanding disability equality issues

What is disability?

It is estimated that up to 20 per cent of children have a disability. This could include:

- a wide range of physical and sensory impairments
- a range of learning difficulties
- a range of medical conditions
- behavioural and emotional problems
- a combination of any of these.

It is important that the difference between disability, impairment and difficulty is understood.

A *disability* refers to the limitations in daily living that a person experiences due to an impairment.

An *impairment* is usually used to describe a physical condition that is not typical or usual. This could be a condition that affects the ability to hear, or see, or walk, or co-ordinate actions.

A *difficulty* is usually the term given to a situation or condition, such as emotional difficulty, that may, with sensitive support and help, be overcome or treated. However some learning difficulties often cannot be overcome.

An impairment can become a disability, but not always. A child with a hearing impairment can wear a hearing aid that will allow that child to function normally, and does not limit or restrict their life. In this case the hearing impairment is not a disability. An impairment or a disability should not be stumbling blocks to meeting a child's needs.

To develop your understanding and knowledge you need to think about your own and other peoples' views of disability and people with disabling conditions. Having a kind and sympathetic nature is a very good quality to have, but it is not enough. It is important that you are able to consider wider issues when caring for children who may have additional needs. A good starting point is to look at two different views of disability: the **medical or individual model** and the **social model**.

1 The medical or individual model (also referred to as the medical/individual view)

The impairment is viewed as the 'problem' of the individual person. If this viewpoint is taken to a logical conclusion, it could be argued that the disability or impairment is the cause of the person's problems. Therefore disabled people should try to be as 'abled-bodied' as possible. Furthermore, the 'solution' to their problems will be found through medical treatment. Often medical and other professionals make decisions about the disabled person's life, such as which school they should attend. The focus for support tends to be on 'care needs' rather than what the person concerned wishes. The focus is therefore shifting away from the person and on to the impairment. The situation that the disabled person finds themself in is regarded with pity and often they are encouraged to 'make the best' of that situation and be brave and courageous. Some people feel that this view is encouraged by the idea of giving awards to disabled people, especially children, for bravery.

2 The social model of disability

The social model of disability sees the problem being with society, the environment and negative attitudes. This viewpoint gives children and people with impairments exactly the same rights as anyone else and is non-discriminatory. The social model aims at changing society, the environment and attitudes, so that the impaired person can have as full a life as anyone else. The medical model aims to 'normalise' the person with the impairment or disability. Most disabled people favour the social model.

Childcare professionals could make statements such as, 'I can't take Jodie out as her adapted buggy is too big for my car.' This is viewing disability from the medical/individual model, as the problem is seen as Jodie and the buggy, regardless of what reason there is for her needing the buggy. A social model of the same situation could be, 'the boot of my car is too small. I need to think of other ways for Jodie and me to go out'. In this statement the 'problem' is not Jodie, but the design of the car.

How you look at this problem will determine whether you see it as a problem of the person or the design of the car

Learning Outcome Activity 61 (ECP)

Recognising the disability model

Read the following statements and then decide which fits the medical/individual model or the social model. Suggested answers are given on page 294.

1 Anna can't go the playgroup because her walking frame won't fit through the door.
2 The door on the village hall can't be altered so Anna can't get in with her walking frame.
3 Your child can't hear me so I can't care for him.
4 The gap between the station platform and the train is too wide so he can't use the trains.

The issues involved in including children with additional needs in your childminding setting

Disabled children and adults with additional needs, and their families, have been subject to various forms of discrimination. This discrimination has included:

- Children being unable to achieve their full potential at school as educational establishments have not had the resources to meet their needs.

- Lack of support to care for the child or adult, or provision of services to make their care easier.

- Lack of access to public places and amenities has restricted their opportunities to socialise, and in some cases take up meaningful employment.

Legislation

There have been several pieces of legislation, particularly since the 1980s, that have been put into place specifically to protect disabled people from discrimination.

The Education Act 1981 set out major changes in the education of children who had special educational needs. **The Children Act 1989** has a section that specifically deals with co-ordinating the services, such as health, education and social services, for children with special educational needs. **The Education Act 1993** built on the previous Education Act but also explained the term 'learning difficulty'. This Act also states that children should not be described as having a learning difficulty simply because their home language is not the language of the school. **The Code of Practice for the Identification and Assessment of Children with Special Educational Needs** was published in 1994 and gave guidance on how to put the Education Act 1993 into practice. A new code was issued in January 2002. The Code of Practice is an important document and you should try to get hold of a copy. Your course tutor should be able to help you, or ask at your local library. In 1995 **The Disability Discrimination Act** set out employment rights for disabled people and also made provision that children with special education needs should have school places which are suitable to their individual needs.

In addition to these pieces of legislation, there is the **United Nations Convention on the Rights of the Child**. This states, in Article 23, that a disabled child has the right to special care, education and training that will allow them to live as independently as possible and take their place within society.

Attitudes

Legislation will not change people's attitudes overnight and you may still come across parents who do not wish to have their child cared for in the company of a child with special educational needs, or an impairment, or who 'label' children in a discriminatory and negative way. Examples of this could be using the terms 'handicapped' and 'special'. Both of these terms are from the 'medical/individual' model.

You may find that when you are in public with a child with additional needs that you become aware of prejudice and discriminatory attitudes. This may be in the form of side-long glances, comments or lack of easy access to certain places. The important thing to remember is that you are caring for a child. This child has exactly the same needs as every other child, and also has some additional needs. Be professional and be prepared to challenge, firmly and politely, insulting and derogatory language and attitudes.

'Special needs' is an expression that is widely used in education and care and often with perfectly good intentions. In reality, using these words implies that children with 'special needs' have different needs or requirements to other children. All children have the *same* needs, but some have *additional* needs at some point in their lives.

It has to be recognised that many of the attitudes of people come from stereotypical images gained from media such as television, films and magazines. Many of these images are negative, and sometimes they are emotive. We are encouraged to feel sympathy and sometimes pity for people with additional needs, rather than focusing on their positive achievements. Attitudes are slowly changing. The Para-Olympics of 2000 brought to public attention many talented athletes who had additional needs. These athletes were able to achieve standards within their particular disciplines that the majority of the population could never meet. Also there are some people in public life, such as politicians, who have additional needs resulting from sensory impairments, for example, and who are working on equal terms with their counterparts.

Your childminding environment

If you agree to care for a child with additional needs, there may be certain things that you will have to alter. It is possible that you will have to consider access to your play areas and main entrance. This could be a wide door and a ramp instead of steps. It could be that you will need to arrange storage of equipment in a different way to clear the floor of obstructions and create more open space. You may want to think about how you label storage boxes for toys and other equipment.

Before you involve yourself in major expense and possible alterations to your home, it is very important that you ask yourself realistic questions about your suitability to mind a child with additional needs. You may consider whether you can cope with the emotion and physical demands that these children will make on you. There may be practical things to consider, such as a tendency to a weak back, which could make lifting a heavy child awkward. You will also need to think about the other children that you already care for. It may be that they will have to adjust to a modified routine.

Other children may not understand the additional needs of the child, so you will have to spend time explaining this and responding to their questions. You should not assume that caring for a child with additional needs always means more work or expense. All children are different with different needs. What is important is that decisions you make about caring for any child are informed and realistic.

All children need to play. You should plan your play activities and experiences for all children, whether or not they have additional needs, on informed observations of what the child can do. It may be that some children with additional needs will respond to the play activities more quickly or more slowly than other children. You will need to consider this when planning your routines.

Do not fall into the trap of thinking about providing play activities for a child with cerebal palsy, or diabetes, or any other additional needs. In the same way there is a danger of creating an environment for a child with additional needs, rather than providing a child-centred care and learning environment.

CASE STUDY

Ellie is a registered childminder with several years experience. She has been asked to care for a six-year-old girl, Jess, before and after school and during the school holidays. Jess uses a walking frame. The entrance to Ellie's home has two steps in front of the door. This means that Jess would have difficulty getting in and out of the door. The only other way in is through the patio doors at the back, but Ellie does not think that this is suitable as it would mean that Jess would have to go all the way around the house and through the garden, not a good idea on a wet day.

Ellie decides to have a ramp made to put over the steps. The local builder is prepared to make one for her, very cheaply, using off-cuts of timber with a non-slip mat on the top. After the ramp is fitted, one of the other parents commented to Ellie how helpful it was for getting in and out with her buggy.

This is an example of how an adjustment to the environment can benefit everyone, not just the child with additional needs.

Your role in working with families of children with additional needs

It is very important that any relationship you establish with the parents is professional. You still need to consider all of the things discussed in Chapter 9, regardless of whether the parents have a child with additional needs or not. All the good practice that you have working with parents should be good practice for *all* parents. Any parent can tell you more about their child than anyone else. In turn, they need information from you about their child's achievements and progress.

However it could be that you may be the first person that parents have dealt with who does not have a medical viewpoint of the child. You could be the first person who is looking at the whole child and not the impairment, or disability, or difficulty. Bearing this in mind, you may find that you will have to spend more time with parents of children with additional needs. Parents may want to share their feelings with you, their concerns, worries and difficulties. Remember, be professional, make sure that whatever you are told is confidential and be prepared to offer support and reassurance, if needed.

Acknowledging parents' feelings

Sometimes parents spend much time and effort on the 'problem' with the child, perhaps with medical professionals. Some parents in this situation may experience many negative feelings about their child, their situation and themselves. They can feel:

- *Fear* – about what the future could hold.

- *Lack of confidence* – in their abilities to cope, or their skills as a parent.

- *Anger* – they may question why they have a child with additional needs.

- *Guilt* – they may consider that it is their fault that the child has these needs. This is quite common in mothers of babies with additional needs, who blame themselves for doing something 'wrong' during the pregnancy which has resulted in the child's need.

- *Blame* – some parents blame other family members for the additional need, especially if it is shown to be an inherited condition.

- *Rejection* – it is not unknown for some parents to reject the child with the additional needs and not want to care for them. They may feel incapable of loving their child. They may resent the amount of time they will have to 'give up' in order to attend hospitals, have treatment and meet with medical professionals.

- *Shame* – this feeling can be linked to any of the others, as parents can feel that they have 'let down' their family, or partner. They may be worried about the attitudes of other people and not know how to cope with prejudice.

However not all parents experience negative feelings, some have positive attitudes and some have negative feelings for a very short time. Each parent reacts differently, so you must respect their individuality.

Practical ways to help and support parents of children with additional needs

- Help the parents to appreciate and enjoy all the positive achievements and characteristics of their child by making it a point to tell them.
- Show parents your records which show the growth and development of their child, as you would do for all children. The growth and development of a child with additional needs may not be as fast, or even in the same way as other children, nevertheless there will be growth and achievement.
- Make sure you have telephone numbers of voluntary organisations and agencies that may be able to offer additional support to the parents.
- Care for the 'whole' child as a unique individual, not as a child with additional needs. Do not try to become an expert on the disability, impairment. Actively try to move away from the 'medical/individual model' of disability and encourage parents to see the child, not the medical problem or impairment; in other words, take the 'social model' approach.
- Be prepared to actively listen to parents when they want to talk. Sometimes the parent may just want you to do more than listen, to be a 'sounding' board. Sometimes parents of a child with additional needs find that there can be extra stresses and strains on their relationship with their partner. Do not try to become a counsellor or advisor. Your professionalism lies in caring for children, not as a marriage guidance counsellor.

Your role in working with children with additional needs

In many ways your role in working with children with additional needs is no different from minding any child. All children learn, develop and grow through play. All children are naturally curious and want to find out as much as they can about the world around them.

Practical things that you can do

- Some children with additional needs may need extra support and encouragement so that they can become fully involved.
- You still need to continue to observe, record and assess all children, and plan and evaluate your play activities and experiences to suit their needs and developmental stage.
- Be realistic in any target that you set for a child. For example, you should not plan for a child with hyperactivity to sit and watch a video for 20 minutes; but don't fall into the trap of expecting too little or not allowing them to watch the video at all.
- Answer the questions of other children honestly, factually and accurately. Teach them to respect differences as interesting facets of another personality.

- Help disabled children to be confident and independent.
- Praise and recognise their achievements, regardless of how small.
- Offer them choices so that they can be part of a decision-making process. You could, for example, ask the child if they want milk or water at lunch-time, rather than just giving them the drink that you think they would like. You would ask any other child, so why not let a child with additional needs also make choices. Look at different methods of communication to enable the child with poor or no verbal communication skills to make positive choices.
- When appropriate, break down tasks or activities into small achievable steps, so that the child can succeed.

Learning Outcome Activity 62 (ECP)

Responding to children's questions

Children are naturally curious and one way they learn is by asking questions. Look at the following questions that children could ask.

- Think of how you would respond to the child.
- Discuss your answers with other childminders or course members.

On page 294 there are suggested answers that you could give.

1 Why does Jenny still wear nappies?
2 I don't want to play with Tom, he is always breaking my models. Why can't he play somewhere else?
3 Why does Amir have that thing in his ear?
4 Why are Lucy's eyes a funny shape?
5 Is Lindy thick, she doesn't talk properly?
6 I feel sorry for Jake, he can't see properly can he?

Working with children with 'special educational needs'

There are many children who, for whatever reason, have difficulties with learning. These children are often referred to as having 'special educational needs' (SEN). The term 'special educational needs' came from the guidance following the Education Acts 1993 and 1996. This guidance is called 'The Code of Practice for the Identification and Assessment of Children with Special Education Needs'. The code states that children have special education needs if they have learning difficulties that require special educational provision. Children can obviously have a wide range of special educational needs, some of which can affect them all their school lives and some of which can be of a temporary nature. It is thought that about 20% of school-age children will have a special educational need at some point in their life, whereas about 2% have a need that is significant. It is this 2% of children that are assessed by their local authority, which issues a statement setting out how their needs should be met. This process is usually referred to as 'statementing', and is clearly set out in the Code of Practice (January 2002).

The revised Code of Practice clearly sets out a 'step-by-step' or 'graduated approach' as to how to set about getting help for children with special educational needs. The graduated approach is basically in three stages:

1 *Early Years Action* (for children under statutory school age) or *School Action*. As you are already keeping records of the children in your care, you could be the first person to identify that a child has an additional need. You will already have good lines of communication with the parents, so together, and using the Code of Practice as your guide, you should devise an individual education plan for the child. This is usually referred to as an IEP, and for children under school age there is no set format for this. This may seem like an additional work load for you, but given that you are regularly observing and recording information about the children, it is just formalising something you are doing already.

2 *Early Years Action Plus or School Action Plus* is the next stage, when other professional and outside agencies, such as an educational psychologist and speech and language therapists, can be called upon to provide specialised help and support for the child.

3 *Producing a statement of special educational needs*. This describes in detail the child's needs and all the special help that he or she needs. It is produced by the local education authority (LEA) after they have made a detailed assessment of the child. The LEA could seek the childminder's views on the child's progress and may want to see copies of records and the IEP.

It is worth noting that children under the age of two very rarely have a statement, but they might be supported by other professionals such as portage workers if they have a medical condition.

Working with children with emotional or behavioural difficulties

In the last few years teachers, parents and childcare workers have reported that more and more children have problems with their behaviour and often have emotional difficulties as well. It is difficult to know if the emotional difficulty results in problem behaviour or the other way around.

It is important that childminders understand that there is not just one or two reasons for emotional and behavioural difficulties. Often it can be very difficult to find the underlying reasons or causes. Sometimes childminders have to accept that they may not find the underlying reasons, but that must not stop them working with and caring for the child.

Childminders need to be sure that there is a problem with the child's behaviour. This you can do by regularly and factually recording everything that the child has done and their reactions and responses to the activities provided. Talk to the parents about your concerns. As a general rule, a problem is not something that is a 'one-off', it is behaviour, responses or reactions that happen frequently.

Once you have decided that there is a problem and talked to the parents, you will all have to decide if there is an underlying reason or cause. This is possibly the most difficult stage as all children react to certain situations in different ways. For example, a new baby in a family can cause some children to behave in ways that would not normally be expected of them; they may become aggressive, withdrawn, possessive or attention-seeking. On the other hand, the child may be excited, proud, or not show any different emotions or behaviour. You cannot generalise. In the same way you cannot jump to the conclusion that a certain circumstance will provoke a certain response in a child, or that the child is reacting in this way because of the circumstance. All children are different.

There is a huge range of strategies and methods to help a child with emotional and behavioural difficulties. Your professionalism will be in deciding which way is the best way to deal with the child.

One way of dealing with anger is to remain calm

Different strategies and ways of dealing with the children will work with different children. It is not a simple case of deciding to use a reward system with a child who shows unacceptable behaviour. Reward systems work very well with some children, with others they are useless. In the same way, distracting a child or offering choices works well for some, for others it can be confusing and add to the 'problem' or 'difficulty'.

It is worth remembering that many children with emotional and/or behavioural difficulties also have a very low opinion of themselves, for whatever reasons. One of the most valuable things that many childminders can do in such circumstances is work to help the child develop a positive view of themselves.

Practical ways that you could do this could include:

- *Praising achievements*, regardless of how small.
- *Allow the child to make decisions* that affect them, such as what they want on their sandwiches, which puzzle to play with, which colour beaker to have a drink from.
- *Make sure that planned activities are achievable* and that there is no risk of failure or 'getting something wrong'.
- Use *positive language*.
- *Make sure that your childminding setting is a calm place*, with no raised voices or aggression.
- *Work with the parents* of the child to make sure that you are all giving the same messages to the child.

Understanding HIV and Aids

More and more children and their families are now affected by HIV and/or Aids. HIV stands for Human Immunodeficiency Virus. Aids stands for Acquired Immune Deficiency Syndrome.

Despite the increase in cases there is still a huge amount of ignorance, misinformation and misunderstanding about these problems. There is also much prejudice and discrimination towards the families and the children affected. Childminders have a duty to combat discrimination and prejudice for all children and to do this effectively they need to have accurate information and be well informed.

HIV

- If found in blood and blood products, amniotic fluid, semen, breast milk and vaginal and cervical secretions in sufficient amounts, it *can* cause infection.

- HIV *cannot* be passed on through faeces, urine, tears, sweat or saliva.

- HIV *can* be passed on through sharing of infected needles and syringes, unprotected sex, contaminated blood or blood products used for infusion and breast feeding.

- Children with HIV *can* lead a normal life.

- Not all children affected by HIV become ill, some remain well and healthy.

- Not all children affected by HIV show symptoms of AIDS

It is also worth remembering that:

- HIV does not survive outside of the body and can be easily destroyed by heat, light, detergents and bleach.
- Children with HIV get normal childhood illnesses but may be affected more.

The issues involved in working with children affected by HIV and Aids

Hygiene

Your home must be a safe and hygienic environment for every child in your care. If you were to treat every child as if they were affected by HIV you would almost guarantee a practice of the highest order. In other words, if you have good safe practices already you would have to make few modifications to your normal routines. You should already be:

- regularly cleaning and disinfecting floors, toys and equipment
- covering up open wounds on your own skin and on a child's (with parents' permission of course, in case the child is allergic to plasters for example)
- cleaning up spilt urine, blood or faeces immediately with a bleach solution
- wearing disposable gloves when dealing with cuts, faeces and urine.

Prejudice

You should have a policy which shows your commitment to equal opportunities and combating all forms of prejudice. This does not mean that you treat every person the same, but that you consider each person as an individual and respond to their individual needs. Children affected by HIV and/or Aids may or may not have additional needs. They are, firstly, children who need to grow, develop and learn. They are children who need to be cared for and encouraged to develop physically, socially and intellectually. They need to be protected from all forms of abuse. They need to play with other children. Children affected by HIV and Aids are, above everything else, children.

Working with parents and issues of confidentiality

Parents have no obligation to tell you, or anyone else for that matter, that they or their children are affected by HIV and/or Aids. If parents do tell you, this information should be treated in exactly the same way as any other confidential information that you are entrusted with. You must respect the parents and the trust that they have placed in you. Confidential information should remain exactly that – *confidential*.

Infection can happen in a variety of ways and you must not make assumptions about how the child may or may not have been infected. Also, you should not assume that because the parents of a child have a particular lifestyle that they or their children are affected by HIV and/or Aids.

Sources of additional information for you, the children and their families/primary carers

- **Sources of information for you**
  - Your health visitor or that of the child.
  - Your network co-ordinator if you are part of childminding network.
  - The National Aids Helpline.
  - The Terrence Higgins Trust.
  - Family Planning Association clinics.
- **Sources of information for children**
  - You.
  - The health visitor.
  - Books from the library or organisations specifically working with people affected by HIV and Aids.
  - The Terrence Higgins Trust.
- **Sources of information for parents/primary carers of the child**
  - You.
  - Their health visitor.
  - Their GP.
  - Books from the library or organisations specifically working with people affected by HIV and Aids.
  - National Aids Helpline.
  - The Terrence Higgins Trust.
  - Family Planning clinics.

Contact details for national organisations are given at the end of the book.

Working with sick babies and children

Children and babies who are unwell or sick have exactly the same needs as healthy children, but they do have additional needs. It is important that you understand how to meet these additional needs. As part of the registration process you will have had first-aid training. You must ensure that you keep this training up to date.

Working with parents

In all aspects of your childminding business you are working in partnership with the parents. Together you want to ensure that the children are in reasonable health. You are helping the children in your care to develop and grow in a healthy and safe environment. One way you can do this is to support the children's parents in the maintainance of regular health screening programmes and developmental checks. Encourage them to keep the appointments and share the information with you.

Children and babies can often become unwell or sick with very little warning. Parents can leave their child with you in the morning and by lunch-time they could be unwell. In most cases children and babies who are sick need to be with their main carer in their own home, if possible. Sometimes this can be a source of guilt and anxiety for parents and can sometimes cause conflict between the parents' employers, the parents and yourself. One way that you can reduce any possible conflict is to make sure that in your contract of services you cover circumstances when children and babies are sick or unwell. You may want to include the following points in your contract:

- You must be able to contact the parents at *all* times.
- If the parents are not able to collect their sick child from your home, they must make suitable alternative arrangements.
- You are not able to give permission for any treatment to be given to a child.
- You have the final decision to decide not to care for a child, if this mean that the health of the other children could be at risk.

You may want to also remind parents that the terms and conditions of your registration do not allow you to care for children who have an infectious illness. You also have a responsibility to the other children in your care to make sure that you provide a safe and healthy environment. If you find out that a child in your care has developed an infectious disease, you must inform the parents of all the other children.

Caring for children who are unwell

Your first-aid kit should include a children's thermometer. One of the first things you can do if a child is feeling or looking unwell, is to take their temperature. It is also very important that you make contact with the parents as soon as possible.

There are four types of thermometer available, the most common being digital, which are easy to read, fever strips, which change colour, and mercury thermometers, which can be difficult to read. It is a matter of personal preference which one you use, but make sure than you can read it correctly.

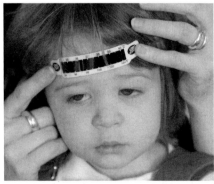

Fever strip

Digital thermometer

267

Normal body temperature is 37°C, so a temperature above this should indicate to you that the body is fighting an infection. A child with a high temperature has an increased risk of convulsions and so you should help the child to get rid of the additional heat.

Practical ways to reduce a child's temperature

- Make sure that the room temperature is not too high, 15°C or 60°F is about right.
- Remove clothing apart from underwear.
- Don't cover the child with a duvet, or blanket.
- Give frequent drinks of cool water.
- You could possibly sponge the child with lukewarm water, especially on the hands, face and upper body.
- If you have the written permission of the parents, you can give the child paracetamol in either syrup, or, for older children, tablet form.

CASE STUDY

Alison left eighteen-month-old Zak with the childminder at 8.30 am. Zak had not slept very well the night before, so Alison mentioned this to the childminder just before she left. By lunch-time Zak's face was flushed and he felt hot. He didn't want any lunch which was unusual. His childminder used a fever strip to take his temperature; it was 38.7°C. The childminder telephoned Alison at work and explained that Zak was not well. Alison's line manager was at lunch and so she couldn't get away immediately. The childminder agreed that she would start to try to cool Zak down and Alison said she would get to the childminder's house by three pm. Alison also said that she would make an appointment with their doctor.

The childminder made sure that the play room was not too hot and then took off Zak's jeans, sweat shirt, socks and shoes and left him in a T-shirt and his underclothes. She wiped Zak's head, face and hands with a cool damp cloth and gave him a drink of cool water. Zak and the childminder sat on the bean bags and looked at books together for a while, then Zak fell asleep. The other children watched a video in the same room. The childminder left Zak where he was, but kept checking on him every few minutes to make sure he was not getting any hotter. When Alison arrived Zak was still asleep, his temperature had dropped slightly, but was not yet at normal body temperature. The childminder had made a note of his temperature, how much water he had drunk and what she had done to make Zak feel comfortable. Alison took these notes with her to share with the doctor. Later that day Alison telephoned to say that the doctor thought that Zak had Roseola infantum, which is very common in under twos, and had prescribed paracetamol. Alison's mum was able to look after Zak for the rest of the week at his home, and, hopefully, he would be back at the childminder's the following week.

1 Do you think that the childminder did the right things?
2 Was there anything else that the childminder should or could have done?

Giving medicines or prescribed drugs to children

Before you can give a child any form of medication, injection or any invasive procedure, it is essential that you have undertaken appropriate and up-to-date training, which enables you to do such things competently. You must be trained by an appropriate medical practitioner who can provide you with written confirmation of your competence. You must never give a child medication unless you have the written permission of the parents. Once you and the parents have agreed that you can give their child medication you will need to know the following:

- Exactly when the child needs the medicine or medication, for example, if before eating, how long before. Some children who take insulin injections for diabetes, need to be injected about half an hour before eating.

- What the point of the medication is, in other words what is it supposed to do. If you don't have this information, you will not know if the medication is working properly.

- The correct dose for the child.

- What to do if the medication does not seem to be working.

- How the medication should be stored.

- The particular way to give the child the medication.

- What you should do if you forget to give the child their medication.

- If there are any side-effects.

It is important that you have a positive attitude when giving children medication. Some children don't like taking any form of medication and may resist. They will need gentle, but firm persuasion. You could make taking medication into a fun experience, or offer something that the child likes, such as a favourite drink or an activity immediately afterwards. Help the child to associate the medicine with good things, not unpleasant ones. Remember to record when you gave the medication, how much you gave and any reactions.

Signs and symptoms of minor ailments

It is not possible to cover all the signs and symptoms of each and every childhood minor ailment in a book such as this. Whilst there are obvious general signs, such as raised body temperature, flushed appearance, rash, or sickness and diarrhoea, each child is unique and can display a wide range of signs and symptoms. There is always the danger that you could jump to the wrong conclusions about a child because they are showing certain symptoms. On the other hand, the opposite could be true; you could decide to not act because the child is not showing certain symptoms. The parents know their child best and you should use this knowledge, together with your own professional knowledge of the child, to decide what course of action you need to take.

Remember:

- keep calm
- inform the parents
- deal with what you can actually see or know, not what you think you can see or think you know
- if in doubt, seek medical help.

Medical centres and doctors' surgeries are invaluable sources of information as many health authorities provide leaflets and booklets about the signs and symptoms of common childhood ailments, more serious diseases such as meningitis, and information about health screening programmes and immunisation programmes. These leaflets and booklets are usually free and contain up-to-date information. It is good practice to collect these and keep them as a source of reference for yourself and the parents.

CHECK YOUR KNOWLEDGE

Are the following statements true or false? The answers are on pages 294–295.

1 A disability, impairment and difficulty all mean that a child has a problem.

2 The medical model of disability tries to 'cure' the person.

3 HIV cannot be passed on through faeces, urine, tears, sweat or saliva.

4 All children have the same basic needs.

5 Lack of access to public places and amenities has restricted the opportunities for children with additional needs to socialise. This is a form of discrimination.

6 Emotional difficulty results in problem behaviour.

7 Every childminder should have access to a copy of 'The Code of Practice for the Identification and Assessment of Children with Special Educational Needs'.

8 A childminder caring for a child with cerebal palsy will need to plan special play activities.

9 Childminders are not involved in the statementing process for a child with special educational needs.

10 Childminders do not need written permission from parents to give medicines such as paracetamol or medication such as an insulin injection.

CHAPTER 12
The professional approach to childminding

Many childminders come into the profession whilst they are at home caring for their own children. It is important to remember that caring for your own children is completely different from caring for other people's children. There will be a wide range of issues that you will need to consider once you start caring for other people's children, everything from insurance and financial issues to how will your own children react to other children playing in 'their' space and with 'their' things. It is important that you take a professional approach to your work from the very first day in order to make your business work.

What is a 'professional'?

If you look up the meaning of the word 'professional' in a dictionary or a thesaurus you will find words such as: expert, specialised, qualified, proficient, skilled, trained.

You should be able to use any one, or all of those words to describe yourself and your attitude to your business.

- You are an *expert* in caring for children.
- You shave *specialised* knowledge about how to plan and provide activities that will help children grow, develop and learn.
- If you are taking the CACHE Level 3 Certificate in Childminding Practice, then you will be *qualified,* or maybe you have gained another childcare qualification in the past, such as the Diploma in Nursery Nursing, the Diploma in Childcare and Education, or the NVQ Level 3.
- OfSTED (or CSIW in Wales) has accepted your application to become a registered childminder; therefore you must have met the criteria for a 'fit person'. This legally means that you are capable or *proficient.*
- *Skilled* people are capable and competent in carrying out their job. This is you.
- To be *trained* means that you have made a deliberate attempt to get the skills needed to do your job, or have decided to develop your skills and knowledge. You must have done this, or else you would not be reading this book!

If you can say Yes to any of those, then you are a professional.

A professional person is not born, nor does it happen overnight. To become a professional can mean a lot of hard work and take time. It is a gradual process that includes every part of your job. It includes the knowledge that you have and can develop. It includes your own skills and how you carry out your job. Being professional also includes your actions, attitudes and behaviour. Being a professional means that you get paid for the work that you do. If you were working for a large company you would be expected to take part in an appraisal system and review your role; as a professional childminder you should also review and evaluate how you work, and take opportunities, such as going on a course, and take extra training to help you do your job even more effectively. If you are working for someone else you would be expected to show some form of commitment to your employer and the company. So you should be committed to your work as a childminder and provide the best possible service that you can. This could mean that you might be inconvenienced at times, but not exploited.

Learning Outcome Activity 63 (ICP, DCP, ECP)

Identifying strengths and weaknesses

Professional people should be able to look objectively at the work that they do and decide which areas they do well, which areas they could do better and which areas would be better if they had extra help or training.

This type of activity is often referred to as identifying strengths and weakness.

Make yourself a chart such as the example shown below and try to identify:

- The things that you think you do really well – your strengths.
- The things that you could do better – your weaknesses.
- Ways that you could develop your weaknesses.

Things that I do well (My strengths)	Things that I could better (My weaknesses)	Things that I could do to help my weaknesses
I am always ready each morning for the children.	My record keeping and observation.	Find a course that may help me be better at observing the children.
I enjoy being with the children.	I am not very sure about the Early Years curriculum.	Find a course that I could go on, ask in the library for a book that I could read.
I help to organise the get-togethers of local childminders.	I am always the one who ends up washing up the coffee mugs.	Suggest that we have a rota for routine jobs.
I have good relationships with the parents.	I am not firm enough about getting fees.	Review my contracts with parents and make sure that I include payment dates. Be FIRM.

Getting registered

Before you can care for other people's children in your own home you must be registered with OfSTED (or CSIW in Wales). From September 2001 the National Care Standards for Under Eights Care and Childminding state that any one who applies to become a childminder must undertake a training course within six months of registration (England only). Many local authorities are using the CACHE Level 3 Certificate in Childminding Practice Unit 1 'Introducing Childminding Practice' (ICP) as the training course to comply with this regulation.

Gaining the ICP is not the only requirement of registration. The registration and inspection officer from the Early Years Directorate of OfSTED (England only) will carry out certain checks on you and your home before agreeing to your registration. These checks include:

- A police check on you and everyone over the age of sixteen years who lives in your house. This is to safeguard and protect the children that you intend to care for. The police check will look for convictions of abuse, child pornography, paedophilia and other related areas. They will not check the number of speeding offences or parking tickets that you may or may not have had. However, any outstanding, unproven accusations may be uncovered and offences of violence and dishonesty are checked.

- A medical check to make sure that you are in good health and do not have any infectious illnesses or diseases that could be passed on to the children.

- A social services check to make sure that you are not known to that department in relation to the care of children; for example if your own children had been taken into care because you as a parent could not cope, this could affect your registration as a childminder.

- A dog check to make sure that any pet dogs you have are not considered dangerous. You may be asked to provide a vet's certificate that your dog is fit and healthy.

- You will be asked for two references, which will be checked, from people you know you well and will vouch for your character. The people who give the references cannot be related to you.

- Checks will be made on your home. Sometimes registration and inspection people may visit your home two or three times before agreeing to your registration. The number of children that you intend to mind will be discussed, as will your routines for making sure that your home is safe and hygienic. These visits will also check whether you are able to offer the children stimulating activities in a warm and safe environment.

- In some case checks are also made by fire prevention officers and environmental health officers.

It is always very good practice to enrol on a first-aid course and gain a recognised qualification.

You will also have to show that you have public liability insurance cover and are committed to providing a service that respects individuality and is non-discriminatory.

This may seem like a daunting number of checks and things that you have to do. What you must remember is that all these checks are to safeguard you, the childminder, and the children that you intend to care for; so it's in your best interests to think of them positively.

Once you are registered you will receive an annual visit from a registration and inspection officer, who will continue to check that all the things required for registration are still in place.

Starting your childminding business

Whilst looking after the children is the most important part of your professional role, there is also a business side to your job. You are self-employed, which means that you do not work for anyone else. This also means that you have full responsibility for:

- Insurance for yourself, your home and your car. You will also need legal insurance cover and public liability insurance.
- Tax and National Insurance contributions for yourself.
- Keeping financial accounts of income and expenditure.
- Being aware of other sources of income such as milk refunds.
- Government initiatives, such as the Children's Tax Credit.
- Keeping accurate and up-to-date records of the children.

It is important that you get the business side of childminding set up in an organised way from the start. Many people worry about the 'paperwork' side of their job and see it as an 'irritating' part of their work. There is a danger that if you think in this way, these worries and concerns could stop you concentrating on the children and possibly affect the way you work with the parents. Be professional and get yourself organised from the beginning. If you get the administrative side of your business well organised from day one you will have more time and energy to care for the children.

Accounts

There is no set way to keep accounts. It is very much a matter of personal preference. Some people set up their accounts on a personal computer, which can be very helpful. There are many straightforward computer software programs available that only require you to put in the headings such as fees, milk refunds, cost of materials and so on. The computer program will then neatly set the items out for you and each time you add an item, the total will be adjusted. However there are many people who do not want to use computers and prefer to keep handwritten accounts. Many high street stores sell account books that are already printed with columns to help people produce logical accounts. The National Childminding Association also has account books that you can buy from them.

You will need, as an minimum, two main headings in your accounts: *Income* and *Expenditure*.

Most people put income on one page and expenditure on the other. Many childminders enter their account details at the end of each day, then add them up and 'rule the accounts off' at the end of each working week. Again it is a matter of personal preference whether you work to weekly accounts or monthly accounts. What is important is that you keep accounts that are accurate.

Below is an example of a double page from part of a childminder's accounts for one week.

This is not a perfect way to keep accounts, but it works for this childminder.

Income			Expenditure		
Week beginning 12.11.01			Week beginning 12.11.01		
Date	Item	Amount £00.00	Date	Item	Amount £00.00
12.11	Fees for		12.11	Toiletries	9.45
	Charley	15.00		Petrol	15.00
	Kerry	15.00		Phone call to NCMA	00.50
	Daniel	9.00		Postage to NCMA	1.19
13.11	Fees for		13.11	Paint	7.50
	Daniel	9.00		Glue sticks	4.50
	Amir	45.00		Books from school book club	19.99
14.11	Fees for		14.11	Food for children's lunches	17.53
	Kerry	15.00		Dry cleaning settee covers	15.00
	Charley	15.00			
	Milk refund for October	12.66			

There will be things such a toiletries, and this includes toilet rolls, boxes of tissues, soap, wet wipes and items for your first-aid box, which will be regular expenditure items each week. If you are not careful these items will become lost in your family expenditure and not your business expenditure. It is important that you make sure that you keep childminding items separate from household items.

Most financial advisors will suggest that you should try to predict what your income and expenditure is likely to be before you start your business. This is important and you should try to estimate your costs. This will help you to set realistic charges for the service you plan to provide. One thing that you do not want to do is work for nothing. You will need to work out how much you are likely to spend working as a childminder. You will need to find out the extra cost of insurance for yourself, your home and contents, your car and your public liability. You will need to work out how much more you are likely to spend on food, toiletries, cleaning costs and replacing equipment, for example, and don't forget to include costs of training courses.

There will also be 'start-up' costs that you will need to consider. These could include:

- Safety equipment such as fire blankets, guards, fire extinguishers, smoke alarms, safety gates, drawer and cupboard locks, harnesses and reins, window and door locks.
- Toys, books and equipment such as child-sized seats, high chairs, low tables, washable floor coverings, as well as consumables like paint, glue and paper.
- Subscriptions to professional organisations such as NCMA.
- Stationery.
- Insurance.

Some areas of the country, but not all, have a scheme where childminders can apply for 'start-up' grants. The situation with start-up grants is constantly changing and you need to check with your local EYDCP if you think that you could be eligible.

Tax and National Insurance

As a self-employed person you must inform your local Inland Revenue office that you are working as a childminder. Their address and telephone number will be in your telephone book, or ask at the Post Office or library. Once you have told the Inland Revenue that you are self-employed, you will be sent a self-assessment form to complete, for income tax. There are very clear deadlines for completing and returning the form; these are included in the guidance notes that come with the form. NCMA can offer guidance on tax and National Insurance.

You will liable for tax on your net income. Your net income is what is left after all your expenses have been paid, in other words, your profit. You will be entitled the usual allowances and you could also be exempt from paying tax if you are classed as a 'low earner'; again this information is in the guidance notes.

There are also different charges for National Insurance contributions if you are self-employed. Depending on which rate you decide to pay, your entitlement to certain benefits will be affected, such as sick pay or maternity pay. Again your Inland Revenue office should be able to help you.

Costs and charges

The charges for childminding vary across the country, there is no set amount. Caring for children is a highly skilled professional job, but many childcare practitioners feel that they do not get the financial rewards in recognition of their expertise. You have to decide for yourself what is an appropriate charge for where you live. When trying to decide what you should charge, you might want to think about:

- The level of unemployment in your area. This could affect how much demand there would be for your services. Areas where there are many dual-income families could mean lots of people wanting childminding services.

- What other childminders in the area are charging. If you try to 'undercut' another childminder it does not necessarily mean that you will make more money. You are restricted by the conditions of your registration in the number of children you can mind, for one thing, and overheads of running your business are going to be very much the same as any other childminder. The cost of electricity and gas does not vary much across the country and you all need heat and light.

- Whether you are going to offer 'discounts' for caring for more than one child in the same family. Many childminders do offer such discounts, but your overheads are still going to be the same, regardless of the relationships of the children.

- Whether you are going to have a different rate of charges. This could be for different ages of children; for example, some childminders have different charges for babies, depending on what they provide, such as nappies. Some childminders charge less if they are caring for children only after school.

- Whether you offer discounts if parents pay a month, or more, in advance.

- Whether you are going to have a different rate of charges for hourly, daily part-time or full-time, weekly attendance.

Some childminders have charges that they think reflect their levels of experience, qualifications and so on. This might be something else that you would want to think about.

Your contract

The importance of the contract has been mentioned in previous chapters. Mentioning it again reinforces the importance of your contract for both you and the families of the children that you care for. Having a contract emphasises your professional status.

Your contract should be written in language that is clear, leaving no room for misunderstandings or misinterpretations. It is essential that you and the parents make time to go through the contract carefully, before you start caring for the child. Your contract should make it perfectly clear what services you will offer. It should make very clear what you are expected to do and what is expected of the parents. You should have a separate contract for each child, even if they are from the same family.

Once you and the parents have agreed every aspect of the contract you should both sign and date it. Once this has been done it becomes a legally binding document. You must keep all your contracts in a safe and secure place. Every contract should be reviewed regularly. Some childminders review their contracts each year, some review them more frequently. Remember each contract will have been signed at a different time and so you will need to make a note of the dates for review. Remember to give the parents notice of the review. Many childminders use the contract review to also review their charges, if appropriate.

If you and the parents have agreed that there will be a 'settling-in' time for the child, you will need to draw up a temporary contract to cover that period of time. This temporary contract must also be signed and dated. Before the agreed settling-in time is up, the parents and yourself will need to agree a permanent contract in the usual way.

Insurance
Buildings, house contents and car

The insurance cover that you will need as you start work as a childminder is different from the usual home, house contents and car insurance policies. You should tell your current insurance company that you are running a business in your home and make sure that you are fully covered. The same applies to your car insurance. Some policies clearly state that your cover is for domestic and social purposes only and not for professional journeys for which you will be paid. If you do not tell your insurance companies that you are working as a childminder, you could find that if you ever needed to make a claim, your policy would not be valid. Some insurance companies regard childminding as a 'high risk' profession and increase their premiums accordingly. However there are companies that deal specifically with childminders and offer acceptable premiums. If you want to find out more about these companies contact the NCMA.

Public liability insurance

It is a requirement of the National Care Standards that all childminders have public liability insurance. This is an important form of insurance, as it should provide you with legal liability cover against:

- accidental injury or death to any person, including the children that you are caring for, caused by your negligence or activities

- any damage that may be caused to other people's property by the children that you are caring for.

Claiming benefits

The rules and regulations affecting benefits claims are getting increasingly complex. If you, or a member of your family, has been claiming benefits before you began your childminding business, your earnings could affect the benefits. It is very important that you inform your local benefits office of your childminding business. Again, NCMA can offer you guidance on this aspect of your business.

Claiming milk refunds

Many childminders are not aware that they are able to get milk refunds. At the present time you are entitled to claim the cost of one-third of a pint of milk for every child under five years old for every day. For the purposes of the claim, a day is anything over two hours. For babies you can claim the cost of one-third of a pint of formula milk made up as instructed on the packaging.

This entitlement can add up to quite a substantial amount of money over a year and you should make sure that you make your claims regularly. You will need to keep receipts to prove that you have bought the milk and also keep accurate records of the attendance of the children. This is definitely a case of 'use it or lose it'. Your local EYDCP should be able to tell you how to get the claim forms.

Keeping your childminding service full

You will not make money if you do not keep your business full. The insurance premiums will not necessarily go down because you have fewer children and vacancies. Many childminders find that having vacancies is not an issue and they have waiting lists. This is obviously an enviable position to be in, but there may be times when you will need to think about the best way of filling vacancies.

Many childminders do not have to advertise. Word of mouth is sometimes quite sufficient. One satisfied parent telling another about you can be a very effective way of filling vacancies. It is unlikely that a parent would recommend you to anyone else if they were not satisfied with the way that you care for their child. Local offices of the Children's Information Service can keep lists of childminders with vacancies. If you have joined a local childminding group it is possible that they will organise a vacancy list. If you do decide to advertise, remember that it is not necessary to put your address. Your telephone number and name should be enough. You must be aware that any advertisement that you place can attract unwanted and 'crank' responses.

You are offering a professional service and you should remember this when you are considering how to fill vacancies. A tatty bit of paper stuck in a shop window will not give a very good impression. You can advertise very successfully in local shops, but you need to make sure that your advert is legible, clear and written or printed on a cleanly cut piece of card or paper.

Learning Outcome Activity 64 (ICP, DCP, ECP)

Design a small advertisement

Mike is a registered childminder. He has a vacancy for a child over two years old for five mornings a week (maximum of four hours). Mike's childminding business closes on Bank Holidays and for three weeks in August. He charges £5 per morning, including a mid-morning snack and a light lunch. His telephone number is 01230 567890, and there is an answer machine.

Using the above information design a small advertisement, about the size of a postcard, that could be put on the notice board of the local health centre.

Sources of information and support

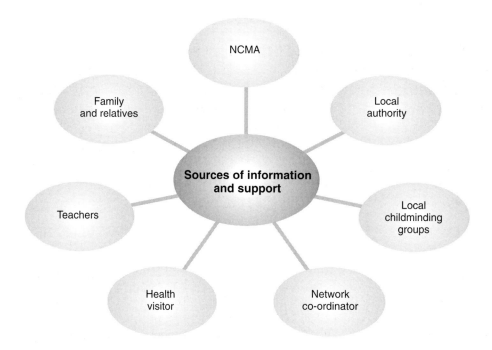

Figure 12.1 *There are various sources that childminders can get information and support from*

All childminders, regardless of how professional they are, will find that at some point they will need support and information. Childminding is a very demanding job and being self-employed can be quite isolating, especially as far as adult company is concerned.

Local childminding groups

Many childminders set up local groups so they can meet one another socially. Sometimes they can meet in each other's homes, depending on the numbers, or in local amenities, such as a sports centre. These groups can be great fun and sources of support. Sometimes people of your own profession are the only people who can really understand some of the issues involved in childminding. The local groups also provide the opportunity to share information and ideas, and to generate new ideas for activities. Remember that you must never discuss with anyone personal information about the children or families that you work with.

Network co-ordinator

Childminding networks are growing all over the country and these can also be valuable sources of information and support. Each network has a co-ordinator who will be able to tell you what training and courses are available in your area.

NCMA

The National Childminding Association (NCMA), is the only organisation in England and Wales specifically for childminders. It is committed to promoting quality of childminding and improving the status and conditions for childminders, children and their parents. NCMA has a national network of development workers and support staff. It is also very effective in liaising with government departments on issues concerned with childcare and childminding in particular. Childminders who join NCMA are provided with a wealth of information, free legal advice, special offers for insurance, as well as training opportunities and the chance to purchase useful publications and stationery, such as account books and sample contracts.

Local authority

In recent years all local authorities have set up Early Years Development and Child Care Partnerships (EYDCP). Many of the EYDCPs have employed development officers with special responsibilities for childminders. These people can put you in touch with other childminders and also provide information about courses that are being run in your area. Your childminding development officer can be a very useful source of support and help. They can often put you in touch with other local authority personnel and social services staff, such as child protection officers.

Health visitors

Health visitors, either your own or those of the children that you mind, can be a valuable source of support and help. Health visitors have a good understanding of children's growth and development, which they often gain through carrying out child health surveillance and developmental checks. They can also put you and parents in touch with other professionals, particularly in the medical world, if you think that there may be a problem.

Teachers

More and more childminders are getting accredited and so are able to accept nursery education funding. This means they must offer activities to four-year-olds that are part of the stepping stones on the Foundation Stage Curriculum in England or Desirable Learning Outcomes in Wales. Teachers can be an invaluable source of support and advice for childminders offering this service and many good professional relationships can be developed along with an exchange of ideas and activities. Teachers can also be supportive with children's learning difficulties and emotional and behavioural problems. It is likely that a child who has such problems at the childminder's home will also have them in school. You should work with the teacher to support the child and hopefully deal effectively with the difficulty or problem.

Family and relatives

Before you started your childminding business you should have discussed it with your family, partner, children, and anyone else who could be affected, such as elderly relatives. Hopefully they will have supported you in your new venture, otherwise you could have problems.

Anyone who works full-time and has family responsibilities and commitments can find, at times, that it is difficult to meet all the demands placed on them. It can be difficult to balance the needs of your family against the needs of your professional life. This may be more difficult for childminders as they are working in their own homes. Many self-employed people work from home, but often have a separate work area, so that their business life does not encroach into their family life. This is not the case for most childminders. There will be other children and partners in their home. There will be changes in the family routine and your working hours may mean that you have less time to spend with your own family. These issues should have been thought of and discussed with your family before your started your business.

If your family understand the demands of your business, then it should not be unreasonable to expect them to support you. This might mean taking a greater share in the running of the family home, such as doing the weekly family shop, or doing the running repairs and DIY around the house that will be incurred with having more young children around.

CASE STUDY

Ameera has decided to become a registered childminder. She stopped working following the birth of her one-year-old son and she has another child who is at school. Ameera and her husband live with his parents. The house has a large garden at the back that is accessible through a conservatory. Ameera plans to use the conservatory as a playroom for her business and will use the big kitchen to serve the children's meals. There is a downstairs bathroom with separate toilet.

At first her in-laws think that the house will be full of other people's children, it will be noisy and they will lose their privacy. Ameera tries to reassure them that this will not be the case and agrees that the children will not have access to any of the rooms upstairs or the family sitting room. Her in-laws agree to see how things go for six months.

Ameera meets an experienced childminder at the pre-registration meeting. She explains her concern to the childminder. The childminder suggests that Ameera brings her in-laws to see how she runs her business, and hopefully that might allay their concerns. Ameera and her in-laws visit the childminder's house and they see for themselves that it is possible to run this kind of business and at the same time keep areas of the house private.

A few weeks after Ameera was registered, she noticed that her father-in-law would often be about as the children were leaving making a special point of using their names when he said goodbye. Her mother-in-law began cooking a few extra sweetmeats 'for Ameera to share with the children'. Ameera now felt confident that she had the support of all of her family, thanks in part to the help of an experienced childminder.

Establishing and developing your business

Any successful business needs time to become established and to develop. A childminding business is exactly the same.

Childminding is a demanding career. You need to be a fit and healthy person, with good social skills, have lots of patience and, above all, love being with children. You could start your childminding business with great intentions and full of enthusiasm. However after a few months you may become weary of having a house full of other people's children; or you may develop a bad back, which restricts what you can do. These things do happen, and in such cases the childminding business may not develop successfully.

Childminding is a flexible career. More and more areas of the country are establishing childminding networks which offer adaptable services. Once you feel confident about your professional skills, you may want to consider joining a network to help you develop your business.

Childminding networks can provide out-of-school care, or become involved with a large company which offers childcare facilities to its employees. Community childminding for children deemed to be 'in need', such as children with additional needs or families in troubled circumstances, is another area in which networks have become involved, and is another way to develop your business. As mentioned earlier childminders can offer early education and receive funding for four-year-olds. All of these are ways in which your business could develop.

However, no business will develop if those running it 'stand still'. As a professional childminder, you need to be always looking for ways to increase your skills and knowledge. In doing this you will develop yourself and your business. It follows that the more skilled you are, the better your childminding service will be. Never think that you cannot learn anything new. We never stop learning.

Updating and refreshing your professional knowledge and skills

Being professional involves continuing to learn, develop and extend your skills and knowledge, and keeping up to date with current trends and thinking. Childcare is a go-ahead profession. It requires people to be lively and self-motivated. It is an exciting choice of career. There is always something new and different to learn and read about, and there are literally dozens of courses and training events that you can attend. It is so easy to say to yourself, 'Well, I've done my pre-registration course, I have got two children of my own, I don't need to do anything more.' This attitude does little to raise the professional status of childminding and nothing for the person who thinks in this way.

CASE STUDY

1   Some years ago it was common practice to cover up a burn or scald. Today we know that the skin and tissue under the burn or scald can go on being damaged for some time after the heat source has gone. Burns and scalds are now treated by putting the injured part under cold running water for several minutes. In such a case if you do not keep up with your first-aid qualifications and read articles, you could do more harm than good.

2   Children with a disability were often referred to as handicapped and people felt sorry for them. Today, children with a disability are encouraged to lead full and active lives, and society is starting to see the child first, not the disability. If you were not

aware of how attitudes have changed over recent years you could not offer a non-discriminatory childminding service, where every child is respected as an individual.

These are two examples of the ways attitudes and care for children has changed in recent years. Unless childminders keep up to date they will not be offering a professional service.

Ways to update and develop your knowledge and skills

There are many courses and training qualifications available to childminders. There are hundreds of books about children, their care and development, as well as many magazines.

Courses and training

Early Years Development and Childcare Partnerships offer many training events which may or may not lead to a qualification. However, they are an excellent way of meeting like-minded people, sharing ideas and opinions and extending your knowledge.

The CACHE Level 3 Certificate in Childminding Practice has three units, Introducing Childminding Practice (ICP), Developing Childminding Practice (DCP) and Extending Childminding Practice (ECP). Each of these units is assessed with written assignments. This qualification is specifically for childminders. It has been developed by NCMA and CACHE (Council for Awards in Children's Care and Education) and is nationally recognised and offered by colleges, NCMA and by distance learning through the National Extension College.

Some childminders go on to NVQ (National Vocation Qualifications) Level 3 in Early Years Care and Education, once they have gained the full Certificate in Childminding Practice – that is, all three units. The new Early Years Foundation degrees will be accessible to people with a Level 3 qualification and will include the opportunity for distance learning.

CACHE also has professional qualifications in Playwork and Professional Development, such as Supporting Children and Families in Toy Libraries, Working with Children and Young People with Special Needs, and Protecting Children. CACHE's address is at the end of the book; you should contact them, or your local college for more information about these and other awards.

Publications

If you become a member of NCMA, you will receive a copy of their magazine, *Who Minds*, at least four times year. This will provide you with relevant and useful articles on every aspect of childminding, from insurance to planning activities to stimulate and interest children on a wet afternoon.

Another useful magazine is *Nursery World*, a weekly magazine written for people who care for young children. There are often very good articles on child development and health issues, as well as up-dates on the latest government initiatives.

Practical Parenting is a magazine written mainly for parents, with very helpful and useful articles on health and development issues and look out for *Practical Pre-school*, another very useful magazine.

CASE STUDY

This is a true story about a group of childminders who agreed to become 'guinea pigs' for a pilot course which was being developed by NCMA. All were registered with their local authority and had many years of experience minding children. However, many of them had not set foot in a classroom for a very long time, and one had no formal 'paper' qualifications. But with tutor support every member of the group successfully completed their written assignments and became the first group of childminders in the country to gain what was then known as the Developing Childminding Practice 2 (now known as the ECP) qualification.

Several of the group 'got the learning bug' and within a short space of time they had gained an NVQ Level 3 in Early Years Care and Education. Some went on to gain a recognised qualification for teaching adults so that they could spread their enthusiasm and professionalism to other childminders in the area.

What does 'being a reflective practitioner' mean?

Part of being professional is that you are able to look critically at every aspect of your work. To be reflective is to think carefully or to give special consideration to something. For professional childminders this means asking yourself questions such as:

- What have I done really well today, or this week?
- What has made these things successful?
- What could I have done better?
- What has made these things less successful?
- Has anything happened today, or this week, that I was not prepared for?
- What has been difficult today, or this week?
- Has anything in particular made me feel more stressed than usual?

It is good practice to set aside some time regularly to think critically about your work. Some childminders do this at the end of every working week, some do it once a month; it very much depends on your own circumstances. To a certain extent it is more important that you make time regularly to reflect on your practice, than to be concerned with how often you do it.

It is all very well and good to ask yourself reflective questions, but it is just as important that you attempt to find some answers. To help you find some answers you might want to think about:

- The ways that you can build on your successes.

- What you might want to do differently in the future and why. This might lead on to looking closely at your personal beliefs and opinions and asking yourself:

  Are these still relevant, up-to-date and appropriate?

- Why did I get especially stressed about things and how can I cope with this stress? What can I do to make me feel better and who can I go to for some help or support if I feel I need it?

- Are there any materials, toys and equipment that I need to get to make my business more successful? Can I afford to buy new toys, or should I go to the toy library?

Being a reflective practitioner is not that easy when you work alone. It is always easier to 'bounce' ideas off other people and share views and opinions. This is where you will find being part of a childminding group or network can be invaluable. You will be with other professionals in the same line of work and who will understand the extent of the job. However, only you can take responsibility for making decisions about your work and business.

If you are not prepared to reflect on your business and make appropriate changes, your business will not develop. You are likely to get 'stuck in a rut' and you will go on making the same mistakes. There are some people in business who have the attitude, 'I've always done it this way, why should I change?' This is someone with a closed mind, who is not prepared to listen to others and who is not willing to take chances and widen their knowledge and experiences. Can you honestly describe such a person as professional?

How to be assertive

A professional childminder who is self-confident and is capable of running a quality service and an efficient business, is likely to be assertive. This does not mean that they are aggressive or that they always want their own way.

Assertive people know their own mind. They have a good self-image and value and respect themselves. They know what they are good at, and what they could do better or more effectively. Assertive people are realistic about themselves and their business.

Learning Outcome Activity 65 (ICP, DCP, ECP)

Are you assertive?

Complete the following quiz to find out how assertive you are.

1 Can you name three things that you are good at?
2 Can you think of something that you have done recently that you were proud of, or something that other people admired?
3 Do you actively listen?
4 How do you react when someone says, 'Childminding isn't a proper job?'
5 How do you react when someone says, 'Children like that should not be taken out into public places, they should be in the home?'
6 How do you deal with a parent who is always late, and so gives you less time to spend with your family?
7 How do you deal with a tutor who you think has given out incorrect information on a training course?
8 What do you do when someone expresses a point of view that you don't agree with?
9 When you talk to people do you make eye contact with them?
10 What do you do when you realise that you have made a mistake?

How did you get on?

Go through the following answers and compare them to your own to decide how assertive you are.

1 Everyone has something that they can do well. Recognising your own strengths is part of your self-image and knowing yourself. This is part of being assertive.

2 Everyone has something that someone else will admire, either in our personalities, physical attributes or skills. Recognising your good points is part of your self-esteem and valuating yourself. This is part of being assertive.

3 Active listening was described in Chapter 9. Do you really listen to what people are saying to you, giving them your full attention. Or do you passively nod or murmur and hope that they won't notice. Being able to actively listen in a considerate way is part of being assertive.

4 Do you stay calm and challenge what is said, using facts to make your challenge? Or do you react quickly and raise your voice, wag your finger and argue? Keeping yourself in control and reacting in a calm professional manner is part of being assertive.

5 Are you prepared to challenge all prejudicial and discriminatory remarks, regardless of who makes them? Do you check that you have heard what they said correctly? Do you stay calm? Or do you ignore what was said, mumble a reply, nod and avoid eye contact?

If you are assertive, you are not afraid to confront prejudice and discriminatory remarks. You can look directly at the person and speak in a clear voice. You appear confident and in full knowledge of the facts. You recognise that people are entitled to their own point of view but you are also entitled to your opinion.

6   A professional childminder will have agreed in the contract with the parents the times for collecting the children. Are you prepared to speak to the parent about the inconvenience that they are causing, not when they rush in late, but at an agreed time when you can talk calmly and firmly? Are you able to express yourself clearly and directly and not be swayed by the emotional side of the parent's problems at work? This is being assertive.

7   Sometimes tutors say something incorrectly to check that everyone is still paying attention! This is not necessarily a good way of keeping everyone awake. Are you prepared to challenge the tutor and are you sure of your facts? Are you prepared to ask questions in a clear and direct way? Or do you delight in the opportunity to prove your tutor wrong and make them feel small, or do you ignore it, knowing that they are wrong but feeling that it is not your place to say so? If you can correctly challenge incorrect information in a calm and direct way, expressing yourself politely and clearly, then you are being assertive.

8   Do you shout them down, interrupt and use fast speech? Do you make them feel stupid for disagreeing with you? If you are assertive you will acknowledge their point of view, but clearly and calmly explain why you don't agree. You don't get into an argument.

9   A confident childminder can look any person straight in the eyes when talking with them, without being threatening, and they use positive body language and facial expressions, such as smiles. A confident childminder is also assertive.

10 A professional childminder is one who regularly reflects on the things that they do, recognises that something could be done better and that sometimes they make mistakes. An assertive childminder acknowledges his or her mistakes and learns from them. An assertive childminder is willing to apologise, without question, if their mistakes have inconvenienced someone else. They learn from their mistakes and improve the quality of their business.

Answers

The following are answers to the multiple choice and true or false questions that occur in some of the Learning Outcome Activity and Check Your Knowledge features in the book. The answers are cross-referred back to the page number where the feature is found.

Check your knowledge, page 101

1   True.

2   False. You should wear gloves to protect both you and the baby from possible infections.

3   False. No one method is better than another, it is a matter of personal preference.

4   True.

5   False. You should avoid wheat-based foods.

6   True. Parents should consult their doctor or health visitor if the problem persists longer than three months.

7   False. All babies can be bathed.

8   False. Mothers can choose to feed their babies as they wish, and it is your job to help them to continue to breast feed if that is what they wish, by either welcoming them to feed the baby themselves or by supplying you with expressed milk.

9   True.

10 True.

Learning Outcome Activity 27, pages 126–127

1	Perception	2	Holophrases
3	Rooting	4	Physical
5	Holistic	6	Sensory
7	Language	8	Balance
9	Nurture	10	Cognitive
11	Cultural	12	Echolalia
13	Self help	14	Bonding
15	Reflexes	16	Coordination
17	Intellectual	18	Emotional
19	Social	20	Grow

Check your knowledge, page 150

1   False. Childminders need to know about children's growth and development so that they can give professional and quality care to the children, regardless of their age.

2   False. Holistic means looking at all areas of growth and development and considering the child as a whole being.

3   True.

4   False. **Spice** stands for social, physical, intellectual, communication (or cultural) and emotional development.

5   False. All children pass through the same stage of growth and development, but not at the same time.

6   True.

7   True, and all the time.

8   False. It is more usual for two-year-olds to have temper tantrums although they can and often do last until the child is older. It depends on what experiences the child has had, how the temper tantrum has been handled and what reaction he or she got from the adult.

9   Maybe. Some two-year-olds have developed control of their bladders during the day, but not at night. Some three-year-olds still can have 'accidents', which is perfectly normal, again it depends on what experiences they have had. Some childminders believe that girls gain control of their bladders earlier than boys.

10   Usually true.

11   Usually true.

12   False. Children of this age are often very possessive about their toys and playthings. They are not able to share and will play alongside and in parallel with other children but not usually co-operatively.

13   True. When this happens you should remember that they want playthings that they have previously discarded or 'grown out of'. Such toys are comforting, familiar and reassuring. They require little effort to play with.

14   False. Four-year-olds usually do start to show concern for the needs and feelings of others, both children and adults.

Check your knowledge, page 184

1   False – very false! Teaching methods are all the things that you do to help the children grow, learn and develop, such as talking with them, providing a range of experiences and play activities, and giving them time and space to play.

2   False. There are nine subjects in the National Curriculum for children up to the age of eleven in England and ten, including Welsh, for children in Wales.

3   True.

4   True.

5   False. You do not have to set aside special time to 'teach'. The normal play activities and experiences that you provide are all learning opportunities for the children.

6   False. You need the parents' permission to keep records about their child and you should get them to agree in writing to this when you first meet, before the child starts.

7   True, absolutely true. Everyone has the best interest of the child at heart and therefore should all work together.

8   True.

9   True.

10   False. Observations of a child should be confidential, which is very different from secret. Any observation you make you should be willing to share with parents.

Learning Outcome Activity 52, page 214

1   Jake needs his glasses to help see things clearly. If he didn't wear them, he could bump into things and hurt himself.

2   Fatima speaks very well, and she is learning to speak two languages. One is English, like you speak at home and here, and the other language is one that she uses at home. Fatima listens very carefully to what we say, so she can learn more.

3   Everyone can play football. There are some very good football teams that have girls in them. Katy can run very fast and she is strong.

4   Look at my hands, they are a different colour to both yours and Amir's. We are not dirty, everyone has different coloured skin.

5   As we get older, some men lose their hair. It is called 'going bald'.

6   Mandy can't walk very well and so using a buggy helps her to get about more easily.

Check your knowledge, page 220

1   True.

2   True.

3   False. You should provide activities for all children that will meet their individual needs.

4   False. Research has shown that children of about three years old are aware of gender differences.

5 False. Equal opportunities is about treating people as individuals and fairly.

6 True.

7 False. Stereotypical attitudes is one of four factors that can and do affect children reaching their full potential.

8 False. This is a case of falling into the 'multicultural trap'. Children could use the material in any way and it will not necessarily help them understand and respect the culture of the women who wear saris.

9 True.

10 True.

Learning Outcome Activity 58, page 234

1 You need to talk to the parent about why they are late. Remind them of the contract that was agreed between you about pick-up times. Explain the problems that this is causing for your own family.

2 Arrange a meeting with the parents to discuss and talk about this more fully. Explain why you think the child is ready, but listen to and respect their views. Do not attempt to assert your view; parents know their own children best.

3 Make time to listen to the parent's concerns, but do not get involved at a personal level. Give the parent a telephone number or address of a support group or organisation that can help both parents. Remember, the parents can ask for advice, but that does not mean they will take it.

4 Explain firmly but politely that you do not want this kind of information from the parent, and tactfully change the subject.

Learning Outcome Activity 60, page 246

1 Record date and time. Charlie has been unsettled and tearful all day. She went to the toilet 7 times before lunch and 4 times during the afternoon. Will telephone Mum tonight after 7 pm to talk about my concerns.

2 Record date and time. Amir came out of school with a lump on his forehead, over the left eye. Asked him how he had done it and he said that he had fallen over in the playground. Spoke to his teacher who said that he had fallen over at lunch-time and that the incident had been recorded in the school accident book. Teacher asked me to pass on the details to his parents. Made a note on the white board by front door to tell Amir's Dad tonight.

3 Record date and time. Katy's Mum had told me this morning that Grandad would be collecting Katy today. Katy's Grandad came to collect her at 1.30 pm today. This is the fourth time he has collected her (see previous notes). As before, Katy started to cry and ran into another room when he arrived. She

shouted 'Want to stay here, go away.' I invited Grandad in and suggested that I telephoned Katy's Mum. Mum spoke to Katy on the phone and persuaded her to go home with Grandad. When they had left I telephoned Katy's Mum and arranged for her to come round tomorrow for a chat.

Learning Outcome Activity 61, page 255

1   medical/individual

2   social

3   medical/individual

4   social

Learning Outcome Activity 62, page 261

1   When you and Jenny are playing together, she sometimes forgets that she needs the loo. She wears a nappy so that she won't have 'accidents'.

2   I understand that you can get cross when Tom breaks your models. Why don't all of us play with something else, and you can make your models when Tom is at school.

3   It is called a hearing-aid and it helps to make sounds louder. Amir uses his hearing-aid so that he can hear what we are saying to him.

4   Everybody has different shaped eyes and different colours too. Look at my eyes. They are a different shape from yours and Lucy's, but we can all see what we are playing with.

5   Some people take longer to learn how to do things than others. Lindy is taking longer than you to learn to talk, but she has learnt how to walk just the same as you.

6   You don't have to feel sorry for Jake, he is not unhappy, he is always laughing and smiling isn't he?

Check your knowledge, page 270

1   False. Don't make stereotypical assumptions.

2   True.

3   True.

4   True, and some children can at some point in their lives have additional needs.

5   True.

6   False. This can be proved. A child with emotional difficulties can have behavioural problems, but not always. Emotional problems are not always the reason for problem behaviour.

7   True.

8   False. All children need to play and a childminder should plan play activities for all children.

9   False. Childminders could be involved in the information gathering stages and the implementation of an individual learning plan, if appropriate.

10 False. Childminders need written permission from the parents before they can give a child any form of medication or medicine.

Learning Outcome Activities

This is a list of the Learning Outcome Activities in the book, with a cross-reference to the pages on which they are found.

The following chart provides a simplified reference to which Learning Outcome Activities relate to which unit.

ICP	DCP	ECP
1, 2, 3, 4, 5, 6, 7, 8, 9, 10, 11, 12, 13, 14, 15, 16, 17, 18, 19, 20, 21, 22, 23, 29, 30, 42, 43, 44, 45, 46, 47, 48, 49, 50, 51, 52, 53, 54, 55, 57, 58, 59, 60, 63, 64, 65	15, 16, 17, 18, 19, 20, 21, 22, 23, 24, 26, 27, 29, 30, 37, 38, 42, 43, 44, 45, 46, 47, 48, 49, 50, 51, 52, 53, 54, 55, 57, 58, 59, 60, 63, 64, 65	20, 21, 22, 23, 24, 25, 26, 27, 28, 29, 30, 31, 32, 33, 34, 35, 36, 39, 40, 41, 42, 43, 44, 45, 46, 47, 48, 49, 50, 51, 52, 53, 54, 55, 57, 58, 59, 60, 61, 62, 63, 64, 65

Useful names and addresses

Every effort has been made to ensure that all details were up to date at the time of publication.

Many of the details below are for each organisation's head office, which should be able to provide local contact numbers.

ADD/ADHD Family Support Group
1a The High Street
Dilton Marsh
Nr Westbury
Wilts BA13 4DL

Alcoholics Anonymous
PO Box 1
Stonebow House
Stonebow
York YO1 7NJ
Tel.: 01904 644026
Web: www.alcoholics-anonymous.org.uk

Association for Spina Bifida and Hydrocephalus (ASBAH)
42 Park Road
Peterborough PE1 2UQ
Tel.: 01733 555988
Web: www.asbah.org

Awdurdod Cymysterau Cwricwlwm ac Asesu Cymru (ACCAC)
Castle Buildings
Womanby Street
Cardiff CF10 1SX
Tel.: 029 2037 5400
Web: www.ccw.org.uk

British Allergy Foundation
Deepdene House
30 Bellgrove Road
Welling
Kent DA16 3PY
Tel.: 020 8303 8525
Web: www.allergyfoundation.com

British Association for Counselling and Psychotherapy
1 Regent Place
Rugby
Warwickshire CV21 2PJ
Tel.: 0870 443 5252
Web: www.bac.co.uk

British Council of Disabled People
Litchurch Plaza
Litchurch Lane
Derby DE24 8AA
Tel.: 01332 295551
Minicom: 01332 295581
Fax: 01332 295580
Web: www.bcodp.org.uk

British Deaf Association
1–3 Worship Street
London EC2A 2AB
Text phone: 020 7588 3529
Video phone 020 7496 9539
Voice phone 020 7588 3520
Web: www.bda.org.uk

British Dyslexia Association
98 London Road
Reading RG1 5AU
Helpline: 0118 966 8271
Web: www.bda-dyslexia.org.uk/

British Nutrition Foundation (BNF)
High Holborn House
52–54 High Holborn
London WC1V 6RQ
Tel.: 020 7404 6504
Fax 020 7404 6747
Email: postbox@nutrition.org.uk
Web: www.nutrition.org.uk

British Red Cross Society (BRCS)
10th Floor Westminster Tower
3 Albert Embankment
London SE1 7SX
Training tel.: 020 7388 8777
Web: www.redcross.org.uk

Child Accident Prevention Trust (CAPT)
18–20 Farringdon Lane
London EC1R 3AU
Tel.: 020 7608 3828
Web: www.capt.org.uk

ChildLine
Studd Street
London N1 0QW
Helpline: 0800 1111
Web: www.childline.org.uk

Commission for Racial Equality
Elliot House
10–12 Allington Street
London SW1E 5EH
Tel.: 0207 828 7022
Fax: 0207 630 7605
Email: info@cre.gov.uk
Web: cre.gov.uk

Compassionate Friends
53 North Street
Bristol BS3 1EN
Tel.: 0117 966 5202
Helpline: 0117 9539639
Web: www.tcf.org.uk

Council for Awards in Children's Care and Education (CACHE)
8 Chequer Street
St Albans
Herts AL1 3XZ
Tel: 01727 847636 or 867333
Fax: 01727 867609
Web www.cache.org.uk

CRUSE Bereavement Care
126 Sheen Road
Richmond
Surrey TW9 1UR
Tel.: 020 8939 9530
Helpline: 0870 1671677
Web: www.crusebereavementcare.org.uk

Diabetes UK (formerly British Diabetic Association)
Parkway
London NW1 7AA
Tel.: 020 7424 1000
Fax: 020 7424 1001
Email: info@diabetes.org.uk
Web: www.diabetes.org.uk

Disability Rights Commission
DRC Helpline
FREEPOST MID 02164
Stratford upon Avon CV37 9BR
Tel.: 08457 622 633
Textphone: 08457 622 644
Fax: 08457 778 878
Email: ddahelp@strasitel.co.uk
Web: www.drc-gb.org

Disabled Living Foundation
380–384 Harrow Road
London W9 2HU
Helpline: 0845 130 9177
Textphone: 0870 603 9176
Email: advice@dlf.org.uk or
centre@dlf.org.uk for advice on
equipment
Web: www.dlf.org.uk

Down's Syndrome Association
155 Mitcham Road
London SW17 9PG
Tel.: 020 8682 4001
Fax: 020 8682 4012
Email: info@downs-syndrom.org.uk
Web: www.downs-syndrome.org.uk

Eating Disorders Association (EDA)
103 Prince of Wales Road
Norwich NR1 1DW
Helpline: 01603 765050
Tel.: 0870 7703256
Email: info@edauk.com
Web: www.edauk.com

Epilepsy Action (formerly British Epilepsy Association)
New Anstey House
Gate Way Drive
Yeadon
Leeds LS19 7XY
Helpline: 0808 800 5050
Email helpline: helpline@epilepsy.org.uk
Web: www.epilepsy.org.uk

EPOCH (End all Physical Punishment of Children)
77 Holloway Road
London N7 8JZ
Tel.: 020 7700 0627
Associated website:
www.stophitting.com

The Food Commission
94 White Lion Street
London N1 9PF
Tel.: 020 7837 2250
Web: www.foodcomm.org.uk

The Foundation for the Study of Infant Deaths (FSID)
Artillery House
11–19 Artillery Row
London SW1P 1RT
Tel.: 020 7222 8001
Web: sids.org.uk/fsid/

Health Development Agency (UK)
Holborn Gate
330 High Holborn
London WC1V 7BA
Tel.: 020 7430 0850
Email: communications@hda-online.org.uk
Web: www.hda-online.org.uk

Health Information Wales
Ffynnon-las
Ty Glas Avenue
Llanishen
Cardiff CF4 5DZ
Tel.: 0800 665544

Health Promotion Customer Services
Tel.:01235 465565

Hyperactive Children Support Group
71 Whyke Lane
Chichester
Sussex PO9 2LD
Tel.: 01803 725182
Web: www.hacsg.org.uk

Kidscape
2 Grosvenor Gardens
London SW1W 0DH
Tel.: 020 7730 3300
Fax: 020 7730 7081
Email: webinfo@kidscape.org.uk
Web: www.kidscape.org.uk/

Macmillan Cancer Relief
89 Albert Embankment
London SE1 7YQ
Tel.: 020 7840 7840
Information line: 0845 601 6161
Web: www.macmillan.org.uk

Meningitis Trust
Fern House
Bath Road
Stroud GL5 3TJ
Tel.: 01453 768000
Email: info@meningitis-trust.org
Web: meningitis-trust.org.uk

MIND (National Association for Mental Health)
15–19 Broadway
London E15 4BQ
Tel.: 020 8519 2122
Fax: 020 8519 21725
Email: contact@mind.org.uk
Web: www.mind.org.uk

MIND (Cymru)
3rd Floor Quebec house
Castlebridge
Cowbridge Road East
Cardiff CF11 9AB
Tel.: 02920 395123

Muscular Dystrophy Campaign
7–11 Prescott Place
London SW4 6BS
Helpline: 020 7720 8055
Email: info@muscular-dystrophy.org.uk
Web: www.muscular-dystrophy.org.uk

National AIDS Helpline
1st Floor
8 Mathew Street
Liverpool L2 6RE
Tel.: 0151 227 4150
Fax: 0151 227 4019
Helpline: 0800 567123
Email: mmclean@healthwise.org.uk

National Asthma Campaign
Providence House
Providence Place
London N1 0NT
Tel.: 020 7226 2260
Fax: 020 7704 0740
Web: www.asthma.org.uk

National Childbirth Trust (NCT)
Alexandra House
Oldham Terrace
Acton
London W3 6NH
Enquiry line: 0870 444 8707 or 020 8886 1625
Breastfeeding line: 0870 444 8708
Web: www.nctpregnancyandbabycare.com/nct-online/

National Childminding Association (NCMA)
8 Masons Hill
Bromley
Kent BR2 9EY

Tel.: 020 8464 6164
Fax: 020 8290 6834
Email: info@ncma.org.uk
Web: www.ncma.org.uk

National Children's Bureau
8 Wakley Street
London EC1V 7QE
Tel.: 020 7843 6000
Fax: 020 7278 9512
Web: www.ncb.org.uk

National Council for One Parent Families
255 Kentish Town Road
London NW5 2LX
Tel.: 020 7428 5400
Helpline 0800 018 5026
Web: www.oneparentfamilies.org.uk

National Drugs Helpline
Helpline: 0800 77 66 00
Email: helpline@ndh.org.uk
Web: www.ndh.org.uk

National Eczema Society (NES)
Hill House
Highgate Hill
London N19 5NA
Tel.: 020 7281 3553
Fax: 020 7281 6395
Helpline: 0870 241 3604
Web: www.eczema.org/

National Extension College
Michael Young Centre
Purbeck Road
Cambridge CB2 2HN
Tel.: 01223 400 200
Fax: 01223 400 399
Email: info@nec.ac.uk
Web: www.nec.ac.uk

National Lottery Funding
Tel.: 0845 275 0000
Textphone: 0845 275 0022
Web: www.lotterygoodcauses.org.uk

NSPCC
Weston House
42 Curtain Road
London EC2A 3NH
Tel.: 020 7825 2500
Fax: 020 7825 2525
Helpline: 0808 800 5000
Textphone: 0800 056 0566
Web: www.nspcc.org.uk

National Toy and Leisure Libraries
68 Churchway
London
NW1 1LT
Tel: 020 7387 9592
Fax: 020 7383 2714
Email: admin@natll.ukf.net
Web: www.natll.org.uk

Parentline Plus
520 Highgate Studios
53–79 Highgate Road
Kentish Town
London NW5 1TL
Tel.: 020 7284 5500
Web: www.parentlineplus.org.uk

Parents Advice Centre
Franklin House
12 Brunswick Street
Belfast BT2 7GE
Tel.: 028 9031 0891
Helpline: 028 9023 8800
Email: Belfast@pachelp.org
Web: parentsadvicecentre.org/

Qualifications and Curriculum Authority (QCA) – for information on Foundation Stage
83 Piccadilly
London W1J 8QA
Tel.: 020 7509 5555
Fax: 020 7509 6666
Minicom: 020 7509 6546
Web: www.qca.org.uk

Relate
Herbert Gray College
Little Church Street
Rugby
Warwickshire CV21 3AP
Tel.: 01788 573 241
Fax: 01788 535007
Web: www.relate.org.uk

Royal National Institute for the Blind (RNIB)
Customer Services
PO Box 173
Peterborough PE2 6WS
Tel.: 0845 702 3153
Minicom: 0856 58 56 91
Helpline: 0845 766 9999
Fax: 020 7388 2034
Textphone: 0800 51 51 52
Email: helpline@rnib.org.uk
Web: www.rnib.org.uk

Royal Society for the Prevention of Accidents (RoSPA)
Edgbaston Park
353 Bristol Road
Edgbaston
Birmingham B5 7ST
Tel.: 0121 248 2000
Email: help@rospa.co.uk
Web: www.rospa.co.uk

The Samaritans
The Upper Mill
Kingston Road
Ewell
Surrey KT17 2AF
Tel.: 020 8394 8300
Helpline: 08457 909090
Fax: 020 8394 8301
Email: admin@samaritans.org
Web: www.samaritans.co.uk

SCOPE
6 Market Road
London N7 9PW
Helpline: 0800 800 333
Email: cphelpline@scope.org.uk
Web: www.scope.org.uk

SENSE
11–13 Clifton Terrace
Finsbury Park
London N4 3SR
Tel.: 020 7272 7774
Minicom: 020 7272 9648
Fax: 020 7272 6012
Email: enquiries@sense.org.uk
Web: www.sense.org.uk

Sickle Cell Society
54 Station Road
Harlesden
London NW10 4UA
Tel.: 020 8961 7795
Email: sickleinfo.line@btinternet.com
Web: sicklecellsociety.org/

Social Security and National Insurance Information
For information on National Insurance contributions –
www.inlandrevenue.gov.uk
Public Enquiry Office (for details of local offices and general help)
tel.: 020 7712 2171
Freeline: 0800 666 555
General information:
www.ukonline.gov.uk
(The Department for Work and Pensions was created in June 2001 from the former DSS and DfEE)

St. John Ambulance
27 St John's Lane
London EC1M 4BU
Tel.: 08700 10 49 50
Email: info@sja.org.uk
Web: www.sja.org.uk

Stillbirth and Neonatal Death Society (SANDS)
28 Portland Place
London W1B 1LY
Tel.: 020 7436 7940
Helpline: 020 7436 5881
Email: support@uk-sands.org
Web: uk-sands.org/

Terrence Higgins Trust (THT)
52–54 Gray's Inn Road
London
WC1X 8JU
Tel.: 020 7831 0330
Fax: 020 7242 0121
Email: info@tht.org.uk
Web: www.tht.org.uk

Twins and Multiple Births Association (TAMBA)
1a Gardner Road
Guildford
Surrey GU1 4PG
Tel.: 0870 770 3304
Email: enquiries@tamba.org.uk
Web: www.tamba.org.uk

Vegetarian Society of the United Kingdom
Parkdale
Dunham Road
Altrincham
Cheshire WA14 4QG
Tel.: 0161 925 2000
Email: info@vegsoc.org
Web: www.vegsoc.org.uk

World Health Organisation (WHO)
Avenue Appia 20
1211 Geneva 27
Switzerland
Tel.: (+00 41 22) 791 21 11
Web: www.who/

Appendix:

Common Dietary Habits

Food	Buddhist	Hindu	Jewish	Mormon	Muslim	Rastafarian	Roman Catholic	Seventh Day Adventist	Sikh
Alcohol	✗	✗	✓	✗	✗	✗	✓	✗	✓
Animal fats	✗	Some	Kosher only	✓	Some Halal	Some	✓	✗	Some
Beef	✗	✗	Kosher only	✓	Halal	Some	✓	Some	✗
Cheese	✓	Some	Not with meat	✓	Some	✓	✓	Most	Some
Chicken	✗	Some	Kosher	✓	Halal	Some	✓	Some	Some
Eggs	Some	Some	No blood spots	✓	✓	✓	✓	Most	✓
Fish	Some	With fins and scales	With scales, fins, and backbone	✓	Halal	✓	✓	Some	Some
Fruit	✓	✓	✓	✓	✓	✓	✓	✓	✓
Lamb/mutton	✗	Some	Kosher	✓	Halal	Some	✓	Some	✓
Milk/yoghurt	✓	Not with rennet	Not with meat	✓	Not with rennet	✓	✓	Most	✓
Nuts	✓	✓	✓	✓	✓	✓	✓	✓	✓
Pork	✗	Rarely	✗	✓	✗	✗	✓	✗	Rarely
Pulses	✓	✓	✓	✓	✓	✓	✓	✓	✓
Shellfish	✗	Some	✗	✓	Halal	✗	✓	✗	Some
Tea/coffee/cocoa	✓ but no milk	✓	✓	✗	✓	✓	✓	✗	✓
Vegetables	✓	✓	✓	✓	✓	✓	✓	✓	✓

✓ will eat or drink ✗ do not eat or drink

Fasting is often a matter of individual choice, however the following times are often observed:
Jews will fast at Yom Kippur, Muslims will fast at Ramadan, Mormons fast for 24-hours once a month. Some Roman Catholics prefer not to eat meat on Fridays.

Index